the
OPEN CLASSROOM

Open and Distance Learning Series

Series Editor: Fred Lockwood

Activities in Self-Instructional Texts, Fred Lockwood
Assessing Open and Distance Learners, Chris Morgan and Meg O'Reilly
Changing University Teaching, Terry Evans and Daryl Nation
The Costs and Economies of Open and Distance Learning, Greville Rumble
Delivering Digitally, Alistair Inglis, Peter Ling and Vera Joosten
The Design and Production of Self-Instructional Materials, Fred Lockwood
Developing Innovation in Online Learning, Maggie McPherson and Miguel Baptista
   Nunes (forthcoming)
E-Moderating, Gilly Salmon
Exploring Open and Distance Learning, Derek Rowntree
Flexible Learning in a Digital World, Betty Collis and Jef Moonen
Improving Your Students' Learning, Alistair Morgan
Innovation in Open and Distance Learning, Fred Lockwood and Anne Gooley
Integrated E-Learning, Vim Jochems, Jeroen van Merriënboer and Rob Koper
   (forthcoming)
Key Terms and Issues in Open and Distance Learning, Barbara Hodgson
The Knowledge Web: Learning and Collaborating on the Net, Marc Eisenstadt and Tom
   Vincent
Learning and Teaching in Distance Education, Otto Peters
Learning and Teaching with Technology, Som Naidu
Making Materials-Based Learning Work, Derek Rowntree
Managing Open Systems, Richard Freedman
Mega-Universities and Knowledge Media, John S Daniel
Objectives, Competencies and Learning Outcomes, Reginald F Melton
Open and Distance Learning: Case Studies from Education, Industry and Commerce,
   Stephen Brown
Open and Flexible Learning in Vocational Education and Training, Judith Calder and Ann
   McCollum
Planning and Management in Distance Education, Santosh Panda (forthcoming)
Preparing Materials for Open, Distance and Flexible Learning, Derek Rowntree
Programme Evaluation and Quality, Judith Calder
Reforming Open and Distance Learning, Terry Evans and Daryl Nation
Reusing Online Resources, Allison Littlejohn
Student Retention in Online, Open and Distance Learning, Ormond Simpson
   (forthcoming)
Supporting Students in Open and Distance Learning, Ormond Simpson
Teaching with Audio in Open and Distance Learning, Derek Rowntree
Teaching Through Projects, Jane Henry
Towards More Effective Open and Distance Learning, Perc Marland
Understanding Learners in Open and Distance Education, Terry Evans
Using Communications Media In Open and Flexible Learning, Robin Mason
The Virtual University, Steve Ryan, Bernard Scott, Howard Freeman and Daxa Patel

the
OPEN CLASSROOM

distance learning in and out of schools

edited by
jo bradley

KOGAN
PAGE

London and Sterling, VA

This book is published in memory of Michael Young, who inspired so many of us to work for the opening up of educational opportunities to young people.

First published in Great Britain and the United States in 2003 by Kogan Page Limited

120 Pentonville Road
London N1 9JN
UK
www.kogan-page.co.uk

22883 Quicksilver Drive
Sterling VA 20166-2012
USA

© International Extension College and the individual contributors, 2003

The right of the International Extension College and the individual contributors to be identified as the authors of this work has been asserted by them in accordance with the Copyright, Designs and Patents Act 1988.

ISBN 0 7494 3131 8 (paperback)
     0 7494 3130 X (hardback)

British Library Cataloguing-in-Publication Data

A CIP record for this book is available from the British Library.

Library of Congress Cataloging-in-Publication Data

The open classroom : open and distance learning at school level / edited by Jo Bradley.
    p. cm.
Includes bibliographical references and index.
  ISBN 0-7494-3130-X (hard) -- ISBN 0-7494-3131-8 (pbk.)
  1. Distance education--Cross-cultural studies. 2. Open learning--Cross-cultural studies. 3. Computer-assisted instruction--Cross-cultural studies. I. Bradley, Jo, 1942-
  LC5800.O63 2003
  371.39'41--dc21

                                                              2003002031

Typeset by JS Typesetting Ltd, Wellingborough, Northants
Printed and bound in Great Britain by Creative Print and Design (Wales), Ebbw Vale

Contents

Notes on contributors   *vii*

Series editor's foreword   *xi*

Introduction   1
Jo Bradley

Part 1. The knowledge society

1.   **Classroom open learning: a case of old wine in new bottles?**   15
     Janet Jenkins

2.   **Living and learning in the information age: from the school**   27
     to e-school to no school?
     Nigel Paine

3.   **The economics of open learning and distance learning in**   39
     primary and secondary schools
     Marianne Bakia

Part 2. Audiences

4.   **From government correspondence schools to parastatal**   55
     colleges of open learning: out-of-school secondary
     education at a distance in central and southern Africa
     Tony Dodds

5. EFECOT: supporting the travelling tradition   67
    Ken Marks

6. Open learning and distance education for displaced   85
    populations
    Michael Brophy

Part 3. Methods

7. Distance learning in India with open schools   101
    Santosh Panda and Suresh Garg

8. Reflections on open schooling and national policy in South   119
    Africa
    Neil Butcher

9. Education by television: Telecurso 2000   133
    *João Batista de Araujo e Oliveira, Claudio de Moura Castro and
    Aimee Verdisco*

Part 4. The future

10. E-learning and the development of open classes for rural   149
    students in Atlantic Canada
    Ken Stevens

11. Virtual high schools in the United States: current views,   159
    future visions
    M D Roblyer

12. From distance education to e-learning: the organization of   171
    open classes at local, regional and national levels
    Ken Stevens and Carol Moffatt

Part 5. Conclusion

13. Open classrooms and globalization: connections and   183
    reflections
    Barbara Spronk

    Index   *193*

Notes on contributors

Marianne Bakia is Project Director for Learning Technologies at the Federation of American Scientists in Washington, DC. She works on the economics of educational technology and was a key contributor to the *Report to the President on the Use of Technology to Strengthen K-12 Education in the United States* (1997) by the President's Committee of Advisors on Science and Technology. She has also worked on major assessments of learning technologies worldwide for the World Bank.

Jo Bradley is Deputy Director of the International Extension College (IEC) in Cambridge, England. She has worked in a variety of countries in Asia and Africa supporting and training materials developers. She has also been involved in sector-level advisory missions, feasibility studies, field-based monitoring and evaluation consultancies and project management and support in distance education. She teaches on IEC courses at postgraduate level, both face-to-face and at a distance. She has experience of refugee education, non-formal education, literacy and post-literacy campaigns, teacher upgrading programmes and alternatives to formal schools, particularly for women and young adults. Jo currently specializes for IEC in materials evaluation, editorial advice and support for course teams at a distance.

Michael Brophy is Director of the Africa Educational Trust in London and is currently responsible for a number of distance education projects in Somalia and southern Sudan. He has worked as an adviser to ministries of education in Africa, Asia and South America, mainly in curriculum development, teacher education and textbook development. He has managed feasibility, mapping, monitoring, evaluation and research studies in formal, non-formal and alternative education, as well as in refugee education. His PhD was on the evaluation of distance learning.

Neil Butcher works with the South African Institute for Distance Education, where he is responsible for research programmes in higher education, technology-enhanced learning, and the planning and administration of education. He is a leading expert in southern Africa on the linking of modern technology, including the Internet, with distance education and open learning techniques. He has run projects across all sectors of education, as well as researching deployment of distance education throughout Africa. He has also been actively involved in shaping national and provincial policy environments in South Africa for the integration of technology into education systems.

Claudio de Moura Castro is a Brazilian economist with a PhD from Vanderbilt University. He has taught at universities in Brazil, Europe and the United States, and has worked as an educational planner in Brazil, as well as at the International Labour Office and the World Bank. Until recently he was Chief Education Adviser at the Inter-American Development Bank in Washington, DC. Currently he is the President of the Advisory Council of Faculdade Pitágoras. His main fields of research are labour markets, social and economic aspects of education, vocational training and science and technology policies.

Tony Dodds has recently retired from the post of Director of the Centre for External Studies at the University of Namibia, where he spent the last six years. Before that he was Executive Director of IEC. He has spent all of his career in adult education, for the last 30 years in open and distance learning (ODL), with special reference to developing countries. His special interests include training for ODL, the planning and management of distance learning institutions and the use of ODL for adult basic and non-formal education. He has worked on long-term assignments in Tanzania, Mauritius, Nigeria and Namibia, and on shorter consultancy and training assignments in many other African and Asian countries. He continues to do short consultancy tasks and research and writing on distance learning.

Suresh Garg is Professor of Physics and currently Pro-Vice Chancellor, Indira Gandhi National Open University, New Delhi. He joined IGNOU in 1989, and became Director of the university's School of Sciences in 1999. He was Commonwealth Distance Science Expert at the University of the South Pacific, Fiji, from 1996 to 1998. He is a member of several national and international professional bodies and serves on academic, research and management boards of several Indian universities. He has co-authored two books in physics, edited three books on distance education, and published research papers in both national and international journals. In 2001 he became an editor of the *Global E-Journal of Open, Flexible and Distance Education* and guest editor of *Staff Educational Development International*.

Janet Jenkins is an independent international consultant in open and distance learning. With over 30 years' experience in around 50 countries, she provides consultancy to promote and support the effective use of the methods, media and technologies of distance learning, in a variety of education and training contexts.

She gained her expertise through working for organizations such as the National and International Extension Colleges, the Commonwealth of Learning and the Open Learning Foundation. Her clients range from international agencies to individual companies. She has published extensively in the field. Much of her recent work has focused on studying the impact of information and communication technologies on classroom teaching and learning, and the implications of ICT for teacher development. She is currently working in the Republic of Uzbekistan as a consultant for the IEC, where her task is to assist the Centre for Secondary Specialized Education to develop a system of in-service training of teachers by distance.

Ken Marks is based in the Department of Educational Studies at the University of Sheffield, where he is a member of the Inclusive Education and Equality Research Centre. His background is in teaching and working with disadvantaged youngsters, and he has undertaken research with both the (former) National Youth Bureau and the Basic Skills Agency. Since 1996 Ken has been actively involved in working with EFECOT (the European Federation for the Education of the Children of Occupational Travellers) to evaluate the various telematics initiatives described in the chapter he has written. His international work in the field of traveller education has involved him with partners in Belgium, France, Germany, Italy, the Netherlands and Ireland. Closer to home he has been involved with evaluating aspects of ICT use in UK schools.

Carol Moffatt is Manager of ICT in Schools with the Ministry of Education, Wellington, New Zealand. Her previous appointment was as Principal of Oxford Area School. Carol was the founder of the Canterbury Area Schools Technology Network (CANTAtech), a network of 10 rural schools in the Canterbury areas of the South Island of New Zealand, of which Oxford was the lead school. She has had an extensive teaching career in New Zealand working in primary, secondary and area schools. In 1997 Carol was awarded the MNZM for services to education.

João Batista de Araujo e Oliveira (or João Oliveira) is currently President of JM-Associates, an education consulting firm based in Brazil. He has worked in over 60 countries as an official of the World Bank and the International Labour Office and consultant to major international organizations. He works in various areas, such as educational technology, evaluation and education management. Besides advising national and regional governments in Brazil, he is currently developing instructional materials for literacy (for children).

Nigel Paine is Head of Training at the BBC and is based in London. Previously he was Director of Science Year, an initiative managed by the National Endowment for Science, Technology and the Arts for the Department of Education and Skills of the UK government. Passionately interested in the power of technology to transform our lives, Nigel is an advocate of lifelong learning. He has written widely on the impact of learning technology and the development of virtual learning environments, and has travelled the world as a keynote speaker on this subject. He has advised governments on learning technology issues and undertaken consultancy in this area.

Santosh Panda is Professor of Distance Education and former Director, Staff Training and Research, at the Institute of Distance Education, Indira Gandhi National Open University, New Delhi, India. In 2003 he is Fulbright Visiting Scholar at the University of New Mexico, USA.

M D Roblyer is Adjunct Professor of Educational Technology, teaching online for the University of Maryland University College's Web-based graduate programmes from her home in Carrollton, GA. A graduate of Florida State University's instructional systems design programme, she has written extensively on educational technology, and taught at school and post-secondary levels for over 30 years. Recent publications include *Integrating Educational Technology into Teaching* (2003, 3rd edition), *Starting Out on the Internet: A learning journey for teachers* (2003, 2nd edition), and *Technology Tools for Teachers: A Microsoft Office tutorial* (2003). Dr Roblyer's current research focuses on identifying factors that contribute to success in online learning and exploring ways to increase interactive qualities of distance courses. Web site: http://polaris.umuc.edu/~mroblyer/MDRpage.htm

Barbara Spronk holds a PhD in Anthropology and worked at Athabasca University in Canada for 22 years. She also served for 10 years on the Board of the Canadian Association of Distance Education, including a term as President. From 1996 until 2002 she was Executive Director of the International Extension College, in Cambridge, England. During this time she carried out consultancies in a wide range of developing countries and taught on IEC's postgraduate courses in distance education, as well as undertaking fundraising and project development. She now lives in British Columbia, Canada, and carries out contract work for IEC and other organizations.

Ken Stevens is Professor of Education at Memorial University of Newfoundland, where he holds the Chair of TeleLearning and Rural Education, a research appointment endowed by Industry Canada. His previous appointments were at Victoria University of Wellington in New Zealand and James Cook University in Queensland, Australia. His research interests are in the education of rural people and the application of telecommunications technologies to education. He has conducted research in schools in New Zealand, Australia (Queensland and Western Australia), Canada (British Columbia and Newfoundland), the United Kingdom, and, through collaboration with other researchers, Finnish Lapland. He lives in Canada and New Zealand.

Aimee Verdisco, PhD, is an Education Specialist at the Inter-American Development Bank in Washington, DC. She is the author of various articles on education and training, and has been involved in the design and evaluation of a number of Bank-financed projects in the education sector throughout the region.

Series editor's foreword

You will have heard the rhetoric – politicians and educationalists, industrialists and social commentators all proclaiming that the major assets of the country are not the natural resources but the people. They make calls for the country to invest in its people if it is not only to survive in the 21st century but also to prosper. For many countries around the world investment is being made in education and training – if not always at the levels that are commensurate with the identified needs nor the demands being made upon their educational systems. In these contexts the potential of distance learning methods, and particularly the use of Communications and Information Technology (C&IT), are often seen as part, often a large part, of the solution. However, as you will read in *The Open Classroom*, although we face formidable challenges, and there are no simple solutions, there are indications from experiments and innovations that the challenges can be met.

Early in this book, we are told there are over 100 million children who do not go to school – and in the foreseeable future have little prospect of doing so. Later we learn that there may be as many as 15 to 20 million children who are 'internally displaced people', or refugees, who could be an asset to their country, their own or adopted country, rather than a liability – if they had skills to contribute to the economy. We learn of large numbers of disadvantaged children, children in remote rural communities and drop-outs from conventional schools – children that represent a potential that is not being realized and which no country can afford to waste. However, we also learn of projects that demonstrate how identified needs have been met both in school settings and outside them. The contributions in this book, assembled from around the world, illustrate that whilst C&IT has enormous potential, 'low tech' solutions can not only be more appropriate to target audiences but also cost effective. The accounts of virtual schools in Canada and the United

States and of online courses in Europe and New Zealand, contrast vividly with accounts from the National Open School in India and southern Africa. Institutions in Central and southern Africa and in South America, which base their teaching on conventional print, radio and television, demonstrate how successful and cost effective teaching can be achieved – teaching appropriate to the cultural context in which it takes place.

The Open Classroom offers an insight into what is happening in distance education among school-aged learners. It reminds us that while we can learn from others we must always seek the solution that is appropriate to our own learners in the cultural context in which they are learning. It provides us with evidence from specific innovations and, hopefully, the incentive to collect further evidence to further inform our decision making.

I thoroughly enjoyed reading this book. It took me back to the classroom, back to central Africa and brought me up to date and outside the classroom. I'm sure you will not only enjoy these chapters but hope you will want to get involved in *The Open Classroom*.

Fred Lockwood
Manchester, February 2003

Introduction

Jo Bradley

This book is about open and distance learning (ODL) at school level. It deals with experiences in schools, and also with programmes for learners out of school. This level of education, and these students, have not been much written about by professional distance educators. We have read and heard a great deal about open universities and distance learning for adults seeking professional qualifications, but not so much about using ODL with children and young people to help them acquire school level certificates.

Now, however, the scene has changed around us and information and communication technologies (ICTs) are revolutionizing the ways in which this level of education can be offered, at least in industrialized countries. Some of the writers in this volume are at the forefront of these developments, experimenting with new approaches to teaching children, and analysing what is happening to schools and teachers in the wake of these changes. Others are part of a movement which predates the new technology, in some cases by a surprisingly long time. Their concern is with young people who do not have access to conventional schools, for reasons which usually originate in social exclusion or economic hardship.

The late Michael Young, to whom this book is dedicated, founded the National Extension College, Cambridge, in the 1960s. He and his colleagues saw the NEC as a prototype for a new kind of distance education: one that would harness the technologies of broadcasting to the techniques of the correspondence colleges to offer a new kind of 'three-way teaching'. NEC has always offered secondary courses leading to nationally recognized school-leaving exams. When Michael turned his attention to distance education further afield, and travelled around Africa in 1970, he became convinced 'that the need for multi-media teaching is much greater there at the secondary level than it is here' (Briggs, 2001: 265).

The International Extension College, which Michael then launched to help address this need, has been supporting school-level initiatives in poor countries and communities ever since. And the observation he made more than 30 years ago is still true, which is why this book is concerned with what is happening in the developing world as well as in the rich countries.

Terminology

In the meantime, technical change has meant that what we call 'multimedia' in 2003 is rather different from what was understood when Young used the term in 1971. So let's start by defining some terminology. Nowadays, multimedia refers to a computer system or computer system product that incorporates text, sound, pictures/graphics, and/or video (Roblyer, 2003: 360). We distinguish this from the older idea, of print and tutorial support combined with broadcast or recorded media, by calling the latter 'multiple media'.

> Nipper (1989: 63–73) describes the evolution of a 'third generation' of [distance education], a generation which enables greater communication with learners and among learners. The third generation is based on the emergence of computer-mediated communication, whereas the first generation is identified with correspondence teaching, and the second with multiple media systems combining print with broadcast media, cassettes and a limited use of computers.
>
> (Harry and Khan, 2000: 124)

There are several other terms to be defined in this field. To follow Perraton and Creed:

> **Distance education** is an educational process in which someone removed in space and/or time from the learner conducts a significant proportion of the teaching.
>
> **Open learning** is an organized educational activity, based on the use of teaching materials, in which constraints on study are minimized in terms of access, or of time and place, pace, method of study, or any combination of these.
>
> **Open and distance learning** is an umbrella term covering distance education, open learning, and the use of [ICTs] in education.
>
> (Perraton and Creed, 2000: 39)

We also need one more definition. **School level**, for the purposes of this volume, means covering education from pre-school up to year 12, in other words what is generally understood by basic (or primary) and secondary (or high school) education. This is 'K-12' in American parlance. It implies a concern with children and young people (the ages vary from country to country), those for whom schools are intended. But it does not mean only education happening in, or organized by, schools. It also embraces organized learning programmes for children and young people not in school.

The knowledge society

The 'knowledge-based' society is an environment of rapid change, and is the focus of the first part of this book. In Chapter 1, Janet Jenkins starts by putting this rapid change into the context of a much longer history of school-level distance learning. She emphasizes the importance of learning from this long experience, even at a moment when many schools are severely challenged by constant and rapid curriculum change, as well as new technology. Using open learning in the classroom raises familiar issues, even if in a new context: the importance of learner support; the need for materials that engage the learner; the cost implications of doing the job effectively. With the inevitable growth of ICT in schools, teachers need new skills. Jenkins lists the barriers European teachers experience in adopting new ICT, and suggests a framework for a professional approach to the challenge. She also presents a vision of the open classroom of the future – with no barriers between school and home, or indeed school and work.

This is also the vision to which Nigel Paine looks forward in Chapter 2. Developing an education system that prepares people for the knowledge-based society, he suggests, requires rebuilding our fundamental concepts of education. The school has to transform itself from an isolated institution into a learning centre in the community, open to adults as well as children. Paine lists 10 ways in which schools can start to prepare themselves for the new demands which the 'knowledge age' brings, all of which are premised on the effective, extensive and transformative use of ICT. As he points out, if countries and education systems fail to meet the challenge presented by the knowledge economy, the consequences will be horrible.

The cost effectiveness of ICTs for school-level learning has been researched by Orivel (2000), Perraton (2000) and Bakia (2000), among others. In Chapter 3 of this volume, Marianne Bakia examines the economics of computer use in classrooms more generally and warns of some of the pitfalls. Like Jenkins, Bakia emphasizes the need for good learning materials and learner support, and points out that these are not cheap requirements. She looks at the differences in costs between different media and technologies, and examines the components that contribute to the costs of computer-based projects: hardware, software, connectivity and maintenance. Her analysis produces some very practical lessons for any educator contemplating such a project. She concludes that researchers still have much to do in establishing cost–effectiveness ratios for instructional alternatives. She identifies a particularly important gap in our information on the economics of computer technology for classroom education, and challenges researchers to tackle the variations in costs between different education systems and regions, different stages of development and particular settings.

Audiences

I began by suggesting that the learners with whom we are concerned in this book are not the audience that has interested most recent writers on open and distance learning. But information about the uses of ODL at school level is certainly growing. The level of international attention is reflected in the activities of bodies such as the Commonwealth of Learning (COL, 1994; Yates and Bradley, 2000), the European Distance Education Network (Open Classroom conferences in 1995, 1997, 1999, 2000; Open Classroom Working Group established in 1998), and the International Council for Distance Education (a participant in UNESCO's working group on secondary education) (*Open Praxis*, 1996).

Distance learning for school-age children in fact has a longer history than one might think. Certainly by 1906 the first primary school in the United States to offer instruction by correspondence was enrolling pupils (Moore and Kearsley, 1996: 22), and Australia, Canada and New Zealand all followed suit within the next 10 to 20 years (Mukhopadhyay, 1994: 1). These wealthy countries have achieved long-term success in using distance education for students unable to attend conventional schools, and are 'the most extensive current examples of current practice in DE at basic education level' (Harry and Khan, 2000: 127). The story in developing countries is one which started later, and has been told by Yates and Tilson (2000).

In Part 2 of this volume, it is taken further by Tony Dodds, in the case of Africa (Chapter 4). Dodds examines the African experience of using ODL for out-of-school education, particularly the history of government provision in central and southern Africa. He argues that the introduction in several countries of a semi-autonomous 'parastatal' organization to replace the earlier government-run programmes has led to better results for the learners and a better reputation for the providers. He identifies the common features of the emerging new model and the main dangers that it needs to avoid. He is confident that these new parastatal institutions have great potential for meeting the target of education for all, by offering more, and more effective, out-of-school secondary level courses.

A rather different experience, with rather different out-of-school learners, is the subject of Chapter 5. Ken Marks reports on European initiatives that address the needs of the children of occupational travellers, by offering them supported distance learning. As he points out, here the open classroom, rather than offering a new element in the school environment, is an alternative for learners who have problems with normal attendance. This approach is based on the use of ICT, or 'telematics', for secondary-age children of travelling families, enabling them to learn with the support of their parents and online tutors. Marks emphasizes that the concerns raised are relevant for all those working with children whose schooling is interrupted or happens outside the normal school environment. They range from pedagogical to organizational issues, and include questions about the child as distance learner, and the relevance of the normal school curriculum in the home and community environment.

Chapter 6 also deals with young people whose education is interrupted, but in this case they are in displaced populations, either in exile or displaced within the frontiers of their own country. The issues facing educational providers in settlements of refugees or displaced people are distinct, but they are relevant to a very large number of learners at or beyond the margins of mainstream education. Here Michael Brophy raises the question of whether it is still helpful to consider ODL and conventional, face-to-face, schooling as completely separate approaches. His argument is that most current programmes in settlements for displaced people fall somewhere between the two, and that features that used to be peculiar to ODL are now found in conventional education as well. Brophy uses the experience of two groups of programmes – one in southern Africa and one using radio for displaced populations in Africa, Asia and Europe – to show that ODL can be used to increase access to education for displaced children and young people. Such programmes can be effective both in rapid responses to emergencies and in longer term post-conflict situations.

The distinction between in-school and out-of-school learning has understand-ably been important to distance educators. In-school programmes are aimed mainly at children, while out-of-school programmes target mainly adults and school drop-outs, according to Yates and Tilson. But the models and approaches that these authors identify do not divide neatly between these two categories (Yates and Tilson, 2000: 8–11). Elsewhere in the same volume, the point is made that the distinction may rest primarily on whether the intended learners are young children, who need a formal institution like a school to learn effectively, or a mixed audience of those who do not have access to conventional education (Dodds and Edirisingha, 2000: 89). Whether this remains a useful or appropriate distinction for the 21st century is a question that arises throughout this book. On the one hand, in developing countries in-school models are rare, even for children. And on the other, in well resourced educational systems, the introduction of ICTs is revolu-tionizing the role of the school, and may well undermine the distinction, at least at secondary level.

In developing countries, ODL has been used at school level mainly to increase access at costs that are affordable. Keeping costs down in distance education requires large numbers of enrolments. It is therefore particularly interesting to see what has been happening in this field in the E-9 countries. These are the nine high-population countries that came together in response to the 1990 World Conference on Education for All (EFA), and formulated an initiative to reach the EFA goals. They attach great importance to distance education as a means of addressing their considerable educational challenges (Creed and Perraton, 2001: 8). According to Creed and Perraton, five of them (Bangladesh, Brazil, Egypt, Indonesia and Mexico) have major distance education projects for in-school and out-of-school children and adolescents. India and Pakistan have such programmes only for out-of-school audiences, China only for in-school, and Nigeria caters only for (out-of-school) nomadic children. Of course, these schemes vary widely in the numbers of learners they serve, but this coverage does indicate a level of commitment to the use of ODL at school level that is more or less universal among these countries.

Such commitment is supported by donors like the British government, whose Imfundo initiative was set up in 2000 to 'create partnerships to deliver ICT-based activities supporting gender equality and universal primary education in sub-Saharan Africa' (http://imfundo.digitalbrain.com). Imfundo's Web site provides information about its partnerships in different aid contexts and its KnowledgeBank database. Papers in the resource bank cover topics ranging from ICT in schools (Selinger, 2000) to the costing of computers in schools (Cawthera, 2001).

Methods

In the previous paragraph I raised the question of whether the in-school/out-of-school distinction is still a helpful one. The rise of the open school movement in the last 25 years seems to me one reason for asking it:

> Open schools are important as an alternative route to basic and secondary school education. They currently represent the foremost evolutionary organizational form in terms of the numbers served and the sophistication of their instructional arrangements. . . Open schools use varying combinations of print, broadcast, face-to-face and, to a lesser extent, other media to deliver their programmes. Where they serve children, their curricula invariably mirror that offered in the state schools; equivalency of quality and the identity of the qualification being offered are of central importance.

> (Yates and Tilson, 2000: 17)

Chapter 7 in this book tells the story of open schools in India, whose National Open School is one of the largest in the world. Santosh Panda and Suresh Garg describe how small beginnings in correspondence secondary schools in the 1960s have led to a network of national and state open schools with a total enrolment of half a million students. These students are mostly employed, and under 25. A significant proportion are from disadvantaged social groups, and enrolments from these sectors are growing. The well tried model of print-based correspondence, with audio and sometimes video as enrichment media, and with networks of study centres, is working effectively and spreading all over India. The National Open School, in particular, is spearheading new initiatives: new institutions for disadvantaged target groups; a national open schooling consortium and network; and an international training programme and *Journal of Open Schooling*.

Neil Butcher, in Chapter 8, offers a very different view, shifting the focus to a policy debate about whether South Africa should set up an open school. He explores the significance of the distinction between open learning and distance education, and argues that the conflation of the two into 'open and distance learning' distorts our understanding of what needs to be done to create openness in educational systems. In South Africa, policy makers are being urged to see open learning as a set of principles that can inform all educational practices with the aim of improving them, rather than as a separate system of projects, initiatives and institutions. The argument which emerges in relation to the idea of a South African open school is that this is neither viable nor desirable at this stage. Indeed, it may even retard the pace of change in the mainstream. Rather, the distinction between distance and contact systems of schooling is being challenged. In Butcher's view, the aim should be to harness the potential of distance methods to open up the mainstream schooling system, and to help improve its quality and effectiveness.

In much the same way as the introduction of postal services brought about correspondence education, the invention of radio made possible the development of multiple media (what Young called three-way) teaching, in which broadcasting – later other technologies as well – and printed materials are used together in a much more effective approach to distance teaching. Educational radio still plays a significant role in school-based learning, although the model has become inter-active (see, for example, the South African Radio Learning Programme, Leigh, Naidoo and Ramofoko,1995; Naidoo, 2001). Revealingly, perhaps, none of the authors in this book deal at any length with the use of radio at school level. For examples and a range of opinions on the subject, readers are referred to Yates and Bradley (2000).

Television too has been used for school-level learning in a variety of ways since its introduction in the United States in the 1930s. Experiments elsewhere in the world really got under way in the 1960s (eg Mexico: see Durán, 2001). Chapter 9 in this volume provides strong evidence for the continuing value of television, particularly for a large-scale programme, in this instance in Brazil. João Batista de Araujo e Oliveira, Claudio de Moura Castro and Aimee Verdisco use the example of Telecurso to draw attention to the potential of a delivery system that many have already written off. It is particularly important for those of us in English-speaking countries to be reminded that Latin America offers a wealth of experience in ODL at school level, successfully using approaches unfamiliar to us, with large numbers of learners. Telecurso 2000 serves older learners than some of our other examples, but the authors report that the programme is attracting an increasingly younger clientele, and is being used in schools as well. The model of an open system leading to public exams, for school dropouts, certainly has relevance for many other contexts. The same television programmes are used for both organized viewing and open broadcast. The cost per student for organized learning is comparable with that of the regular school system. The numbers are large, yet the dropout rate is low. Oliveira and his colleagues conclude that its innovative curriculum, paired with high quality programmes and support materials, gives Telecurso 2000 its edge. There may not be many other countries in the world of the right size and at the right stage of economic development now to use educational television success-fully. But this experience certainly casts the potential of television in education in a new light.

Looking to the future

The technology that has now captured the attention of educators, as well as others, is, of course, information and communication technology. ICTs are dominant in the activities, the research, the literature and the conferences of the international distance education profession. All the conferences held by the European Distance Education Network between 1991 and 2001 focused on them (EDEN, 2001). Of the 11 titles published by the Commonwealth of Learning in its Knowledge Series in 2000–01, only two do not deal with them (COL, 2002). And every chapter in this book acknowledges their central importance in one way or another.

Online learning for school-age learners is a topic dealt with in Chapter 5, where the target audience is out of school, though of school age. The chapters in Part 4 of the book, by contrast, are all concerned with online learning as part of main-stream schooling, rather than for excluded learners. In Chapter 10, Ken Stevens looks at the Canadian experience of using electronic learning for senior students in rural schools, who would otherwise have to move to urban or boarding schools to complete their education. The introduction of district Intranets has made it possible to organize open, or virtual, classes. This in turn has policy implications for the teachers and managers concerned, as well as for the future of education in rural Canada. Stevens argues that this experience challenges the traditional, closed, model of the school, thus supporting the thesis presented in Chapters 1 and 2.

The establishment of 'virtual schools' in the United States and elsewhere harnesses the power of the Internet for secondary level learning. Since 1996, 'a virtual high school (VHS) movement has been thriving in the United States. . . . However, as with other types of distance learning programs, VHS courses have proven to have comparatively high dropout and failure rates. . . Successful online students seem to need more than the usual degree of organization and self-motivation' (Roblyer, 2003: 212–13). These observations are, as M D Roblyer points out, familiar to practitioners of the more traditional forms of distance education. The VHS movement is thriving in the United States, and Roblyer's chapter in this volume (Chapter 11) highlights many concerns of the school district superintendents who have oversight of them. She identifies economic survival, access and equity as challenges that will shape its future.

In Chapter 12, Ken Stevens and Carol Moffatt present a case history of distance education in New Zealand, focusing on what is happening at the beginning of the 21st century in rural school districts. With similar conditions to Canada, New Zealand is also using Intranets to link rural schools. The result is that competing models of open learning are offering some learners a choice between enrolling with a national distance teaching institution or joining a regional electronic classroom. A range of national strategies to support e-learning in schools, and pilot programmes evaluating different options, are building the basis for new electronic teaching and learning structures. New Zealand education is becoming more open, not just regionally, but also nationally and internationally.

Issues

These chapters range widely, and they present the reader with a similarly wide range of issues to think about. The 'digital divide', for example, lurks everywhere. Is it realistic to expect openness and flexibility to be achieved at low cost? Writers on the use of technology in schools have for some years now been voicing concerns about the issues raised for developing country schools by the introduction of computers (see, for example, Jo, 1996; Brandenburg and Dudt, 1998). And there is the powerful temptation to turn our backs on more familiar media, which still have not exhausted their potential to widen access. 'A concern for the newer technologies should not divert attention from the known and demonstrated strengths of broadcasting in education' (Perraton, 2000: 4).

This is a particularly interesting time, when divisions between North and South are starting to shift, at least in terms of technology in the classroom. Here is a story which appeared on the front page of a north Indian local newspaper in 2002. In it are encapsulated several of the practical and political issues raised by such developments.

Click M for Maths

The students rush for their seats, the excitement runs high and so does the imagination. But why? It's time to get going for the maths class. No longer dull and boring, students of DAV Public School in Sector 8 are logging in to a whole new medium of teaching. 'It's all about e-education,' explains principal Sarita Manuja. Students, says Manuja, study mathematics and science entirely on a giant screen in their multi-media room. And as geometry, trigonometry, animal life, organic chemistry comes alive on the colour screen, these subjects are dull no more.

Lapping it up, chapter by chapter, are the students themselves. Manvin Clair, one of the students, says the software saves time since the teacher does not have to scribble on the blackboard. 'The audio-visual lessons are much more interesting,' he says. Divya Sharma, however, feels the subjects have become much easier to grasp, and it's like watching them on television.

The innovative learning is courtesy Classtech, the software made for these subjects by Saral Academics whose director Ruchi Relhan says she studied dozens of books on each subject to develop the software which is totally compatible with the CBSE [Central Board for Secondary Education] requirements. The result: information that works wonders for students. The principal agrees. 'People tell me it is strange that I am experimenting with this new method for Class X. But you have to see the enthusiasm among the students to know how motivated they are now,' smiles Manuja.

Not surprisingly, the concept has proved to be a hit with the teachers too. Chemistry teacher Akhila Mittal tells you that even the usual 'back-benchers' are now totally focussed in the class. Biology teacher Dr Mamta Goyal says much more time is available for interaction between teachers and students. 'If a teacher changes mid-session, children won't suffer as the software remains the same.' And just as you plug in to the class, your seat's taken. You see, the chemistry class just got underway!

(Rajni Chopra, *Chandigarh Newsline*, 2002)

Are these children in the mainstream, or the margins? Are they part of a trend towards global integration? What about their teachers? In Chapter 13, Barbara Spronk challenges us to look beyond the issue of openness in school-level open and distance learning. In her analysis of the impact of globalization and its associated neo-liberal agenda, she argues that we need to make connections between global restructuring and the impact of the technological revolution on education – economically, politically, materially and culturally. The dynamics of globalization operate in education in complementary and connected ways. The goal of quality in education is couched in the rhetoric of flexibility, opportunity, efficiency, diversity and equity. But the contributors to this book raise questions about costs, privatization, marginalization and going to scale. The digital divide is not going to be bridged without continued public investment and government commitment.

References

Bakia, M (2000) *The Cost of Computers in Classrooms: Data from developing countries*, mimeograph, World Bank, Washington DC

Brandenburg, M and Dudt, K (1998) Technologies for learning and working: an assessment of the use of technology in schools of Belize, Central America, *International Education*, Fall, pp 42–56

Briggs, A (2001) *Michael Young: Social entrepreneur*, Palgrave, Basingstoke

Cawthera, A (2001) *Computers in Secondary Schools in Developing Countries: Costs and other issues*, Department for International Development, London

Chandigarh Newsline (2002) *SimpliCITY*, 1 (405), Thursday 25 July

COL (1994) *Open Schooling: Selected experiences*, Commonwealth of Learning, Vancouver

COL (2002) *Expanding Learning Horizons* (CD ROM), Commonwealth of Learning, Vancouver

Creed, C and Perraton, H (2001) *Distance Education in the E-9 Countries*, UNESCO, Paris

Dodds, T and Edirisingha, P (2000) Organisational and delivery structures, in *World Review of Distance Education and Open Learning, Volume 2*, ed C Yates and J Bradley, pp 87–109, Commonwealth of Learning and RoutledgeFalmer, London

Durán, J (2001) The Mexican Telesecundaria: diversification, internationalization, change, and update, *Open Learning*, **16** (2), pp 169–73

EDEN (2001) *10th Anniversary 1991–2001 Collective CD of EDEN Conference Proceedings*, European Distance Education Network Secretariat, Budapest

Harry, K and Khan, A (2000) The use of technologies in basic education, in *World Review of Distance Education and Open Learning, Volume 2*, ed C Yates and J Bradley, pp 122–37, Commonwealth of Learning and RoutledgeFalmer, London

Jo, M (1996) Computer use in Korean schools: instruction and administration, *Computers and Education*, **26** (4), pp 197–205

Leigh, S, Naidoo, G and Ramofoko, L (1995) South Africa: Designing multichannel options for educational renewal, in *Multichannel Learning: Connecting all to education*, ed S Anzalone, pp 119–32, Educational Development Centre, Washington DC

Moore, M and Kearsley, G (1996) *Distance Education: A systems view*, Wadsworth Publishing, Belmont, CA

Mukhopadhyay, M (1994) Open schooling: an introduction, in *Open Schooling: Selected experiences*, Commonwealth of Learning, Vancouver

Naidoo, G (2001) South Africa: English in Action – a radio learning project – how effective?, *TechKnowLogia*, Nov/Dec

Nipper, S (1989) Third generation distance learning and computer conferencing, in *Mindweave: Communication, computers and distance education*, ed R Mason and A Kaye, Pergamon, Oxford [Online] http://icdl.open.ac.uk/literaturestore/mindweave.html/

Open Praxis (1996) *Open Praxis: the bulletin of the International Council for Distance Education*, **1**, special issue on the opening school

Orivel, F (2000) Finance, costs and economics, in *World Review of Distance Education and Open Learning, Volume 2*, ed C Yates and J Bradley, pp 138–51, Commonwealth of Learning and RoutledgeFalmer, London

Perraton, H (2000) *Information and Communication Technologies for Education in the South*, report prepared for the Department for International Development, International Research Foundation for Open Learning, Cambridge

Perraton, H and Creed, C (2000) Applying new technologies in basic education, *TechKnowLogia*, May/Jun, pp 39–42

Roblyer, M (2003) *Integrating Educational Technology into Teaching*, 3rd edn, Merrill Prentice Hall, Columbus/Upper Saddle River, NY

Selinger, M (2000) Information and communication technology in schools, *Imfundo KnowledgeBank* [Online] http://imfundo.digitalbrain.com

Yates, C and Bradley, J (eds) (2000) *Basic Education at a Distance: World review of distance education and open learning, Volume 2*, Commonwealth of Learning and RoutledgeFalmer, London

Yates, C and Tilson, T (2000) Basic education at a distance: an introduction, in *World Review of Distance Education and Open Learning, Volume 2*, ed C Yates and J Bradley, pp 3–26, Commonwealth of Learning and RoutledgeFalmer, London

Part I

The knowledge society

Chapter 1

Classroom open learning: a case of old wine in new bottles?

Janet Jenkins

School-level distance learning is an old story. It first hit the headlines with the foundation of the Schools of the Air in Australia in the 1920s. It continues to be used, and it works well. But in the last quarter century it has received little attention in comparison with university distance education. The spotlight has been on the supermarket open universities with their mass market, the tailor-made distance programmes of traditional universities and – most recently – e-learning initiatives aimed at the global market.

In contrast, the old story of school-level distance education is half-forgotten. Classroom open learning is often thought to be something completely new, stimulated by information and communications technologies (ICT) and inspired by open and distance learning (ODL) in higher education. This chapter attempts to redress the balance by reviewing the past – the long tradition of school-level ODL – and describing its renaissance in the emerging 'open classroom'.

The notion of 'open classroom' requires some elaboration. The traditional view of ODL is one of physical distance between teachers and learners. So what has distance education to do with the classroom? The reality is that, with the advent of new learning technologies, the boundaries between distance and traditional education are becoming blurred. School-level ODL is no longer simply an alternative mode of curriculum delivery for two major client groups: school-age children out of school, and adults wanting to catch up with missed schooling. The scope of ODL is much enlarged. It is expected to enhance teaching and learning for people of all ages – lifelong, from infant to elderly – and in a variety of contexts ranging from the traditional classroom to virtual classroom environments. It is this new enlarged scope which suggests that the moment has come to re-launch school-level distance learning under a new brand name – the 'open classroom'.

The beginning

Mention 'open learning' or 'distance education' today, and many people are familiar with the terms. Over the last quarter century, ODL has become well established almost everywhere. But for most people it is associated with university learning, and many understand it to mean the use of the Internet to take a university course. Whether they are the huge distance learning institutions, now known as 'mega-universities' (Daniel, 1996),[1] or traditional universities offering specialist distance learning programmes to niche markets, it is universities that have caught the limelight in ODL.

Now ODL is established as part of the mainstream of education, more attention is being paid to its potential for school-level learning. In 1996, for example, EDEN (the European Distance Education Network) launched the Open Classroom movement with the first of a series of international conferences under this title. But few are aware of the long history of school-level distance education, and of the extensive body of experience that has been accumulated. The idea that children could benefit from distance learning is often seen as a novelty, perhaps greeted with suspicion or even sheer disbelief.

But there is nothing new about ODL for young people (except, perhaps, the name). Absent parents have used letters to teach their children for centuries past. In the 15th century, for example, Thomas More continued his daughter's education by letter, after the English King Henry VIII had thrown him into prison. However, the early 20th century saw a new development, organized school-level distance learning, in several countries (Young *et al*, 1991). In probably the best known case, the Australian Schools of the Air, children in isolated farms study at home. In the 1920s they learnt from specially designed study materials and used radio to communicate with teachers and fellow pupils. Today, children in similar environments still study at home, but the technologies used for delivering learning have changed with the times. In such cases, doubts about the effectiveness of ODL for children have long disappeared.

There are other, less well known, chapters to this history. In France, for example, a state distance learning institution was established during the Second World War to ensure that displaced children continued their school education uninterrupted. Today the National Centre for Distance Education (CNED – Centre National d'Education à Distance) is one of the largest ODL operations in the world. It now caters for adults as well as children and, besides the school curriculum, offers a broad range of vocational and technical subjects and professional courses at all levels (Daniel, 1996).

Other distance education institutions that were originally established to teach children have now, like CNED, added adults to their rolls. Yet others were established specifically to provide school-level courses for adults. In Britain the National Extension College (NEC) was set up in 1963 to offer a 'second chance' to adults who had not completed school successfully. It used the methods that we now call ODL to provide a high-quality alternative to correspondence colleges, after a review by the National Consumers' Association found they gave poor value for money (Jenkins and Perraton, 1980).

NEC soon discovered another market for its courses – schools. One of its earliest projects was a GCE O-level course in physics. Weekly lessons were presented on television, accompanied by a specially designed textbook, a correspondence course and a home experiment kit. The course was intended for adults, but transmission during school hours meant that pupils could view the programmes in class, and a number of schools without specialist physics teachers enrolled groups of pupils for the course (Ingleby, 1967).

Soon many NEC courses were being used to help schools introduce new subjects – for example an O-grade course in Scottish Gaelic commissioned by the Gaelic Society was used by schools in Scotland as well as by adults at home. The high-quality learning materials set new standards for educational texts. Although designed for mature students studying at a distance, NEC's O-level English language course, *A New English Course*, was a best-selling school textbook over several years. Teachers liked the structured and comprehensive approach, and pupils liked independent study. Just as Open University texts have influenced the design of university textbooks, good ODL texts have probably also influenced school textbooks.

Long experience has thus laid the foundations for open learning in the classroom. Over the years school-level ODL has developed its own distinctive flavour and modes of operation. Today the environment is changing rapidly, as new ICT applications help to create new opportunities to learn. Learning in ordinary schools can no longer be constrained within the bounds of a static curriculum or within the four walls of the classroom. It is increasingly open to all, whatever the age. These new opportunities are in line with the three strands of long-established school-level ODL:

● to teach children out-of-school;
● to provide adults with school-level learning;
● to extend the range of learning for pupils in-school.

At this critical moment of change in school, much can be learnt from this little documented but solid tradition and experience.

The context today

The moment is indeed critical. The crux of the issue is that greater demands are being made on school education. So much is said and written about change in education that it is easy to overlook the heart of the matter. To start with, basic education for all is seen as a human right. Despite international effort to provide basic education for every child, there are still more than 110 million children in the world today who do not go to school. Further, it is one of the tasks of education to prepare children to work in the adult world. There is strong pressure on schools to do better – to reform the curriculum so that school graduates are better fitted for employment. There is much debate about how best to achieve these two ends. The potential contribution of distance education as an alternative methodology for curriculum delivery is widely recognized.

But there is a further complicating dimension. The school curriculum can no longer be seen as static. The global store of information and knowledge is increasing faster than ever before. This affects schools, not only because they are responsible for passing on knowledge to children, but also because the demands of employers change fast. It is expected that education will adapt the curriculum to meet demand. It is generally assumed, with some truth, that developments in information and communications technology bear much of the responsibility for this turbulence.

Can the selfsame tools of technology both set the challenge and provide the solution? In all probability, yes. Education ministers everywhere are convinced that they must promote the use of computers in education, not only so that children develop information technology skills, but also to harness the power of new technology applications to enhance the quality of teaching and learning across the curriculum. Many teachers, too, are eager to familiarize themselves with ICT, in some cases even when they have little opportunity to use a computer.

But the case is not yet proven. The ICT revolution has been full of surprises. A few years ago there was no World Wide Web, and the possibilities now at our fingertips were unimaginable. We do not know what new surprises the future will bring. Will online learning ever displace schools? Probably most of us will believe not, indeed hope not. And yet there is a need, indeed a moral imperative, to consider how we can use the resources of the rich world to address the problems of our poorer sisters and brothers.

However, we do not yet know much about how best to use these new possibilities in our schools. Can the new technologies genuinely help to reach that pot of gold of every child achieving his or her full potential at school? Can they help to deliver learning that is flexible and responsive to changing demand? And what of the teachers? How can the new learning technologies best be used to support teachers? Will they displace teachers?

It is too early to answer such questions. Moreover present developments are not only rapid but also multi-faceted and complex – a difficult environment for research and evaluation. But the long experience of school-level distance education could offer some useful lessons. This chapter does not attempt to provide a full account of that experience, as that is available elsewhere (Jenkins and Sadiman, 2000). Instead it touches on some of the key issues that affect the new environment of the 'open classroom'.

Lessons on quality

School-level distance learning can be a quality product. As in any education, there are bad examples, but there are also some successes. We know from these what makes for good practice.

First, effective ODL depends on meticulous learning design, systematic organization and high-quality learning support. These principles apply equally to forms of ODL that use traditional technologies and those that use new ICT.

The starting point for all ODL is the learner. The essence of distance learning is independent study, the guiding principle that each learning system is designed to enable learners to learn effectively. In order to achieve this end, ODL has to be designed carefully. Learning technologies and learning support are systematically combined to create an interactive and flexible learning environment, designed to achieve a specific purpose.

The first step is to consider the learners and their environment. The choice of technology comes afterwards. The range of technologies available for distance education is far greater in some environments than in others. One of the strengths of ODL is its ability to use a wide variety of technologies. One size does not fit all. ODL needs to be designed systematically to maximize the potential for learning of the individual in a specific environment. It is essentially demand-driven, not supply-led.

Good ODL materials are self-instructional. Content is selected and elaborated in a way that is interesting and relevant to the learners. Different presentation formats and media are packaged together to suit different subjects, as in the NEC physics course which used television and experiment kits as well as printed materials. Materials, whatever the medium or technology, are carefully structured, interactive, and provide frequent feedback to facilitate independent learning.

This does not mean that ODL is simply a matter of self-instruction. (Unfortunately, it is often assumed that it is. Learning support is neglected. The result is poor performance, leading to renewed mistrust of the methods.) Good ODL includes systematic support for learning, such as communication and interaction between learners and teachers. A striking acknowledgement of this fact was the decision by the Massachusetts Institute of Technology (MIT) in 2001 to make all its teaching material openly available on the World Wide Web. MIT has not closed down as a result! The material is only part of the process of education.

Teachers thus have a place in all ODL. Moreover – and this surprises many unfamiliar with distance education – in almost all good quality ODL there is some face-to-face contact between teachers and learners. Teachers facilitate learning, organize group interaction, evaluate achievement, and provide feedback. In some subjects and contexts they may be responsible for delivering practical components of the curriculum or for supervising practical work.

One unusual feature of ODL is that the teachers who prepare the learning material and those who interact with the learners are often different. On the one hand this means that the very best teachers can develop the materials. On the other, the teachers who interact with the learners are not responsible for delivering content, although they may elaborate or supplement as necessary. This apparent loss of one of their core responsibilities can lead to teachers feeling threatened. However in practice their role changes to one of facilitating and supporting learning. Less mature learners and those with lower levels of prior learning need more support. This team approach – material developed by the best teachers, class teachers supporting learning – can result in better quality.

Why open the classroom?

There is a clear case on grounds of equity for providing ODL opportunities for people outside the classroom, whether adults or children. But ODL is a demanding method of teaching and learning. What, then, do we know about effectiveness of classroom open learning? The jury is still out on a number of critical issues.

Is it good for children?

The long experience in Australia and similar countries demonstrates that ODL works with children. As we have seen, experience also suggests that older pupils can cope well with learning materials designed for adults. But independent learning requires good motivation. School-age pupils may not be highly motivated, in part because they are young, in part because they are often not learning from personal choice. Younger people also lack experience and skills. The younger the pupils, the less developed is their underlying general competence. Overall, they lack maturity.

Perhaps the experience of using ODL helps young learners to mature. But it is also possible to ask too much of them. We do not know enough about using ODL methods on a large scale for school-age pupils. Until we know more, it is important to create a highly supportive learning environment for any ODL for children.

Does it work for basic education?[2]

All learners who use ODL to study at basic levels, whatever their age, need a high level of support. While children lack the maturity to cope alone, older people often lack self-esteem and confidence. They may also lack the basic skills that make effective distance learning possible. ODL systems can however work for basic education. The New Zealand Correspondence School, for example, has devised a system to teach adult literacy which relies on mentors, trained peers who provide support on a one-to-one basis (Gamlin, 1999).

One effective strategy is to use special learning centres. In Britain, such centres, often in a further education college, sometimes in a library or shopping centre, are places where individuals can learn independently from a wide choice of ODL courses, all available in the centre. Centres offer a quiet place to study, access to equipment and other resources, and a high level of personal support and guidance from a learning facilitator.

At the most basic levels, children and adults need different learning materials. Literacy and numeracy materials need content and examples that engage each learner. Young children like fun, family and fantasy. Adults tend to learn for a purpose, to cope with form filling, income tax or family accounts. There is often a direct link between learning and work. There are differences in culture too. Calculating the odds on the horses is a good starting point for number work for many men in countries where racing is popular, but a non-starter for those from a culture or religion that prohibits gambling. Such issues make the design of ODL for basic education difficult indeed. The open classroom does not have a simple curriculum or a clear-cut shape.

Is it cost-effective?

ODL is often used for school education because it is seen as a cheap alternative to school. But good ODL is not cheap. There is normally a trade-off between quality and cost. In some poor countries where attempts have been made to use ODL to provide alternative secondary schools, it has not been possible to invest enough in materials and learning support. The result has been poor quality, indicated for example by disappointingly low graduation rates. In other cases, where investment has been adequate, the results have been satisfactory as well. In Mexico, for example, there are no traditional secondary schools in some rural areas. Instead, children attend special learning centres and learn through a television-based distance learning system called Telesecundaria. Established in 1968, it now has over 14,000 centres. Costs are much the same per pupil as those of the regular secondary system, but less than it would cost to provide quality schooling for rural children. The system provides these children with access to education of equal quality to children in other areas of the country. This is in line with government commitments to equal opportunities in education for all children.

Classroom open learning, likewise, is not a cheap alternative. But will it give value for money? In the short term, the answer is negative. It will be some while before there are demonstrable returns on investment. Initial costs of integrating learning technologies into school are inevitably heavy. There are four principal elements. First, there are high development costs for materials. Costs vary according to technology choice, but a major and unavoidable cost is the time of teachers and other experts in creating the material. Second, teachers have to learn to use the materials effectively. Then there is the cost of supplying schools with the necessary equipment and establishing and maintaining the communications infrastructure.

Finally, there is the cost of innovation. As each new learning technology emerges, there is need for a period of exploration and experiment.

The open classroom emerges

In one sense, it is too late to ask basic questions about whether we should use the new learning technologies. They are already here and their increasing use is inevitable. The arrival of the Internet is turning school-level ODL inside out. Once ODL was used mainly to reach people outside schools. Now, any pupil can try learning over the Internet. With connectivity, ODL arrives in class. The issue is rather how to use ICT to deliver quality.

Used well, computers can enrich teaching and learning. New learning technologies are more interactive, a feature that impacts on learning in a number of ways. Most pupils enjoy working with computers and find such work highly motivating. Computers in the classroom bring new opportunities both for individualized learning and for collaborative work. They act as a stimulus for the development of a range of personal and interpersonal skills (Socrates, 1998; Jenkins, Lieberg and Stieng, 1998).

To illustrate, here is an example from one Scottish primary school, a pioneer in the use of new learning technologies. In its first year of connection, the whole school took part in a project where pupils used the Internet to present information about themselves to other schools. The dossier they prepared, using hypertext, was comprehensive and highly illustrated, with photographs and drawings of themselves and their community. They wrote a song to go with the project. Every child made a contribution.[3]

In their work on this project, the pupils learnt a great deal. For example, they collected knowledge about their community and its history. But much of their learning was about themselves. The project required team work, with different pupils in different roles. They learnt to work collaboratively, and to take personal responsibility for tasks assigned to them. At computers, they could work at a pace that suited them, thus developing their capacity for self-instruction. Older pupils with better literacy and technical skills helped younger ones. Each found a task that was within his or her capability. For example one pupil with learning difficulties had an excellent visual sense and became the 'official' photographer for the project, wielding the digital camera and then inserting photographs into the presentations. To see their work on the Internet was, for each child, an enormous boost to self-esteem.

ICT brings many other new possibilities for more effective curriculum delivery. For example, multimedia applications model chemical processes, simulate volcanoes, look inside the human body. Such 'virtual reality', on CD ROM or over the Internet, can make learning more effective. Online communication brings a whole range of further possibilities – the immediacy of talking to explorers on their way to the North Pole, e-mail that brings different cultures into school, collecting and analysing fresh data from across the world (see examples in Jenkins *et al,* 1998 and Ehrmann, 1996).

Towards open teaching

How can this whole range of possibilities be exploited effectively in classroom open learning? Pupils using ICT rapidly become relatively autonomous learners, ready to seize and use opportunities offered by the new learning technologies. Teachers as a result have a new role. First, the pedagogic approach is different, centred on facilitating learning. The traditional role of transmitting content takes a back seat. Then, teachers also need a range of specific skills related to learning technologies, comprising competence both in handling the technology and in its use for learning (Jenkins, 1999).

But new skills are not enough. A recent study conducted across several European countries identified the barriers teachers experience in adopting new ICT:

- large psychological barriers to trying out and using ICT;
- underlying pedagogical beliefs that resist change;
- deep-rooted mental structures on the 'art of teaching';
- fear of losing authority and control of the class;
- 'technical paralysis': teachers and schools cannot keep up with changes in ICT;
- blocking factors at institutional and government level;
- under-estimation of effort required of teachers to master new technologies (Dillemans *et al,* 1998: 227–28).

This study underlines the deep and complex change being demanded of teachers. They are expected to use technologies with which they are, in many cases, ill at ease. They are asked to make these changes with no immediate payoff, with no guarantee of success, with no guarantee of continuity, with no additional rewards. Teacher attitudes and teacher development are major factors in the open classroom.

I suggested earlier that the principles of design used in traditional ODL apply to classroom open learning. But in traditional ODL, courses in their entirety are designed in advance, while in classroom open learning the class teacher has to mediate or even create the design – a new and challenging role. A recent European project, MAILBOX, observed teaching and learning in schools in six countries. *The Connected Teacher,* a publication resulting from this project (Jenkins *et al,* 1998), attempted to analyse the implications for teachers and suggested a framework to guide their use of ICT – the four Ps:

- *purposeful:* one or more specific learning objectives underpin any use of learning technology;
- *planned:* the use of technology is part of the lesson plan;

- *possible:* the plan is realistic – avoiding, for example, time-wasting activity;
- *productive:* tangible learning outcomes result.

Two supplementary Ps were also proposed – partnership and professionalism. Partnership relates to the style of work required for in-school ODL. As openness blurs boundaries between disciplines, place, curriculum, so the importance grows of collaborative work between teachers across the school, and with other teachers in other schools. Partnership and collaboration are also important means for disseminating innovation. Teachers need to share their experience, learn from others, reflect and apply. Thus:

> Professionalism relates to the need for responsible and reflective exploration of the new communication possibilities. Ready made answers and guidelines are not available. It is thus a matter for every teacher to design their practice with care, to reflect on its value, and share their experience to the benefit of the professional community.
>
> (Jenkins *et al*, 1998: 40)

Convergence

At this early stage in the development of the open classroom, it would be premature to propose conclusions on the new configurations that will emerge. However, the signs are that a different approach – 'open teaching' – will be necessary. The Internet – the principal driver of openness – has only recently invaded the classroom but already new actors, outside school, can enter the open classroom door, and what goes on inside is potentially open to all. So the open classroom has two dimensions – open from inside to outside, and from outside in. Who can tell what this means? Barriers down between school and home, school and work; age, place and time less of an issue; the end of a set curriculum; the possibility, even, of global learning – the development of the open classroom is likely to be multi-faceted and complex.

It would be nice if we could take just one step at a time. But that is not in the nature of the Internet. Dynamic, anarchic, exciting, it sets the pace and demands that we use it, now, in a variety of learning settings, from traditional to virtual classroom environments.

This chapter has laid emphasis on the importance of personal contact in ODL, between teacher and learners, and among peers. Group learning has an important role in ODL, particularly for basic education for adults. As the open classroom develops, it will be important to retain a balance between centralized provision and personal support for individual learners. There is a risk that the quality of learning may suffer as a result of over-reliance on technology. Today there is growing recognition that the teacher has a role in classroom open learning, but widespread uncertainty concerning the nature of that role.

Open teaching could bring a merger of the methods and institutional structures of ODL and traditional education, creating a single set of methods within a new framework for learning. Both traditional and non-traditional learners will be able to enter the open classroom. If this convergence is indeed possible, the open classroom will be a powerful agent for lifelong learning.

Conclusions

To conclude, a vision of the open classroom: reliable and easy access to school learning for all; consistently high quality learning material and learning support; and a framework to enable learning on the scale necessary for cost effectiveness.

The elements of the open classroom exist. It remains to find good ways to put them in place. There is much to learn from experience. Good wine changes and improves as it gets older. So it is with the techniques we still call ODL. A blend of the best ingredients is maturing well. But we must now use new bottles – the new learning technologies. We have yet to understand fully how this transforms the product.

Notes

1 The term was coined by John Daniel (1996) to describe universities with over 100,000 students. All existing mega-universities happen to be distance learning institutions.
2 See Yates and Bradley (2000) for a full treatment of this issue.
3 See ' Chips with everything', monograph on Richmond Park School published on Socrates Mailbox site, http://tecfa.unige.ch/socrates-mailbox; link to school Web pages from that site.

References

Calderoni, J (1998) *Telesecundaria: Using TV to bring education to rural Mexico*, Education and Technology Technical Notes Series, World Bank, Washington DC

Daniel, J (1996) *Mega-universities and Knowledge Media*, Kogan Page, London

Dillemans, R, Lowyck, J, Van der Perre, G, Claeys, C and Elen, J (1998) *New Technologies for Learning: Contribution of ICT to innovation in education*, Leuven University Press, Leuven, Netherlands

Ehrmann, S (1996) *Adult Learning in a New Technological Era*, OECD, Paris

Gamlin, M (1999) Delivery of basic literacy skills by distance education in New Zealand, *Open Praxis*, **1**, pp 26–30

Ingleby, J (1967) *Physics by Television*, National Extension College, Cambridge

Jenkins, J (1999) *The Impact of ICT on the Role of the Teacher*, paper prepared for Council of Europe

Jenkins, J, Lieberg, S and Stieng, I (1998) *The Connected Teacher*, National Centre for Educational Resources, Oslo

Jenkins, J and Perraton, H (1980) *The Invisible College: NEC 1973–79*, International Extension College, Cambridge

Jenkins, J and Sadiman, A (2000) Open schooling at basic level, in *Basic Education at a Distance*, ed C Yates and J Bradley, pp 205–26, RoutledgeFalmer, London/New York

Socrates (1998) *Socrates Mailbox Project Synthesis Report, August* [Online] http://tecfa.unige.ch/socrates-mailbox

Yates, C and Bradley, J (eds) (2000) *Basic Education at a Distance*, RoutledgeFalmer, London/New York

Young, M, Perraton, H, Jenkins, J and Dodds, T (1991) *Distance Teaching for the Third World: The lion and the clockwork mouse*, 2nd edn, International Extension College, Cambridge

Chapter 2

Living and learning in the information age: from the school to e-school to no school?

Nigel Paine

Introduction

Every nation is striving for a world-class education system. As we move into a new millennium many countries are putting programmes in place that they believe will lead to a fundamental transformation of public education systems and a significant rise in educational standards. They all believe that they have the key to educational improvement. The Australian academic Brian Caldwell has analysed these programmes and clustered them in three parallel tracks. These are 'building systems of self-managing schools', 'an unrelenting focus on learning outcomes' and 'creating schools for the knowledge society'. They are not mutually exclusive. He has identified that some countries have moved faster along one track rather than the other two, but all three are recognized as defining the scope and thrust of the current educational moment (Caldwell, 1998). In this chapter I will focus on track three: developing an education system that locks in with, and prepares people for, the emerging knowledge-based society. There is, however, an underpinning assumption that the other two tracks, school autonomy and a focus on educational outputs, are significant complementary developments that are almost precursors for real progress to be made in the third area.

Context

Here are three recent statements. The first is from the world's largest software company, Microsoft. Microsoft has produced a number of thoughtful papers on a range of key issues including education. In his foreword to Microsoft's white paper on the digital nervous system in education, Bill Gates announced that 'New technologies can offer unparalleled opportunities to enhance the educational environment for students, teachers, and administrators' (Gates, 2000).

Consider that together with a statement by the former British Cabinet Minister Peter Mandelson, who claimed in a 1999 lecture that we had to readjust our vision of the Internet in the light of the digital television revolution. Instead of accepting 20, 30 or even 40 per cent of homes gaining Internet access via a PC, we need to consider the moment – not too far distant – when the analogue television signal is finally switched off. At that point all homes will have either digital televisions or digital set top boxes. Internet access is, potentially, ubiquitous through the television rather than the PC. Every family will be connected. We will be living in a wired world (Mandelson, 1999).

This sentiment complements an interview comment by Sir Peter Bonfield, former Chief Executive of BT, Britain's largest telecommunication company, in the *Financial Times* (London) 25 March 1999, that access to bandwidth would not be an issue in a year's time. In other words anyone who wants to will be able to afford broadband access to the Internet, thus demolishing at a stroke issues about the speed of Internet access and the viability of media content online. Each quotation is potentially a 'he would say that, wouldn't he' statement. Add them together, however, and they point to an inexorable shift in the way we work, play and learn. I will follow through the implications of the second and third quotations and set them in the education context. There is not the slightest chance that the kind of momentous shifts in access to technology that Mandelson and Bonfield predict will leave education unscathed. The American academic Dr Jeff Brand summed this up when he said, 'communications media are so fundamental to a society that when their structure changes, everything is affected' (Brand, 1999).

Indeed for the new economy to work, we need educated adults able to cope with a technological future. School is the best place to introduce these fundamental principles, and the best time to develop the habit and the building block skills for lifelong learning. The inevitable corollary to a global economy is the development of world-class standards. World-class standards demand, almost by definition, world-class education. Everyone will need to be 'highly literate, highly numerate, well-informed, capable of learning constantly, and confident and able to play their part as a citizen of a democratic society' (Barber, 1997).

What Barber omitted to say is that to be literate, numerate and well-informed in the next century must take for granted a high degree of comfort with technology and a ubiquity in its use. Gates, Mandelson and Bonfield, however, are drawing similar underlying conclusions: the summation of the changes happening all around us inevitably is a lifestyle/workstyle change. Technology will impinge not just on the periphery of our lives but the very core of our being. Just as our parents and grandparents in the UK grew accustomed to life with electrical domestic appliances; light and power at the flick of a switch; and clean water on demand; our children will demand the right to access an information utility wherever it suits them to access it. The difference is that it took a generation or more for us to get used to electricity, radio, telephone and television. In the UK, to build a user base of 50 million for the radio took half a century. To have 50 million televisions in use took 37 years. In comparison, the Internet revolution will be upon us in an instant. The 50 million Internet-user target was breached in four years.

Wireless, seamless networking of devices as disparate as mobile phones, PCs, personal organizers and televisions will be the norm, and the expectation will be that this works well and that it happens as if by magic. Access will be everywhere; at home, in the workplace, on holiday, in both public (public sites will vary from Internet cafes to public libraries) and private (home access, subscriber clubs). It will be as 'natural' for them to access information as it is for us to access electricity. If there is a dull inevitability that – for at least a proportion of our consumption – we will buy from the Internet, then it is equally inevitable that we will learn from the Internet.

Ultimately it is very simple: we will be able to directly access and process the information that will enable us to make more intelligent choices about our lives. Scale that up and we will live in a society able to define its place within the new global order. But the underlying corollary to that is that we have to compete and survive in a global economy where our creativity, skills and competencies will define whether our economy wins or loses. Intelligence is the key natural resource of an economy built on knowledge, services and products; and every country, potentially, has that in equal measure. It is the application and development of intelligence that will make the difference. If we fail to make the grade, and success in the first Industrial Revolution does not necessarily define success in the second, the resultant national decline will offer less choice to everyone. For the first time in our history, education moves from the periphery to the cutting edge. This presents a tremendous challenge.

Whither education?

Our school systems, as we currently know them, grew up shoulder to shoulder with the first Industrial Revolution. In other words the first Industrial Revolution generated the wealth to contemplate, speculate upon and ultimately deliver free universal education. It created the need for a disciplined, ordered and largely unskilled or semi-skilled workforce where brawn was more important than brain. That industrial system demanded basic levels of literacy and numeracy, and disciplined behaviour. This began to define what was taught in the new school system. Only a tiny elite was educated past elementary school level. And remember that we have had barely 100 years of universal education.

In the UK only 3 per cent of the age cohort went on to a university education at the turn of the 20th century. That remained more or less unchanged until the 1960s where it edged up to 6–7 per cent. It is now 30 per cent in England and Wales and 35 per cent in Scotland. In the United States it is 56 per cent, in Russia it is over 70 per cent. Developed societies have not yet established the natural level of higher education penetration.

The new economy drives forward the need to rebuild our fundamental concepts of education. We always need to maintain the synchronicity between the nature of learning we feel it is appropriate to build in our society, and the aptitude and skills we require in the population to generate wealth for the future. In a fascinating book, Mark Ward (2000) applies the logic of biological development to technological development, and draws attention to the symbiosis between social development and education systems. Ward claims that 'life is a self-sustaining system. Once life gets started it is tenacious and tries to build a world fit for itself . . . living things work to keep themselves going but, at the same time they are unconsciously altering the world to make it more habitable for them.'

The world impacts upon, and forces change in, our systems of education, and our systems of education produce individuals capable of developing specific kinds of world. It is a complex and interrelated symbiosis.

Future models for education

Let us take a radical view. The current dominant features of the high school – sealed off from the world around it; focused only on children from the ages of 11 to 18; and structured around age cohorts moving though vast amounts of predefined curriculum at lock-step pace – are not going to deliver adults with the intellectual resilience and creativity to work successfully in the new economy. They will be unprepared to learn throughout life or even discouraged from doing so. They are unlikely to become enthusiastic independent learners.

What we need is a new paradigm that takes us away from the concept of a school, to an outward-looking, community-facing, lifelong learning centre. This is open, if not all night, most of the night as well as on most days in the year.

These centres may, perhaps, begin with a majority of young people during the day and end with a majority of adults in the evening. They will act as hubs for face-to-face encounters and the base for access to information and online learning. It is likely that these centres will be places saturated in technology, where children learn not so much in classes as in project teams centred upon learning stations. These are places where teachers intervene to structure, support, enable, guide and inspire. Their aim is to enable young people to work it out for themselves, while adult learners will expect intervention when they ask rather than as the basic mode of learning delivery.

This may be the kind of working environment where teachers work three days equivalent with young people, two days equivalent with adults. A teacher may spend at least one working day equivalent online, supporting those unable or unwilling to attend face-to-face. It may even be a place for the portfolio career, where the teacher is self-employed, offering so many days to the centre and running an independent business or working for someone else for the rest of the week.

Here, a young person registering in such a centre will begin a lifelong contract where his or her learning is not time delimited, but grows richer and deeper throughout life. In the same way that a parent's role is ultimately to prepare a child for independent living, the schools' role should be, ultimately, to prepare a student for independent learning.

Going global

Even more than before, the global economy creates a need to belong. As our connections to the rest of the world extend from the economic to the social, the links become stronger, and the world shrinks in our perception. Somewhat ironically, at that point we need to belong to our local community and accept common value systems that allow us to live and work together.

The school needs to redefine itself as the hub of a learning community, not just a learning community for those students who spend part of their lives going through the school system, but a learning community within the wider community, that is 'leaky'. In other words, it must communicate with the whole community and be seen as a community resource and community centre of expertise. The *Financial Times* of 16 August 1999 published comments suggesting that by 2050, 40 per cent of the working population in Britain will be self-employed. Bill Gates has stated that he feels the figure in the United States will be at or above 50 per cent. It is, therefore, possible to surmise that at least some of the professionals working in schools will be self-employed. The knowledge expert will be a valuable commodity, able to teach for part of his or her career and undertake other paid work, perhaps in separate learning institutions or in companies. We may not be able to afford the luxury of dedicating such an expert to one institution for the whole of his or her career.

What will learning look like?

Two 12-year-olds were asked to give their view of learning in the next century. (North-Eastern Education Consortium USA Web site http://21stcenturyschools. northcarolina.edu/center/). Their own words are extremely illuminating:

Most work in schools will be done as projects. Kids will have to be good problem solvers, very responsible and make lots of decisions themselves, be superb communicators but good thinkers.

Teachers will have to become coaches and helpers and learn together with the kids. Kids will be able to learn any time. . . school hours will be more flexible.

The factors that the 12-year-olds have isolated are very important. They include:

● Project work: the ability to apply learning and focus on a particular issue or theme. Project work is often extended, drawing on information and resources from various places, which allows conclusions to be reached. It is often collaborative.
● Problem solving at the heart of the curriculum: looking for solutions, testing available evidence, and drawing conclusions. These are core skills for the world of work.
● Autonomous learning: allowing students to develop independent learning skills and helping them see themselves as capable learners. Emphasis has to be on the process of learning as well as the end product.
● Communication of knowledge will be as important as the knowledge itself: helping develop excellent communication and presentation skills in different media.
● A changing role for the teacher as facilitator and coach: shifting the teacher's role so that he or she becomes the organizer of the learning environment. He or she will be the person who shapes and defines the knowledge base, but not necessarily the person who delivers the learning. The teacher becomes an enabler and support person who generates a safe but demanding environment.
● Lifelong learning will be critical for teachers as well as young people: teachers will not be able to escape the demands of the changing world outside the classroom. In other words teachers will increasingly have to be learners too, able to adapt both process and content to their changing world.
● Anytime, anywhere learning: the school as a hub able to connect into homes and the community. Students will all need and demand the skills of online learners for at least part of the time. Students and teachers will be connected permanently into their learning resource base, and will be able to access 'the school' at any time from any computer. Parents will have the opportunity to be more involved and actually see what their child is learning and creating, as well as what the school has achieved, by 'virtually' entering the school. There will be no limits to learning. The relationship between home, school and work will inevitably blur.

Unwittingly, the young people quoted earlier have pulled together an agenda which defines the parameters for school evolution.

The radical continuum

Don Tapscott (1997) tried to track the impact of technology on schools in the diagram in Figure 2.1. He showed that to get to transformation rather than mere efficiency gains was a complex, detailed and radical process. It involved changing the way courses and curriculum are designed, changing the way the school relates to the world, and making the individual student more efficient and effective as a learner. Only at the most radical level, where we have moved, technologically, from the use of stand-alone multimedia computers, past local networks, and on to fully embrace the Internet as a source for information, communication and delivery, will we be building learning communities able to complement and support the information age. Most schools and most countries are still at stage one. What is misleading in the diagram, however, is its implication that there is a natural, linear progression which moves seamlessly from one level to another. In reality, each has to be tackled simultaneously. We have never seen such radical change necessary in such a short period of time, nor such a challenge to fundamental assumptions about the nature of learning and the role of the school in our society.

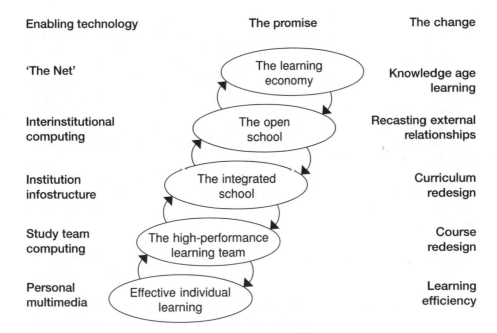

Figure 2.1   *The transformation of formal education*

The broader role of the school

Charles Handy spelt out the new relationship between education and work. The old model, 'well prepared but empty mind', where you learnt at length how to actually do useful, productive things once you started work, fitted both the vocational apprentice and the aspiring manager. Time was available in bucketloads to prepare the young person for an entire career of applying those skills. After five or six or more years, training was complete for life. Handy contrasts the demands of employers now as:

> They expect you to come fully equipped. And fully equipped means not only having these basic skills and 'A' level and maybe degrees even, but all kinds of other qualities. They want you to be self-confident. They want you to be self-disciplined. They want you to be trustworthy. They want you to be honest and open. They want you to be good with people. They want you to be courageous and imaginative. They want you to be able to take risks and to learn when the risks go wrong. These are things that are hard to teach in a classroom.
>
> (Handy, 1995)

We have entered a period of dislocation where what schools produce is only part of what is necessary to survive in the world outside. If Handy's list is 'hard' to teach in a classroom, it is 'easy' to teach as part of the ethos in a school. Handy is essentially referring to emotional intelligence (Goleman, 1996). This is something that can be taught and is appropriate for schools to teach; it should be a critical part of the new school and the new curriculum.

In a recent publication James Tooley (1999) lists the seven fundamental characteristics that differentiate effective schools from the rest. He defined these by visiting 10 outstanding specialist schools in England. He concluded that what they did was entirely replicable in any school, but not divisible. In other words, to be highly effective you needed all seven characteristics, not five or six. Tooley was drawing upon Stephen Covey's 1990 book *The Seven Habits of Highly Effective People*. His conclusions were:

1. **Focus on school ethos** with high and consistent expectations of teachers and staff, strong pastoral care and a disciplined environment obtained through student commitment.
2. **Strong leadership and management** with a clear mission and a focus on leadership in learning that generates both teachers' and students' commitment.
3. **Focus on students' learning** with diagnostic information, target setting, regular assessment and feedback, extensive complementary use of ICT and attention to all students' learning needs.
4. **Innovation to promote school goals** in areas such as teaching and learning, administration, relationships with parents, improving schools' finances.

5. **Quality control** manifested in external awards, teacher appraisal, setting realistic targets and setting a quality ethos.
6. **Organizations and structures in empathy with ethos** so that teacher effectiveness is ensured, a minimum disruption to learning, and good parental communication are maintained.
7. **Parental and community links** with regular reports to parents, home, school technology links and links with primary schools and local employers; as well as making school resources available to the community.

Tooley is implying that much of the context for successful learning happens outside the classroom, just as many of Handy's 'fully equipped' characteristics are based on an approach to teaching and learning and the nature of the whole school environment, rather than simply changing the teaching. Both authors point to the significance of the school as a community and microcosm of society rather than as a grade factory. Achievement in the classroom is both the baseline of excellence on which great schools build, and the natural corollary for schools demonstrating the seven habits above.

The 10 features of openness

There are 10 ways in which schools can begin to make themselves ready for the demands that the knowledge age will make. Running through all 10 is the effective, extensive and transformative use of information and communications technology – not as a way of passing information round a building faster, but as the critical link between students, teachers, parents, other experts and the world outside. As schools become physically more fortress-like, the demand to reach out will be sublimated into the technology. The school will have to choose whether to exploit the infrastructure that exists or contain it; allow the transformation or work against it; deliver an exciting and highly resource-intensive learning environment or stick to the dull classroom model. It is the choice of an autonomous institution. However, what that means in reality is that the choice exists to postpone, but not really to prevent.

The first openness quotient is to *be international in outlook*: whether the school chooses to use technology to form serious learning partnerships with other schools in the same country or all over the world, to encourage the 'what if' experience of sharing other people's lives, and the free exchange of information and ideas. This applies equally to teachers and students. A teacher who is part of an international network of teachers who share particular ideas, projects or interests, is more likely to want his or her students to do the same. No young person should leave school without the virtual experience of life in a different culture or having shared learning across normal geographical boundaries. No young adult should leave university without having actively collaborated with students from a different culture.

All schools should aim explicitly to *build independent learning skills* in everyone they teach. Every student should be a conscious learner, confident in his or her learning ability.

Schools should *build a network of experts* who are prepared to devote a small amount of time to answering questions and offering a new perspective from the world outside the school. This could be from inside a university or business or government, but it should smack of the real world. Only extensive use of e-mail and bulletin boards can deliver this. We need wired schools plugged into the wired world.

Schools should *consciously build learning communities*, where learning is part of the ethos and teams of interest groups are developed. Like a miniature paradigm of the Internet itself, schools will build Intranets covering each and every area of interest in and around the curriculum. These will change and evolve as communities develop and grow.

Schools should share: publish as much as possible, be willing to discuss openly what they do, and take the idea of their community role seriously. They should *be open to parents and accept parents into the learning community* of the Intranet.

Part of the learning programme should involve the opportunity to *develop integrated projects* that require input from groups across the whole school working in mixed age cohorts.

Emotional intelligence should be part of the curriculum. All of Charles Handy's 'fully equipped' requirements should act as the checklist for inclusion: self-confidence; self-discipline; trustworthiness; honesty and openness; being good with people; being courageous and imaginative; taking risks and learning when the risks go wrong.

Schools should be *ambitious for their students.* The concept of maintenance of standards, and a belief that we are doing quite well, should be banished forever. Whatever is achieved can be improved upon. Finally, schools should have an agenda of constant improvement.

Towards the open school

The concept of openness cannot be disengaged from the concept of building the learning environment. For the first time it is now possible to deliver openness through the nature of the learning environment. It is also possible to offer a learning experience that encapsulates more than one mode of learning and multiple approaches to knowledge acquisition. One size never did fit all. It simply guaranteed that a majority would never fit and would therefore fail.

It is clear that this chapter argues that we should do things differently. The models of innovation that have been discussed have hardly been tested on a broad scale. We need new paradigms that stretch and focus new ideas. But we also need to do different things, and perhaps this means, ultimately, that we ought to challenge the concept of the school as a self-contained unit and look at the role of the school as a community resource that leaks into the adult environment and the world of work. Such a school not only attempts to meet the educational and intellectual needs of the community, but has a stake in knitting together the social fabric as well. It is a holistic view of school in a holistic view of the community.

Thomas E Stewart's recent book *Intellectual Capital* (1998) opens with the sentence, 'Information and knowledge are the thermonuclear competitive weapons of our time.' Stewart means 'thermonuclear' in both senses: critical and destructive. The point he makes forcefully is that the knowledge economy is here, and to survive we have be make step changes in the way we do business and educate our citizens or face the horrible economic consequences of failing in the 21st century. In the words of John Chamber, the CEO of CISCO systems, 'Are you ready?'

References

Barber, M (1997) *The Learning Game*, Orion, London

Brand, J (1999) Educating children for the global information society, *Values*, Summer, pp 7–9

Caldwell, B (1998) *Beyond the Self-managed School*, RoutledgeFalmer, London

Covey, S (1990) *The Seven Habits of Highly Effective People*, Simon and Schuster, New York

Gates, B (2000) Digital nervous systems, in *Business @ the Speed of Thought*, Penguin, Harmondsworth

Goleman, D (1996) *Emotional Intelligence*, Bloomsbury, London

Handy, C (1995) *The Empty Raincoat*, Random House, New York

Mandelson, P (1999) *Digital Future*, Independent Broadcasting Authority Annual Lecture, London

Stewart, T (1998) *Intellectual Capital: The new wealth of organisations*, Nicholas Brealey, London

Tapscott, D (1997) The digital economy, chapter 8 in *Learning in the Digital Economy*, McGraw-Hill, New York

Tooley, J (1999) *The Seven Habits of Effective Schools*, Technology Colleges Trust, London

Ward, M (2000) *Virtual Organisms*, Pan, London

Chapter 3

The economics of open and distance learning in primary and secondary schools

Marianne Bakia

Introduction

Because educational resources consume a significant percentage of public resources, and because educational budgets are never infinite, determining the most efficient means of accomplishing goals can have significant impact within and beyond educational systems (Tsang, 1997). Cost analysis is an important tool for identifying opportunities for increasing institutional or system efficiency. This chapter briefly presents cost analysis terminology and procedures, followed by a review of what is known about the economics of open learning in primary and secondary schooling. Because the choice of media and delivery systems in open learning programmes will impact on the cost of the programme, these are then discussed in greater detail. Here the focus is most intensely on the use of computers, because the understanding of the economics of computer use in classrooms is not commensurate with the degree of use around the world.

A brief introduction to cost analysis

Cost analysis relies on the systematic compilation of various types of programme variables and related costs. Number of courses, number of students a year, and life of course are essential details. All costs should be identified through a systematic process that values all resources necessary to replicate a programme (see Levin and McEwan, 2001). Even donated resources are included in the cost analysis since these have some value, regardless of who paid (or didn't). Costs are usually categorized as either capital or recurrent, and fixed or variable. Capital costs are goods with an expected life of more than one year. Capital costs are 'annualized' to determine the cost per year (Jamison, Klees and Wells, 1978: 32). Capital cost, C, is multiplied by an annualization factor determined by the following function:

$$a(r, n) = [r(1 + r)n]/[1 + r]n - 1]$$

where $a(r, n)$ is the annualization factor
r is the social discount rate
n is the lifetime of capital.

Recurrent costs refer to goods and services consumed immediately (labour, electricity, etc). Fixed costs are not dependent on the scale of the programme, and variable costs are directly related to the number of students served.

The relationship among types of costs – capital or recurrent, fixed or variable – and the allocation of costs across either functions (eg curriculum development, instruction, administration and assessment) or expenditure category, eg salary, rent, supplies (Rumble, 1997), are referred to as a 'cost structure'. Economists compare cost structures to examine total costs, per unit costs, or impact on costs if a programme is expanded or contracted. Total cost, average cost and marginal cost are typically reported.

Cost analysis has some practical difficulties. Information on the full range of costs for a programme is rarely available. While some data about prices can be found in budgets and expense documents, planning, administrative and capital costs are frequently overlooked or difficult to determine. Goods and services that are donated by sectors of government or the private sector may also be difficult to determine. The method of incorporating capital and investment costs is not always well understood, creating errors in the analysis. Finally, comparisons of projects across countries carry all of the inherent difficulties of currency conversion and generalizability. Nevertheless, better empirical information on the costs of educational technology projects, particularly those in developing countries, is essential.

Cost structure of open learning projects

The structure of costs has important implications for programme planners and managers. Projects with low capital costs and relatively high recurrent costs might be easily started but difficult to maintain. A low proportion of costs that vary with enrolment will probably be more easily scaled than a high proportion. In traditional, classroom-based education, costs tend to increase in a stepped function with the number of students. This is because the bulk of costs (teachers' salaries and classroom space) tend to vary according to enrolment.

Many open learning projects, however, design and produce specialized materials. These materials are typically only relevant to individual projects and are rarely developed at a national or international scale, as mainstream textbooks are. Therefore, individual open learning projects must budget differently for open materials than they would for textbooks traditionally.

Traditional textbooks can often be 'costed' with a simple algorithm multiplying market price by number of units, which is based on enrolment. The market price is set by the publisher on the basis of fixed and variable production costs. Since open learning programmes must design and produce materials there is usually a wide variety of associated costs, both fixed and variable. The design of the materials is usually both fixed and substantial. When materials can be used to substitute for teacher time and/or classroom space, the fixed costs of material design substitute for the variable costs of teacher salary and rent. In projects that fit this characterization, per student costs will decline as the project is expanded, up to a particular point, and thus demonstrate economies of scale. In practice many open learning projects have high variable costs as well. This is typically caused by higher levels of student support (the number of instructors or tutor hours devoted to individual students), which are often viewed as a necessary component of quality education. This is particularly true at the primary and secondary levels because students often require physical proximity to a teacher and regular, timely feedback. In these cases open learning might cost as much as or more than traditional education, but the additional costs may be justified if either completion rates or average learning outcomes are improved beyond what could be expected in a more traditional arrangement.

Impact of media and technology selection on costs

Media and technology costs vary considerably depending on production and implementation characteristics. For example, a book may cost $5.00 or $200. The same book can be used differently in classrooms, and the design of particular books can facilitate types of use. For this reason, precise costs of media and technology have only modest utility conceptually or practically without their implementation characteristics. What is more useful is an understanding of 'cost drivers' – predictable factors that will typically propel the costs up or down. Simplified examples of cost drivers for book production include production quality (paper quality and number of colours), length of book, and number of books to be produced. The discussion below focuses on the general cost structures and relationships of costs across media and technologies, as reported in several volumes (see for instance Bates, 1995; Daniel, 1996; and Rumble, 1997). After a brief discussion of text, audio, and video costs, computing costs are considered in some detail.

Text

Text is generally considered the cheapest of media to deliver (Bates, 1995). These materials typically have a significant text-based component that may be delivered either via printed books or more recently, across the Internet either in e-mail or by the World Wide Web. The design of the materials is a fixed cost, independent of enrolment. On the Internet, most costs of production and distribution are also fixed independently of enrolment. Production and distribution of print materials, however, usually vary according to enrolment. In a tightly controlled study, Inglis compared the direct costs of print delivery with online delivery on a per course basis. 'The results of the comparison indicate that online delivery was less economical, when measured on a cost per student basis, than print-based delivery for all intake levels,' in Australia (Inglis, 1999: 231). The difference was caused mainly by two factors: ISP charges added about $30 per student, and written communication was assumed to take twice as long as spoken communication, and so an additional $23 per student was added for individual academic and administrative support. These comparisons were based on print documents of 200 pages. Doubling the print component adds shipping costs and narrows the cost gap between distribution methods.

Audio

The technology used to deliver audio sharply influences the cost structure. There are three dominant methods for transmitting audio for distance education: cassette, broadcast or telecommunications.[1] Choosing among these alternatives should be based on several factors, and one of the most important is number of enrolled students at a given time, in addition to other pedagogical and logistical concerns. For instance, use of an audio cassette may have educational benefit because a teacher or student has great control over the medium. Audio can be stopped, started or repeated. These actions are not possible with radio transmissions if the broadcast is not recorded onto tape. Telecommunications technologies also often allow two-way audio. They therefore are synchronous and allow for more immediate feedback than the other two alternatives.

Video

Much of what was said about the costs of audio is also true for video. Cassette, broadcast technologies, video conferencing, and more recently computing technologies such as CD ROM and the Internet principally transmit video. Videos distributed by CD ROM and the Internet are discussed in the computing section below.

Probably no other teaching medium varies so much in its costs, in almost every facet, but especially in production of learning materials and distribution. While simple lectures are the easiest (and cheapest) to produce, these are often the most limited pedagogically and do not take full advantage of the medium. In areas where television is familiar, students may have expectations about production quality and may dismiss productions that are not up to par.

Use of television implies one-way, broadcast communication. Educational television projects were studied considerably up to the mid-1970s. Telesecundaria in Mexico is an example of a modern use of television in primary and secondary classrooms. Telesecundaria is a government-sponsored programme that tries to compensate for the lack of experienced maths and science teachers throughout Mexico (Calderoni, 1998). Today, television is viewed as a costly medium that is generally most appropriate where television infrastructures exist and there are large numbers of students enrolled. Television transmission costs are reported to be much higher than those of radio transmission, although this is dependent on geographic coverage and number of broadcast hours (Rumble, 1997: 105), and production costs of audio-visual materials are typically higher than the transmission and reception costs, especially when an existing broadcasting network is available. Overall, television appears to be 3 to 10 times more costly than radio (UNESCO, 1982; Bates, 1995).

Economies to scale are most apparent in the broadcasting technologies of radio and television, and with these technologies the marginal cost of an additional student tends to be very low. Orivel (1987) reports that there are two essential conditions for lower costs in radio-based courses.[2] First, staff costs must be lower. Second, sufficient numbers of students must be enrolled to benefit from economies of scale. One common use of radio in primary and secondary education is interactive radio instruction (IRI). IRI projects 'are front-loaded – that is, they have higher initial fixed costs associated with creating management and training systems, and producing audio and print programmes, when compared to conventional systems. At the same time, they have far lower recurrent costs associated with permanent staff, dissemination, training and maintenance' (Bosch, 1997: 4).

Computing

Computers challenge many of the existing constructs used to classify media because of their tremendous flexibility compared with other technologies and the ensuing range of educational applications they can support. Computer-based applications can include any media and multimedia; provide a vast store of information, particularly through CD ROMs and the Internet; facilitate productive activities including word-processing and calculation; and support asynchronous or synchronous communication. Because computer use in education is evolving and relatively new, analysts are always aiming at a moving target, and even precise estimates of the costs of computer use are unlikely to be valid and reliable across projects and across time. Media selection, production quality, intensity of use, implementation scale and staff time all play a major role in determining total and student costs. Schools today often take for granted print resources, blackboards and other technologies, which have collectively had dramatic impact on pedagogical practice and curricular content in classrooms around the world. However, until computer applications are as thoroughly accommodated and integrated, computers are likely to add to the costs of schooling and may not have any immediate impact on teaching and learning.

Estimating the total costs of computer projects

Total cost of ownership (TCO) is a concept used among American businesses today to estimate what a computer is likely to cost over the life of the investment, and it has also been applied to technology projects in education.[3] Components of a computer project for education will inevitably include hardware, off the shelf and/or specially developed software, Internet connectivity and maintenance costs. Each of these is discussed individually below.

Hardware

Hardware costs typically include computers for students, teachers and/or administrators; printers, CD ROMs and scanners. Issues that affect the exact cost of hardware include functionality of hardware, total number of computers, and the configuration of computers.

The functionality of a computer – processor speed, hard drive space and memory – affects its unit cost. Age indirectly affects costs because older computers often have lower functionality. The kinds of computers that are necessary for a given project depend on the type and intensity of use. High-powered computers cost more, although high-powered computers are not always necessary. In fact, the typical use of computers in K–12 (elementary and secondary) schools does not require state of the art hardware. Although the computers being purchased today for $1,500 may be more powerful than the computers purchased five years ago for $1,500, off-the-shelf software applications often require newer hardware without providing measured educational improvements. Two alternatives to this dilemma are emerging, although neither has been widely tested: software that takes advantage of lower-grade computers, and 'networked computers'. One programme, called New Deal Software[4] has developed software that reportedly delivers the functionality of newer software on 'legacy' computers – computers that have been used and then donated – thereby sidestepping the need to upgrade hardware.

Others are focusing on developing lower cost hardware that needs to be upgraded less frequently, as in the case of network computers (NCs, also known as thin clients and dummy terminals). Network computers do not have hard drives, so are unable to store data or applications on the computer. Instead, NC users access these through their local server or, in some cases, the Internet. NCs have three major advantages:

- they cost less than personal computers;
- they require very little maintenance or technical support, since they are much simpler machines;
- they do not need to be discarded and replaced by newer, more powerful computers every few years. Instead, upgrades are simply provided to the server.

There are three main drawbacks to network computers:

- there is need for more technically proficient network administrators, although fewer network administrators may be needed overall;
- processing speeds of terminals are greatly reduced when network traffic is heavy, as is likely to be the case when a class goes to the lab for an organized computer session;
- should the server go down, all computers connected to the server lose almost all functionality, rather than just networked services.

The impact of NCs on project costs is not yet well documented, although several projects are underway. A South African distance education consortium has started using Sun NCs for its computer centres, and Sun is also working with a number of school districts in the United States to pilot their NC systems.

Number of computers

The total number of computers purchased also influences the magnitude of total project costs, and the largest proportion of hardware costs typically goes to student computers. Therefore, student-computer ratios will often drive the total and per student cost of hardware. There are few guidelines available to help determine optimal computer–student ratios. A general tendency has been 'the more the better.' Administrators can estimate the likely need for computers by assessing what students will do with computers, how long it will take them to do it, whether students will work alone or in groups, and the number of hours that computers will be available in a school day or week. Where only a few computers are to be deployed in a school, administrators and the library are generally the first recipients. Where these few computers are used for instructional purposes, they are generally used as presentational aids.

In addition to the specific type and number of computers, how computers are configured will impact on cost. The choice is typically between a centralized 'laboratory' model and the more diffuse 'classroom' model. Computer labs typically have 10–50 terminals. They are well suited to centralized instruction, maintenance and security. It has been argued that a centralized model does not encourage curricular integration among classroom teachers and so many valuable uses are lost. McKinsey & Co (1995) found that a classroom model with a computer for every five students and a high-speed T-1 connection would cost about four times as much as a computer lab model in up-front investments and a little more than three times the per student recurrent cost.

Beware of donations

It is important to note that donated computers are not free. Donations are likely to generate expenses, although very little has been documented in this area. Many donated computers are likely to require memory and hard drive upgrades to run newer software. Such upgrades can be expected to cost $50–$500 per computer. Further, at least one country in Africa has charged as much as $200 per donated computer for import duties.

Software and content

The intended uses of the computer will also dramatically impact software costs. A library of software resources can allow teachers greater flexibility in their use of technology. But hosting a wide range of software applications can increase not just the amount spent on software, but the amount needed for training and support as well. At one end of the spectrum, 'freeware' (for generic applications) exists. Much of it can be found on the Internet at little direct cost to potential users (except telephone charges for downloading material as they may apply in specific countries). At the other end, there is custom-made and/or specialized software. Specialized software, such as that for scientific purposes, is typically very expensive, with some packages costing thousands of dollars. Similarly, software in languages other than English is more difficult to obtain. Countries interested in using computers in other languages may face linguistic hurdles, and thus incur additional costs for translation and new programming. Economies of scale can be realized by organizing the storage of CD ROMs and other resources in a central place, such as a library, for use by many classrooms or sometimes across schools.

In the United States, experts have recommended that school systems allocate approximately $100 per student for software (President's Committee of Advisors on Science and Technology, 1997). Schools typically fall well short of this figure. Quality Education Data report that the average school in the United States spent about $11 per student on instructional software in the 1998–99 school year. Other research in the United States suggests that 10 per cent or less of a school's technology budget is typically spent on software (Melmed et al, 1995; International Data Corporation: www.apple.com/education/k12/leadership/LSWTF/IDC1. html). Costs in developing countries for software also appear to fall within this lower range.

Relatively simple uses of computers for text, as in the discussion of text above, are likely to be less expensive than more robust uses. Very little is known about the costs of developing computer content for primary and secondary schools.

Individual teachers may devote their personal time to developing materials for their classrooms. There is also a 'virtual high school' model evolving in the United States. The Concord Consortium runs one of the largest programmes, which acts like a cooperative. Schools pay annual fees, and teachers from participating schools agree to offer content. Although there are reports that this type of practice is widespread and growing (Lizardi, 2002), studies of the costs of these programmes have not been published widely. In fact, there have been very few studies of computer-based material development of any sort at the primary and secondary levels.

Lessons emerging at the tertiary level appear likely to hold true in primary and secondary education as well. Whalen and Wright (1999) attempted to compare three Web-based delivery platforms (two asynchronous, one synchronous) with classroom instruction. Synchronous and asynchronous Web-based courses and classroom instruction all demonstrated different cost structures. Asynchronous Web-based courses had considerably higher fixed costs than either synchronous Web-based or classroom courses. Course development costs for asynchronous Web-based instruction were higher than course development costs for classroom-based teaching in all three instances. In the synchronous Web-based course, however, course development costs were actually only 37 per cent of the classroom costs.

The amount of multimedia used in these courses was the primary determinant of development costs. The only course using video (and only five minutes of it) had the highest development costs of all. 'The synchronous course, however, required far less development time, primarily due to less use of multimedia' (Whalen and Wright, 1999: 137). In addition to development time, estimated duration of the course also dramatically influenced the findings of the study. A two- or four-hour Web-based 'course' was considered equivalent to 12 hours of classroom instruction. Further, it was company policy to pay students for two complete days at seven hours a day. Thus, classroom instruction was saddled with a cost of $614 per student, compared with just $110 or $176 for Web-based instruction. This accounts for a significant portion of the 'savings per student over classroom delivery'. And so, assuming 200 students a year over five years, Web-based courses were found to be cheaper than classroom instruction by between 44 per cent and 77 per cent.

Unfortunately, the reliability of the study is in question, because many variables were left uncontrolled. Entirely separate development teams worked on each of three different courses. No explanation is offered for why a synchronous course takes four hours but the three asynchronous courses take two hours; nor is it entirely evident that these two- and four-hour courses would be equivalent to a two-day training seminar, as the authors assume. As a result, there may be a confounding of subject matter, development team, platform and type of media use. In addition, many costs were also left uncounted. Facilities, operating costs and other indirect expenses for classroom-based teaching are assumed to equal the tuition charged, yet no facilities or indirect costs are calculated for the Web-based platforms, including the computers students use to receive instruction. No cost is assigned to the computers used by students because all employees already have computers at their desks. Nor are any delivery costs attributed to Web-based instruction: no costs for Internet connectivity or delivery of physical materials.

Despite these limitations there is the hint, at least, that synchronous communications have lower fixed costs and higher variable costs than asynchronous communication. This study also reinforces findings from earlier studies that video is an expensive medium, and more intensive uses of video cause project costs to escalate.

There is not yet enough cost information about computer use for text, audio or video, to compare computer and Internet delivery with other technologies. Without providing any evidence, Cukier asserts: 'Once a network is in place and terminal equipment established, some of the new telelearning technologies, such as computer conferencing, can have quite low fixed costs and quite high variable costs. Others, such as networked multimedia, can have a more equal mix of fixed and variable costs' (Cukier, 1997: 140). While this is the hope, it is yet to be determined if it is in fact true.

Connectivity

All projects include funds to connect computers within a school and to connect computers across schools through the Internet. The costs of connectivity depend heavily on three factors: the cost to prepare a building for connectivity, the costs of equipment and installation, and recurrent connectivity charges. Budgeters and planners must also keep in mind the need for network software. Although smaller, administrative software costs are not negligible.

Preparing a school for connectivity will often require renovations within a building. A building must have sufficient electrical capacity, from available power to number of outlets, adequate temperature control and ventilation, and security. 'Several studies [in the United States] have projected the cost of building local area networks and wiring classrooms to the Internet to be roughly about $500 per student per year. However, many factors, including the age of physical plant and previous technology investments, [school size and computer student ratio] will determine the precise figure' (*Taking TCO to the Classroom*, available at www.cosn. org/tco). These costs can often be reduced if they are considered when new buildings are being constructed. There is also a wide range of wireless solutions emerging, which could further reduce the burden of some wiring costs.

Equipment costs associated with connectivity depend heavily on the type of connectivity made available to schools. Low-bandwidth connections are generally less expensive but by definition reduce the capacity of the network and how it can be used. Downloading materials in a slow network can be very costly in staff time. The California Department of Education has produced a document to help planners determine the level and costs of connectivity called 'Going Beyond your Local Area Network' which is available at http://www.cde.ca.gov/ftabranch/retdiv/k12/ISDN.html.

Telephone companies charge for the use of a telephone line in many countries, even for a local call. Thus schools will be paying two different types of charges: one for the use of a telephone line and another for Internet service provision. Where telecommunications are still operated by monopolies, these prices can be quite steep. The additional cost of the telephone line can dramatically influence total costs. For instance, in Turkey, a single, dedicated telephone line per school is likely to cost $80 per month, resulting in an estimated total cost of $2,400,000 per year (or 4 per cent of total annualized project costs). The World Links Project in Ghana reports that schools are paying an average of about $86 a month per school in telephone dial-up charges for the Internet, in addition to an Internet subscription fee of $100 per school. Planners in contexts such as these must think carefully about how many telephone lines per school are needed, and balance cost and performance issues.

Strategies to provide low-cost Internet access are emerging. Some costs may be mitigated, at least in the short term, during the bidding process. For instance, firms supply free Internet service for one year as part of an arrangement in Turkey. Further, the major investment necessary for access – country gateways and university nodes – already exists in most countries.

Wireless is also emerging as a viable solution. Wireless systems can be terrestrial, when radio frequencies are used, or satellite-based. High-speed data links can cost less than $2,000 for a simple point-to-point connection over a mile or two, and these links can cost less for lower bandwidth (IDRC, 1999). Cost components of a wireless system include capital costs, recurring costs, and usage costs. IDRC offers the following checklist to 'ensure the success of a project including wireless':

- How much traffic needs to be transported?
- How reliable does the link have to be?
- Are there any other potential users of the system in the area that can help defray the set-up or operating costs?
- What are the characteristics of the terrain where the equipment is to be used?
- What is the required distance of the link?
- Is a licence required?

Support and maintenance

Once computers are installed in schools, users will need regular support. Also, hardware and software will require regular maintenance. The number of support staff required depends on several factors, including the number of computers, the number of software applications, and the ability of users. Schools and ministries have often been innovative in the way they provide support and maintenance. In Chile, an engineering school faculty from a nearby university largely provided technical support. Students and their parents also have a role to play in maintaining equipment. For instance, the role of the PTA (Parent Teacher Association) is typically to raise funds for computer upgrades, computer personnel and supplies.

In both Chile and Costa Rica, 'parents and other private individuals or locally based companies have provided telephone lines, air conditioning, and other equipment free of charge to the schools' (Alvarez *et al*, 1998: 9). In addition, students have contributed to basic trouble-shooting and can be trained to participate in the upkeep of computers. 'The Chilean computer program has encouraged schools to appoint older students with a special interest in computers as "monitors" or computer assistants' (Alvarez *et al,* 1998: 15).

Inadequate support costs schools too. A detailed cost analysis was undertaken in Fairfax County in the United States:

> Fairfax County is a large district in the suburbs of Washington, DC, with 155,000 students and 26,000 employees. It calculated that if every teacher spends at least one hour a week trying to fix their own computer problems, that equals 307 full-time equivalent positions, at a cost to the district of $15.3 million in lost teaching time. In addition, if 5 per cent of teachers are regarded as 'technical wizards' by their peers, and are asked to provide 1.5 hours a week of informal support, that equals 23 full-time equivalent positions, at a cost of $1.2 million. Thus, the district concluded that its 'hidden' costs for technical support could amount to an estimated $16.5 million.

> (http://www.cosn.org/tco/checklist/support.html)

Conclusions

Researchers have much work to do – not just by increasing the number of studies exploring the costs of various uses of open and distance learning, but also in the use of hard technologies to support these practices. Most importantly, researchers must begin to relate the resource requirements of programmes to anticipated learning gains and completion rates in order to establish cost-effectiveness ratios for instructional alternatives. Policy makers everywhere need more solid information about models of technology deployment in education, their effectiveness, and their related costs. There is a particular dearth of information on the economics of computer technology for classroom education, especially with regard to development time and resources and providing interactivity for students. This presents a challenge to researchers since computer technologies are particularly difficult to cost, because of their multiple functions and protean nature. Research activities ought to seek answers to three primary questions. What are the investment and recurrent costs associated with the use of learning materials in formal education systems around the world today? How are these costs likely to vary across regions and countries at different stages of development? What do we know about the relative cost-effectiveness of learning materials in particular settings?

Notes

1   Computing technologies such as the Internet and CD ROMs also allow for the delivery of audio. The costs of computing for all media are discussed under a separate heading below.
2   While the exact numbers may change compared with television, television costs are likely to behave similarly because of the many similar properties between radio and television (broadcast, expensive transmitters and relatively inexpensive receivers, etc).
3   See, for instance, the TCO Project at www.cosn.org/tco. Much of the analysis for this section is based on another work by the author, which can be found at www.cosn.org/tco/cic.pdf.
4   See http://www.newdealinc.com for more information.

References

Alvarez, M *et al* (1998) *Computers in Schools: A qualitative study of Chile and Costa Rica*, Education and Technology Series: Special Issue, World Bank, Washington, DC

Bates, A (1995) *Technology, Open Learning and Distance Education*, Routledge, New York

Bosch, A (1997) *Interactive Radio Instruction: Twenty-three years of improving education quality*, World Bank Technical Notes, **2** (1), World Bank, Washington, DC

Calderoni, J (1998) *Telesecundaria: Using TV to bring education to rural Mexico*, World Bank Technical Notes, **3** (1), World Bank, Washington, DC

Consortium for School Networking (1999) *Taking TCO to the Classroom: A school administrator's guide to planning for the total cost of new technology*, Consortium for School Networking, Washington, DC

Cukier, J (1997) Cost-benefit analysis of telelearning: developing a methodology framework, *Distance Education*, **18** (1), pp 13–52

Daniel, J (1996) *Mega-universities and Knowledge Media: Technology strategies for higher education*, Kogan Page, London

IDRC (1999) *The Wireless Toolbox: A guide to using low-cost radio communication systems for telecommunication in developing countries – an African perspective*, International Development Research Centre [Online] http://www.idrc.ca/acacia/03866/wireless/ (accessed 29/9/2002)

Inglis, A (1999) Is online delivery less costly than print and is it meaningful to ask? *Distance Education*, **20** (2), pp 220–39

Jamison, D, Klees, S and Wells, S (1978) *The Costs of Educational Media: Guidelines for planning and evaluation*, Sage, Beverly Hills, CA

Levin, H and McEwan, P (2001) *Cost-Effectiveness Analysis: Methods and applications*, 2nd edn, Sage, Beverly Hills, CA

Lizardi, A (2002) Virtual education: development, trends, and issues, *Techknowlogia*, **4** (2)

McKinsey & Co (1995) *Connecting K-12 Schools to the Information Superhighway*, McKinsey & Co Inc, Palo Alto, CA

Melmed, A et al (1995) *The Costs and Effectiveness of Educational Technology*, RAND, CA [Online] http://www.ed.gov/technology/Plan/RAND/Costs/ (accessed 29/9/2002)

Orivel, F (1987) *Analysing Costs in Distance Education Systems: A methodological approach*, IREDU, Université de Bourgogne, Dijon, France

President's Committee of Advisors on Science and Technology (1997) *Report to the President on the Use of Technology to Strengthen K-12 Education in the United States*, Panel on Educational Technology, Washington, DC

Rumble, G (1997) *The Costs and Economics of Open and Distance Learning*, Kogan Page, London

Tsang, M (1997) Cost analysis for improved educational policymaking and evaluation, *Educational Evaluation and Policy Analysis*, **19** (4), pp 318–24, American Educational Research Association, Washington, DC

UNESCO (1982) *The Economics of New Educational Media, Vol. 2: Cost and effectiveness*, Imprimerie des Presses Universitaires de France, Paris

Whalen, T and Wright, D (1999) Methodology for cost–benefit analysis of Web-based tele-learning: case study of the Bell Online Institute, *American Journal of Distance Education*, **13** (1), pp 24–44

Part 2

Audiences

Chapter 4

From government correspondence schools to parastatal colleges of open learning: out-of-school secondary education at a distance in central and southern Africa

Tony Dodds

Introduction

This chapter is not really about open schooling. It is about out-of-school secondary education at a distance. Many of the projects described are far from open as regards curriculum choices, or even in some cases entry requirements. Some set fixed or closed requirements about time, place and pace of study. They are open only in so far as they have opened up opportunities for thousands of students who would otherwise have been deprived of them to continue their secondary level studies after they were unable to do so in formal schools.

Distance education in Africa, as we know it today, really started with out-of-school secondary education by correspondence. Initially it was largely in the hands of private correspondence colleges from the metropolitan countries of the west, usually the home of the colonial authority, and was used by individual Africans to get qualifications they had had no earlier opportunity to achieve, as they sought positions in politics or in the rapidly Africanizing civil services of their countries. After independence, this pattern was often adopted by the new governments to meet the demand for increased secondary education. This demand came both from adults, and increasingly, as universal primary education produced more primary school leavers who could not get places in conventional secondary schools, from young adults and adolescents.

The curriculum offered was exactly the same as that offered in the normal full-time secondary schools. The courses led to the same O-level and junior secondary certificates, as these were the qualifications that marked out success for secondary school children. With few exceptions, no attempt was made to adapt that curriculum to suit people whose future did not lie in academic progression to tertiary education, but who needed or wanted formal education beyond primary school. While self-study methods seemed to work for working adults who were motivated by prospects of job advancement, the self-discipline needed proved harder for adolescents, who would have preferred to be in conventional schools anyway. The courses also did not develop skills for immediate employment or self-employment. As this younger group came to dominate the audience for such courses, the drop-out and failure rates grew to unacceptable levels and doubts about the suitability of the system grew.

A search began for new ways of organizing and managing out-of-school secondary education. One important outcome of this search, at least in central and southern Africa, has been the creation of institutions such as the Malawi College of Distance Education (MCDE), the Namibian College of Open Learning (NAMCOL) and the Botswana College of Distance and Open Learning (BOCODOL). The latter two have since been reorganized as parastatal institutions.

This chapter examines the history of out-of-school secondary correspondence education programmes run by government departments in this sub-region, and the emergence of the parastatal model. (By a parastatal, I mean a semi-autonomous organization set up by legislation, under the ultimate policy control of a government ministry, but with a large degree of autonomy in its day-to-day management.) It seeks to explore what is different between the former and the latter, and what evidence there is to date that the new model is attacking and overcoming the problems of the earlier one. Its conclusion is that there is such evidence, and that results, and even reputation, are beginning to improve. It ends by trying to answer the question 'Why?', by suggesting ways whereby the model might be replicated elsewhere, and by examining the prospects for doing so.

It is important to declare biases: I played a minor role in the support programme for the Malawi College of Distance Education referred to below in the 1980s; I played a more major consultancy role in drawing up plans for the Namibian College of Open Learning in the early 1990s, of which I was also Vice Chairman of the Board of Governors from 1999 to 2002; I also played a consultancy role to the National Education Commission which recommended the establishment of a Botswana distance education college in 1993, and in 1997, on the development of implementation plans for the Botswana College of Distance and Open Learning. The views expressed in this chapter reflect that experience as well, perhaps, as the biases derived from it.

A brief and potted history

By the early 1960s, when many of the countries of east, central and southern Africa were emerging into independence, correspondence courses were an established way for people whose opportunities for formal schooling had been limited to obtain qualifications that gave them access to jobs or prospects for advancement within their jobs. Many of the first generation of African political leaders and civil servants obtained a significant proportion of their secondary qualifications in this way.

The courses were mainly offered by private commercial correspondence colleges from the metropolitan countries, such as Wolsey Hall and British Tutorial College of Britain, International Correspondence Schools of the United States and Rapid Results College of South Africa. They were geared towards qualifications in the country where they were based and were often irrelevant to local needs. Their materials were often of poor quality, and primarily designed to make profits from drop-outs rather than to advance education in the colonial countries. Many such courses led solely to qualifications of the colleges themselves, which were unrecognized both in the UK and by the colonial authorities in the African countries.

My own first contact with distance education consisted of being asked in the mid-1960s, as a university adult education tutor, to advise South African refugees in Tanzania about the quality and acceptability of courses that they had seen advertised and wanted to enrol for. After making enquiries I had to advise them that they might well be wasting their or their sponsors' money on courses of poor quality leading to unrecognized qualifications. At the same time these criticisms were emerging in Britain, and were leading to the revolution in distance education brought about by the creation of the National Extension College as a pilot project for an open university.

The new independent governments of African countries recognized the advantages of being able to offer increased educational opportunities in this way. As early as 1964–65 both Malawi and Zambia, encouraged respectively by educators from New Zealand and Australia, set up government correspondence colleges. (As they offered almost exclusively courses leading to secondary school qualifications, these were really correspondence schools.) The next 10 years saw a rapid expansion of similar initiatives in the east, central and southern African sub-region. Most were government or university initiatives, and aimed to provide adults, usually working adults including un- and under-qualified primary school teachers, with opportunities to obtain secondary-level qualifications. They were established with the encouragement of international educational support agencies such as the Swedish International Development Agency, the University of Wisconsin, the International Extension College of the UK, and of individual Australian and New Zealand distance educators. By 1975 such programmes existed also in Botswana, Ethiopia, Kenya, Lesotho, Mauritius, Swaziland, Tanzania and Uganda. In addition to the correspondence courses on which they were founded, many began to use additional media such as radio and audio cassettes, as well as occasional face-to-face tutorials, in line with developments taking place internationally at the time.

Nearly all these programmes were set up, as indicated above, to serve the needs of adults who wished or needed to get qualifications they had been unable to obtain when younger and of schoolgoing age. During the 1970s, nearly all these countries saw a dramatic increase in the number of students completing primary school without a parallel increase in formal secondary school places (Murphy and Zhiri, 1992). In response, first the Malawi Correspondence College and then the Zambia National Correspondence College were led by their governments to enrol primary school leavers who could not find places in conventional secondary schools, and junior secondary school students who had not done well enough in Junior Certificate exams to win places in senior secondary classes. This opening up to younger students led to huge increases in enrolments but sadly not to parallel increases in the resources, both financial and personnel, made available to the colleges. Correspondence education, or distance education as it was gradually becoming known, was being promoted to ministries of education as a cheaper alternative to conventional schooling: why increase the resources of the institutions providing it? It became a useful political safety valve: so long as the chance was there for such youngsters to enter secondary level, that was the main concern. If the revolving door threw out almost as many as it let in, that was the fault of the learners, or of their tutors or mentors. There was a recognition, however, that these younger students needed more support and supervision than their adult fellow students, and in both countries the supervised correspondence study-group became an integral part of the programme.

The same approach was followed in many of the other countries that had initiated correspondence programmes, especially in southern Africa: in Botswana, Lesotho, Swaziland and, as they moved towards independence, in Namibia and Zimbabwe. In the last two cases the study groups were organized for students studying the courses of private, as opposed to government, institutions.

In the 1980s economic decline hit the region, and educational budgets suffered seriously. Resources available to distance education institutions, as to all out-of-school programmes, fell particularly sharply. Many of the institutions were prevented for political reasons from limiting student intake, as their reason for existence was to offer an alternative path to secondary education to the conventional – and expensive – secondary school. The result, inevitably, was a decline in the quality of the service offered. It became harder and harder to meet the demand for learning materials and to maintain the level of tutorial support. It was increasingly being recognized that approaches to distance education designed for self-motivated adults, seeking career advancement, were not adequate to meet the needs of adolescents who through no fault of their own were unable to complete their secondary studies at conventional schools (Dodds and Mayo, 1996). But resources were not available to experiment with new ways of using traditional methodology for the adolescents and young adults who were now the majority student body. Staff whose careers had been diverted from the conventional full-time schools into distance education, often with little or no training, were eager to return as they saw the depressing results of their efforts. The result was a serious decline in the reputation of the new approach, which had been introduced with such fanfare 10 years earlier. In one of the countries under discussion a government educational official was heard in 1992 to describe the distance education structure for school leavers as 'education for failure'.

The emergence of a new model

In spite of this growing scepticism among government education officials about the effectiveness and quality of what was being provided, there was a recognition that economic decline in most countries made it impossible to meet the level of demand by replacing these distance teaching bodies with traditional secondary schools. Led by the World Bank, which developed an economic perspective of structural adjustment as the way forward for developing countries, several studies carried out in the late 1970s and 1980s showed the cost advantages of distance education provision of out-of-school secondary education (Perraton, 1979; Perraton, 1983; Murphy and Zhiri, 1992; Dodds and Mayo, 1996). While these studies recognized the problems of quality faced by the institutions, they argued that the approach remained sound, but the structures and services provided by the institutions must be improved. To do this required strengthening the professionalism of the personnel and their ability to make decisions based on student needs assessment, and providing the additional resources needed without jeopardizing their economic advantages. The studies sought ways to strengthen the commitment of governments to this approach, while allowing greater professional autonomy to the institutions in their day-to-day management. Murphy and Zhiri (1992) sum up these arguments, in the final chapter of their report on a seminar held in Zimbabwe in May 1990 entitled 'Distance Education in Anglophone Africa':

> For second-level education the participants recommended that organizations have autonomy with regard to staffing, finance and decision-making. At the start-up stage, adequate resources should be provided and attention given to ensuring that the quality of the instructional materials is high and that the public is made aware of the importance and status of distance education. Staff also need appropriate training in the tasks expected of them.

This gave impetus to a movement that had already started in Malawi to find a new model for out-of-school secondary education at a distance. The rest of this section looks at how this movement has worked itself out in Malawi, Namibia and Botswana.

The Malawi College of Distance Education

The Malawi Correspondence College was combined with the Schools Broadcasting Unit in 1973 and renamed the Malawi College of Distance Education (MCDE) in 1988. It remained a department of the Ministry of Education with no control over its staffing, its budget, its fee levels or even its enrolment numbers. Student numbers increased dramatically from the late 1980s till they exceeded the national enrolment in conventional secondary schools, but financial and personnel resources were not increased to match this growth. However, the change in the college's name seems to have reflected an attempt to improve its public status and a continuing government commitment to this form of educational provision. MCDE attracted considerable international notice, especially from the World Bank, and the name change coincided with a decision to invest considerable sums of money in MCDE from a newly negotiated World Bank education loan. A significant part of this investment was to build study centres for the MCDE students; a second element was to provide a new purpose-built central MCDE headquarters; a third was to upgrade the professional skills of staff and assist them to revamp and improve both materials and student support. As part of this third element, attempts were made to redesign the MCDE organizational structure to give it more internal self-management and more control over its own finances. For reasons that are not entirely clear these elements of self-management were resisted by the Ministry of Education and failed to materialize.

In the late 1980s and early 1990s major improvements in MCDE's services were attempted, though many of these were thwarted by a lack of understanding of the nature of distance learning in the Ministry of Education, and by the increase in enrolments, despite warnings that the college could not cope with them. It appears that there were eventually significant improvements in the exam results at the junior certificate level, up to an 88 per cent pass rate (Perraton, 2000, quoting Laymaman) in 1996–97. This was at a time when total enrolments with MCDE at that level significantly exceeded those in all the formal schools put together. Very important staff capacity building activities were undertaken, and plans were under discussion to provide career development for the study centre supervisors and tutors. Sadly this support project was brought to an end before the plans had been realized, and the promise of change and improvement was not fulfilled, because of a lack of autonomy and the necessary management skills.

An important feature first introduced by MCDE was its learner support system. This recognized that young learners (many of primary school age or just above) needed more supervision than adult learners. Study centres were set up all over the country, many involving the local community, to provide supervision and help on a daily basis. However, these centres suffered in several ways that reduced their ability to provide the support needed. They were usually staffed by primary school teachers, with little training or help in supporting secondary-level learners. The students and their parents, and the supervisors themselves, had expectations of face-to-face teaching, not guidance on self-study; and the severe shortage of the printed course materials often meant that the students were dependent on the supervisors/teachers for course content. As a result the study centres (which opened during school terms, kept normal lesson times, had school uniforms and generally appeared to be conventional schools in all but name) were seen and often functioned as second-rate conventional schools. They never developed a philosophy, methods or status which marked them out as different but effective providers of secondary education.

After the change of government in Malawi, for reasons that are also very unclear, MCDE was drastically reduced in size and importance and its study centres were mostly turned into conventional secondary schools (Perraton, 2000).

Thus the MCDE story is one of ambitious plans, considerable promise and initial success, and ultimate failure. But many of the ideas developed at MCDE were influential in shaping the thinking that informed the planning processes for similar successful developments in Namibia and Botswana.

The Namibian College of Open Learning

Namibia's distance education history is very different from that of Malawi. First, serious government investment and interest in it took place only after independence in 1990. Second, the Namibian educational authorities had experimented in exile with distance learning to attack the backlog of access to education at secondary level, and were ready to take it seriously. With international assistance they had set up a distance education unit in Lusaka, called the Namibian Extension Unit, to provide education to their young people in exile in both Angola and Zambia. Third, from the outset of the post-independence reconstruction of the education system, proposals for a semi-autonomous or parastatal national institution for distance education at pre-tertiary level were on the table. Eventually such a college was created out of the Directorate of Adult Basic Education's division of distance education and its continuing education evening-class programme, which had absorbed the Namibian Extension Unit on its return from exile. It thus began its life with both a large number of part-time face to face learners and a body of learners studying at a distance. The fourth difference is that NAMCOL has received the full political support of both the Minister of Basic Education and the Minister of Higher Education since its inception, and has therefore been treated as a political priority. Its parastatal status has been accepted by the government in ways that have ensured continuing political and financial support.

NAMCOL is governed by a board of governors appointed by the Minister of Basic Education, representing a range of educational, government and private sector interests. The board and its committees oversee policy formulation and implementation, but day-to-day management is in the hands of the college's management committee, consisting of senior officials both at headquarters and from the regions. College administration has been divided into three main sectors: programme and material development; administration and finance; and the regional administration. Under this structure a major programme of staff development has been put in place, and great emphasis placed on improving the quality of the materials and the efficiency of the delivery system. After considerable research and experimentation, at the time of writing NAMCOL is preparing to introduce a new and unified system of learner support, ensuring that all students, both those who previously studied mainly through evening classes and those who studied entirely at a distance, receive all the study materials and significant face-to-face tutorial support.

Two administrative reforms have been implemented. First, the college has set up a strong publicity and public relations section, which is working hard, with some success, to improve the image of distance education from the unfortunate reputation it inherited. Second, a funding formula has been hammered out with the Ministry of Finance and the Ministry of Basic Education, so that each year's government subsidy can be predicted on the basis of the previous year's student enrolment. Together with a realistic student fee structure and a growing programme of income-generating courses, for example through the Computer Training Centre, this funding formula seems set to ensure a sound and self-sustaining financial basis for the college's further development.

The result of these changes can be seen in rapidly growing enrolments, making NAMCOL by far the biggest educational institution in Namibia, and a marked improvement in examination results. Since 1994 enrolments have gone up 500 per cent, drop-outs (or incomplete marks) appear to have halved, exam results have steadily improved (NAMCOL, 2001), and these trends are confidently predicted to continue. The status of the college both in the public eye and in the view of education officials is clearly rising, and the pride of its staff in their work and achievements is clear.

The Botswana College of Distance and Open Learning

Distance education at out-of-school secondary level has a long history in Botswana, dating back to the establishment of the Botswana Extension College as a government department in 1973. This was absorbed into the Department of Non-Formal Education when that was created in 1978. Its history reflects the generalizations about the development of such programmes made earlier in this chapter, from great expectations to low reputation and poor results. In 1992–93 a National Commission on Education reviewed the whole education sector and put forward policy recommendations for the future. It commissioned a study 'to contribute to its consideration of options for the future development of distance education' (Dodds, 1993). The recommendations made in that report later formed the basis for the development of plans to set up the Botswana College of Distance and Open Learning (BOCODOL). By 1996 this decision had been taken; it would absorb the Distance Education Unit of the Department of Non-Formal Education, but would be a semi-autonomous parastatal institution. The college formally came into being by Act of Parliament in December 1998. Though the pre-history of BOCODOL is very different from that of NAMCOL, the transition from government department to parastatal body is very similar. This similarity has been emphasized by the fact that both have benefited from support projects funded by the British Department for International Development, through partnerships with the University of Bath, which have enabled significant exchanges of experience to take place through study exchanges between staff and members of the boards of governors.

Like NAMCOL, BOCODOL has undertaken a complete revamp of its study materials, making the print materials much more student friendly as regards appearance, language and layout, and introducing properly integrated audio cassette and radio programmes. It has also inaugurated a pilot project in two regions for a new learner support system which incorporates a more comprehensive though decentralized support model, and a well publicized 'learners' charter'. It has restructured its organization, with a directorate and four departments, for course development; learner support; media production and ICT; finance and administration; and the regional offices. Its board of governors came into being in November 2000 under the chairmanship of the Permanent Secretary of the Ministry of Education, a sign of the commitment of the ministry to the new body.

BOCODOL is at a much earlier stage in implementing its new plans than NAMCOL. It is not therefore possible to assess the impact on student exam results of the new dispensation. There were signs of an increase in enrolments, even before the serious marketing drive in 2002. There are also clear signs of an improvement in staff morale compared with the previous distance education unit of the Department of Non-Formal Education, even though nearly all the unit's staff have joined BOCODOL. This appears to be due partly to good leadership, effective management and vigorous staff development plans, and partly to the resulting growth in the staff's professional and career confidence. Finally, as in NAMCOL, BOCODOL is developing plans to diversify its course offerings, adding vocational subjects to its traditional academic secondary programme. Efforts are still under way to find a secure but flexible funding formula with the Ministry of Education, to give BOCODOL the ability to plan ahead financially.

Common features of the new model

This assessment of an emerging new model for out-of-school secondary education at a distance is based on the three examples described above. MCDE failed to sustain the momentum created by the changes it was trying to initiate, largely, it would appear, for political reasons. Both NAMCOL and BOCODOL benefited from its experience and have been saved from its political disappointments. The following summary of the main features of this new approach draws on the MCDE experience, but is mainly based on NAMCOL's and BOCODOL's development over the last decade.

These features seem to fall into eight categories:

- The creation of a parastatal organization with management autonomy, within the limits set by government priorities, and accountable to the parent ministry.
- Firm leadership and effective management.
- Strong support from the parent ministry, and a realization that out-of-school secondary education will always require substantial financial subsidies if equity and quality are to be preserved.
- Improved cost awareness, effective financial management, the strengthening of the skills of the financial management staff, and a firm and secure formula for both government subsidies and alternative fund-raising activities.
- A recognition of the need to diversify the programmes beyond the traditional core academic out-of-school secondary courses.
- A commitment to provide quality materials and media support.
- A recognition of the importance (and added costs) of student support services for out-of-school adolescent learners, and the researched needs of other students. This includes a commitment to a sensitive public relations and marketing strategy.
- The development of clear career paths for staff within the organization, matched by vigorous human resource development plans. The aim is to produce within the institutions a higher level of professionalism in the practices of open and distance learning.

Lessons for replication and the future

Out-of-school secondary education by distance learning methods has a long, but not always glorious, history in southern Africa. In terms of educational equity, the need for such programmes in one form or another seems set to remain for the foreseeable future. In the near future, universal conventional secondary schooling, even with the flexible use of new technology to supplement the teachers, seems a pipe-dream for most African countries, where there are doubts even about the achievement of universal primary education by 2015. As universal primary education (UPE) comes closer, the need for alternative forms of secondary provision will grow. Distance education methodologies, and a structure that opens access as wide as possible, will almost inevitably be part of those alternatives. It is therefore vital to learn the lessons of the past and the present about how such structures and methodologies are most effectively organized. The NAMCOL/BOCODOL experience, though still quite young, offers one of the most hopeful pointers for this future.

It is necessary to recognize certain dangers in the model and to suggest precautions that need to be taken. The greatest risk is that, once established as a parastatal agency, such a college will become detached from government involvement and be forced to become increasingly self-financing because starved of government subsidy. To avoid this fate it is crucial to retain government commitment and policy involvement. This is probably best ensured by maintaining ministerial responsibility for the appointment of the board of governors, and by establishing funding formulas whereby government buys from the college priority services, such as the provision of out-of-school secondary education, at favourable but agreed prices.

A second risk is that parastatal status may become a barrier to involvement with the formal system and may restrict access to government-owned educational resources. Continuing government involvement in such colleges and their policy-making structures is necessary. Part of this continuing commitment must be agreement that such resources are at the disposal, at an agreed cost-recovery price, of out-of-school learners as well as school students.

A third danger seems inherent in educational institutions, namely the tendency towards an academic drift upwards, or the urge to be seen to offer ever more advanced academic qualifications. Such colleges must avoid the temptation to become tertiary education providers, when such services are provided elsewhere and the need is to open up distance learning opportunities for people deprived of learning opportunities at the lower end of the educational scale. An ethical commitment to educational equity must underwrite their mission statements.

If these dangers can be avoided, the potential of a semi-autonomous distance and open learning institution at pre-tertiary level is almost unbounded. We have already seen that the demand for out-of-school secondary level courses is set to grow, not diminish, over the next few decades. To be able to experiment with the most effective ways of meeting those needs, freed from the restraints of civil service regulations and practices, is a challenging and exciting task for the most imaginative educators and managers. Part of this process should be to develop a wider range of courses, including vocational courses relevant to the needs of this particular young adult student body. Some such courses undoubtedly have the potential to be cost-covering or even profit-making. In addition, the need to experiment with making distance education available to adult students who have just achieved literacy is of vital national importance if the target of education for all is to be achieved in the next two or three decades. The experience and freedom of such parastatal colleges to experiment makes them well suited to meet this task as well. Finally, as more flexible learning methods, including those made possible through new ICTs, are incorporated into conventional school systems, specialist distance and open learning institutions, such as NAMCOL and BOCODOL, which can respond to government educational priorities, could provide important services and materials for the secondary school system.

The essential characteristics of an institution set to tackle these challenges are as follows:

- the size, skills and professionalism to be able to operate on a scale that allows for the development of quality materials and services at economic costs;
- a management structure that promotes and encourages initiative and the taking of responsibility;
- a philosophy and working practice that thrives on innovation;

- a learner/client-oriented approach by staff at all levels;
- a human resource development policy that enables staff to develop professionalism and rewards them for exercising it;
- an ability to operate across the normal educational sub-sector boundaries;
- agreed funding formulas with government for services provided in response to government educational priorities;
- sound financial management and entrepreneurial skills, and a preparedness to contract out work where cost and quality advantages apply;
- strictly accountable, but nevertheless autonomous, financial management procedures;
- research capabilities to ensure quality of service, to identify new programmes and to develop innovative approaches to open and distance learning.

References

BOCODOL (2001) *Annual Report for BOCODOL for 2000/2001*, BOCODOL, Gaborone

Dodds, T (1993) *Report on a Feasibility Study on the Establishment of a Distance Education College for Botswana*, International Extension College (IEC), Cambridge

Dodds, T and Mayo, J (1996) *Distance Education for Development: The IEC Experience 1971 to 1991*, IEC, Cambridge

Murphy, P and Zhiri, A (1992) *Distance Education in Anglophone Africa: Experience with secondary education and teacher training*, World Bank, Washington, DC

NAMCOL (2001) *NAMCOL Annual Report for the Academic Year 2000 and the Financial Year ending 31 March 2001*, NAMCOL, Windhoek

Perraton, H (ed) (1979) *Alternative Routes to Formal Education*, World Bank/Johns Hopkins University Press, Baltimore

Perraton, H (1983) *The National Correspondence College of Zambia and its Costs*, IEC, Cambridge

Perraton, H (2000) *Open and Distance Learning in the Developing World*, Routledge, London

Chapter 5

EFECOT: supporting the travelling tradition

Ken Marks

Introduction

The European Federation for the Education of the Children of Occupational Travellers (EFECOT) was set up in 1988, as part of a response to the needs of travelling children, following an initiative by the European Parliament. The remit of the organization includes the exploration of ways of addressing the challenge of interrupted schooling within highly mobile communities. This chapter describes EFECOT experience in the area of supported distance learning for children and, in particular, the evolution of approaches that have involved ICT. Here the 'open classroom' is not a concept to add a new dimension to the school environment, but rather offers a radical alternative where normal attendance is problematic. A distinctive feature of the initiatives described is the wireless nature of communication, as travelling families have limited access to fixed telephone lines or cable facilities. However, much of the experience reported is independent of this constraint.

The main purpose of the chapter is to outline the user context of the challenge, and then to describe interrelated developments in both telematics and pedagogy. It will conclude with a brief listing of some of the main issues that are emerging in this area of work, some of which have a broader relevance to all those working with children whose schooling is interrupted or necessarily outside the school environment.

The user context

'Occupational travellers' are defined by the European Parliament as the bargee, circus and fairground communities across Europe, seasonal workers, and others who travel as a direct consequence of their trade or profession. Indicative estimates suggest that there are something of the order of half a million such travellers across the European Union (EU). There is also an overlap with other travelling cultures, such as those within the Gypsy/Romany tradition.

Such cultures and communities have established histories and ways of life, and pose two overlapping challenges in terms of schooling and educational opportunity. The first is an ingrained pattern of negative perception and prejudice, often unspoken or masked but part of everyday reality for travellers and their children, and which in the schooling context can all too easily fail to recognize, celebrate and draw on the strengths of the families and communities. The second is the mobile lifestyle which, in itself, poses formidable practical problems for both parents and school systems designed essentially for sedentary populations.

Where families travel, schooling is necessarily interrupted, and this is particularly marked within parts of the 'occupational' sector. Fairground and circus families travel from site to site throughout a season which can run from March to November, and movement may be on a weekly basis, so that their main contact with schools is during the short over-wintering period. Bargee families are mobile throughout the year, with only short stops to load and unload cargo.[1]

Traditional responses to this challenge are very variable across Europe, but have included outreach initiatives (mobile schools, tutor visits to families and sites, and other ways of 'bringing the teacher to the community') as well as the development of distance learning packs. Where structured supportive services exist, some progress has been made within the pre-school and primary sectors, although the children will usually still miss out on a full and varied curriculum, and there is an increasing attainment gap as they move through the primary years. However, in parts of Europe there are no systematic attempts to provide a service, with children left to attend primary schools where and when they can.

The secondary age group poses a major challenge, and a recent EFECOT survey identifies this as a fundamental concern even in countries with developed support services (EFECOT, 1999: 44–50). There are here two underlying causal threads which become entwined and reinforce each other. First: the older 'children' increasingly see themselves as young adults within the family business and the community, question the value of formal education, and react to the ethos of school. Second: it is very difficult for schools, with their subject segmentation and specialized staff, to organize and support responsive and effective distance learning activity, so that children rapidly fall behind their peers.

EFECOT is in essence a network of partners, served by a small core team based in Brussels, which was set up to share experience and encourage new approaches to meet such challenges. In setting a context for the remainder of this chapter it is also important to appreciate that its work is based on presuppositions which reject the notion that 'the problem' lies with travelling families who should be left with the responsibility of finding ways to accommodate to schooling systems. Rather the EFECOT mission statement emphasizes the importance of working to complement education systems that were designed for sedentary populations, and to establish new approaches 'which create positive opportunities for access, which are sensitive to the lifestyles of travellers, and which encourage the celebration of cultural diversity' (EFECOT, 1999: 9). It is from this perspective that EFECOT first began to explore the potential of telematic approaches which would provide both practical solutions and a foundation for culturally sensitive pedagogy.

Evolving approaches to the challenge

Since its inception EFECOT has taken an active role in exploring distance learning as part of a strategic approach to providing education for travelling children. The early text-based work was culturally sensitive and highly imaginative in its mix of materials and activities, but suffered the now well-documented limitations of traditional methods, including those that Moore has drawn together in his discussion of 'transactional distance'. In particular, Moore highlights the 'psychological and communication space' between tutor and learner, and the potential of narrowing the gap by increasing dialogue and by taking more flexible/responsive approaches to learning-programme structure (Moore, 1993).

The EFECOT move towards telematics-based approaches can be seen as a direct response to targets which involved addressing tutor/learner distance by working at these two dimensions, as well as making good use of the potential strengths of multimedia assets and interactivity. There have been three major initiatives (TOPILOT, FLEX and Trapeze) and latterly, as wireless communication has become more secure, a developing focus on collaborative learning.

Before describing the approaches and experiences of each project, it will be helpful to outline briefly the underlying pedagogy that informs the work of EFECOT, and some of the issues this raises; also to look, again briefly, at the developing use of wireless technology. Hopefully these introductory notes will be a useful backcloth to understanding evolution within and across the projects; an evolution which has been dependent on the art of the (technologically) possible and on increasing understanding of applied pedagogical principles.

EFECOT: an underlying pedagogy

EFECOT has been supported by a Pedagogical Advisory Committee, which drew expertise from a range of specialist institutions, and nailed its colours quite firmly to the mast of the cognitive and constructivist perspectives. These have been fairly well summarized by Elen under the headings of active orientation, goal orientation, (learner) construction of meaning, cumulative processes and self-regulation (Elen, 1996). Such perspectives have, of course, to be applied to working with traveller children, and to working at a distance. The goals are clear, but application raises important issues for designers and the (teacher) practitioners who are to provide tutorial support.

Perhaps first and foremost comes the challenge of creating a necessarily active orientation to learning. In the EFECOT context, learning has been seen as involving a significant degree of 'compulsory schoolwork'[2] which raises questions about intrinsic (goal orientated) and extrinsic motivation. Leading on from this comes the related target of working towards the ideal of the autonomous learner; or in practice perhaps shifting the balance of the teacher/pupil relationship towards learner control.

Distance is a major consideration, and raises important questions about preparing learners and their families, ongoing communication, and the supportive/ mentoring role of parents (and/or other members of the family or wider community). Parental oversight is crucial, particularly at the early learning stage, and Bruner's metaphor of 'scaffolding' is a useful reminder of the part parents can play in encouraging movement towards learner control (Bruner, 1968: 10–11).

The constructivist perspective has also found expression in the major shift in distance education generally, to embrace collaborative learning, and this is also reflected in the development of EFECOT initiatives. Here the challenge is not just 'shared schoolwork' but the development of contextualized community-based approaches. These can ground learning and motivate children by drawing on their everyday priorities and realities within what Moll and Greenburg (1990), building on the work of Vygotsky, have referred to as 'zones of possibility'.

Developing use of wireless technology within EFECOT initiatives

Broadly speaking EFECOT has explored two major strands of wireless technology, mobile telephony and satellite, as well as being involved with enhanced digital radio communication. The first efforts were planned in 1995 (for TOPILOT), and were focused on the use of GSM data transmission,[3] which would allow narrow-band monitoring and management of disc-based multimedia learner materials, and some constrained tutor/learner messaging. Given the limitations of GSM bandwidth, this was an imaginative approach, and proved fairly successful (see below). However, the reliance on (necessarily specially designed) discs was a restraint, and the subsequent FLEX project set out to use satellite to broadcast a wider range of server-based multimedia materials. The GSM route was still used as a return, learner to tutor, link for monitoring progress and to support a full e-mail-based messaging facility.

One weakness in these approaches was the reliance on GSM networks and their coverage. Although this is improving, as are options for bandwidth capacity, the necessary infrastructure costs mean that investment in areas of lower population density remains uncertain. Given EFECOT's travelling target population this is a fundamental issue, and the problems were highlighted in part of the TOPILOT acceptance trials.[4] This was the impetus for an exploration of other options, starting with a brief involvement with trials for an enhanced digital radio system (E-DSRR) with broadband capacity and automatic switching to two–way satellite if radio connection signals proved inadequate.[5] The trials involved young fairground and bargee children, and took place in Rotterdam early in 1999. They were very successful in showing the potential of synchronous tutor–learner activity and real-time communication (Marks, 1999). However, they are not further described in this chapter as their main outcome for EFECOT was as a precursor to Trapeze, a leading-edge initiative supported by the European Space Agency (ESA), which essentially involved a broadband Intranet concept using two–way satellite to link tutors and learners.

The projects

TOPILOT: First steps in the use of information and communication technology (ICT) with travelling children

TOPILOT (To Optimize the Individual Learning Process of Occupational Travelling Children) was set up within the Telematics Applications Programme of the EU Fourth Framework and ran from January 1996 to November 1998. It involved 22 partners from four countries, with technical expertise provided by Expertisecentrum voor Digitale Media (EDM) based at Limburg University Centre in Belgium, working with Philips Interactive Media.

The development of a pedagogical approach, as well as specific ideas for the multimedia materials, was undertaken with practising teachers from a number of schools and services working with traveller children, and these efforts were supported by two Dutch organizations: the Centrum voor Innovatie van Opleidingen (CINOP) and Educaplan.[6]

As noted above, the approach involved disc-based materials, and these were designed for the then newly developed CD-interactive (CD-i) platform (which at the time offered a potentially popular, robust and transparent environment). Three discs were produced, one aimed at young learners in the 4–6 age grouping, and two aimed at the 14+ grouping, which contained relevant, vocationally orientated materials, supplemented by text-based work books (see Fig. 5.1).[7]

The final disc contents were designed as a series of 'units' and were put together by EDM. As well as being culturally sensitive, they used a range of multimedia assets and made good use of the interactive platform and features such as full-screen video. However the unique feature of the discs was that each contained a 'control and communication package'. This was able, one, to use the CD-i memory to store information about work done with the materials, and the results of specific exercises; and two, to initiate GSM-based data communication between the (CD-i) learner workstation and a remote server based at Limburg University. The communication process was initiated automatically each time a learner logged on or off, and was effected via a radio modem attached to the CD-i player. This

Figure 5.1 *A menu screen from one of the TOPILOT discs*

enabled monitoring information and short, pre-set, student-to-teacher messages to be uploaded to a specially designed database, and tutor-to-learner messages to be downloaded together with management instructions (see below).

Tutors were able to access the database to review student progress through a series of Web pages, and could use the same pages to set up messages to be sent to their learners when the communication link was next activated. They could also use this interface to set up management instructions which would open up new units of work on the discs, and in the case of 'Rollerball' (the disc designed for the young learners), to change the levels of difficulty of the exercises.[8]

The other special design feature of 'Rollerball' was a separate 'Parent Programme', located on the same disc, which allowed parents to monitor some aspects of progress, as well as giving information on the objectives and contents of each unit, and ideas for practical activities to reinforce learning (see Figure 5.2).

Looking at the underlying pedagogical features of the approach as a simplified model, it is possible to highlight a number of key features:

- Experienced teachers were involved throughout the design process, and could select a variety of approaches, with a mixture of interactive (disc-based) and traditional materials and activities.
- Materials were developed as units, and wherever possible within the logic of design, learners could choose their own routes.

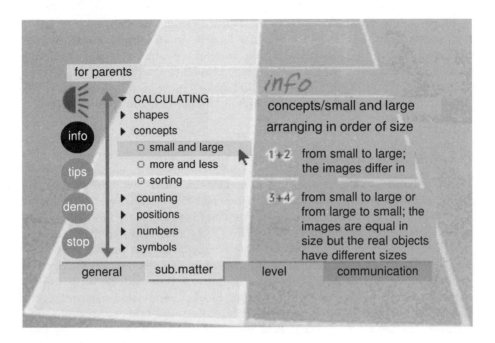

Figure 5.2   *Part of the parent menu within the TOPILOT environment*

- The discs were designed with in-built corrective and supportive feedback, which encouraged learners to progress within the materials open to them at any particular time.
- Supported learning was provided in a one-to-one tutor/learner environment, with parental involvement for the younger learners.
- Tutors were able to monitor progress at a distance via a WWW interface. They could also control the materials by opening new units and changing levels of difficulty.
- Tutors could also send simple feedback and short supportive messages.
- Learners and parents were able to select and send short, pre-set, messages to their tutors.
- The system was asynchronous, allowing learners and tutors to choose convenient times to engage with the educational process.

The project trials reinforced the growing body of evidence that well-designed interactive multimedia courseware can enhance motivation, as well as enabling improvements in learning within a self-paced, supportive environment. They also gave strong support to Moore's suggestions that responsive tailoring of the learning programme, and (in this case very basic) tutor/learner dialogue, can have a positive impact within the distance learning context (Marks and Pullin, 1998). The integrated parent programme was also a successful innovation.

However, the major constraint of the TOPILOT approach was the necessarily heavy investment in professional expertise to develop a relatively limited amount of material for the CD-i discs, and there were also frustrations with the limited messaging facilities, as well as the coverage problems noted above.[9] These considerations set the context for the EFECOT involvement in the subsequent FLEX project, and led to the exploratory involvement with the E-DSRR system described above.

FLEX: A library concept

FLEX (The Flexible Learning Environment eXperiment) was initiated in late 1998, as a two year project within the special EU Educational Multimedia Taskforce programme. It was again coordinated by EFECOT, and many of the partners had been involved with TOPILOT. As an interdisciplinary theory/ practice venture, it set out to explore a more systematic application of constructivist principles, with specialist input from the Centre for Instructional Psychology and Technology at the Catholic University of Leuven. From this basis the project worked to develop the concept of 'learning blocks', and related standards, as the foundation for a library of materials. Details of the applied theory are outlined in a report from the Centre (Utsi, Bellens and Lowyck, 1999). At the same time, from the technological perspective, the project set out to explore the potential of satellite broadcast as a means of delivering learning materials from the library directly to learners and their families, while maintaining and enhancing the GSM return link from learner to tutor.

The major objective, as the project title indicates, was to focus on flexibility by encouraging the cost-effective development and distribution of a range of server-based and culturally sensitive materials. In essence the library was a specially designed database, with a Web site interface. The interface allowed tutors to submit, or draw on and edit, existing units of material. These units were classified within the library for ease of access, and could be used to build up individualized learning modules and learning packages, which could then be broadcast to learners and parents, along with instructions and messages, via a one-way broadband satellite link. At the learner/receiving end, data were selected and stored via a specially designed (Mediaspot) device, which could identify and download (only) materials and messages uniquely coded to each individual. These could then be transferred to the family's laptop workstation, to appear within a specially designed and transparent learning environment.

Practising tutors were again central to the approach, and could add to the library by designing their own units, which could remain 'private' or become publicly available to colleagues via the classification system provided they satisfied agreed quality criteria. Materials could have a multimedia format, and/or could be designed within the framework of any Microsoft Office software, PowerPoint proving the most popular. There were also special 'wizard' template tools to create interactive options with built-in feedback, like matching and multi-choice exercises. Tutor training was central to the project, and covered aspects of asset

Figure 5.3 *A FLEX menu screen with five modules open to the learner*

design as well as related ICT skills. It also encouraged the creation of holistic packages, built on agreed pedagogical principles, with activities stimulated from and within the learning environment, and also using tasks and resources away from the computer interface where appropriate to learning objectives (see Figure 5.3). As with TOPILOT, tutors could monitor the progress of individual children via a Web-based interface; for FLEX separate from, but linked to, the library interface. This stored the results of interactive exercises and also open-ended work, such as text files and drawings, submitted as a response to specific tasks. It also stored e-mail messages from both learners and their parents.

Simplifying the main features, the evolution from TOPILOT is clear. This is again a one-to-one tutor/learner approach, which encourages parental involvement, and which has an asynchronous design. But here:

- tutors became more central to the process of creating materials;
- these materials were held within a classified system which encouraged editing and re-use, and could also act as a resource library for additional materials, for example materials bought in from other sources;
- monitoring and content management features were extended, and the constraints removed from tutor/learner/parent messaging;

- there was a more systematic and detailed attempt to apply learning theory to content design, rather than working within broad principles.

As indicated in its final report (Marks, 2001), the project proved successful in achieving its main educational objectives, with positive feedback from the fairground, circus and bargee families involved with the project trials. However there was one important proviso, and a fundamental change to the technological approach. The proviso relates to tutors (all practising teachers) and the difficulties they encountered in uploading/downloading large amounts of material from the database, and in working within the database environment. New processes had to be introduced, and these incorporated levels of expert support that had not been envisaged at the outset.

The technological change came as a direct result of experience from the field trials. There were problems with the broadcasts, which suggested that available one-way satellite broadcast reception/storage systems were currently not sufficiently technically robust and easy to use in the highly mobile environment of traveller families. In the event, satellite broadcasts were backed up by CD ROMs, duplicating the content of individualized parts of broadcasts and delivered to families within one week of the original transmission. The unexpected consequence was that families preferred the new delivery arrangements; receiving regular CD ROMs was much easier than erecting and trying to tune special satellite reception equipment each time they moved from site to site. As a consequence, FLEX proved much closer to an extended version of the TOPILOT approach than had been envisaged. However it was interesting to note that, in Moore's terms, both dialogue and learner-programme flexibility were significantly enhanced, and the softening of the effects of distance was reflected by evaluative feedback from the parents and young learners.

Trapeze: online virtual classrooms and collaborative working

As noted above, Trapeze was a venture into the world of two-way broadband satellite communication, and was to an extent stimulated by the experience gained from the E-DSRR project. Satellite expertise was provided by the Italian company Telespazio. Participating tutors were based in the Netherlands and the UK, and the development of the learning environment, and associated interactive materials, was supported by a Belgian company, @iT, as well as the audio visual section of the Catholic University of Leuven.

The project was supported by ESA and involved the development of a state-of-the-art VSAT-based system[10] to facilitate delivery of materials, return of completed work and enhanced communication between teachers and learners. Pupils could also be given access to selected Web sites via a proxy server. The pedagogical design was based primarily on synchronous activity within a virtual classroom environment. For the purposes of the field trials there were actually four separate classes using the system. (In effect each class had its own Intranet.) In the Netherlands tutors worked with two fairground groups aged between 10 and 13,

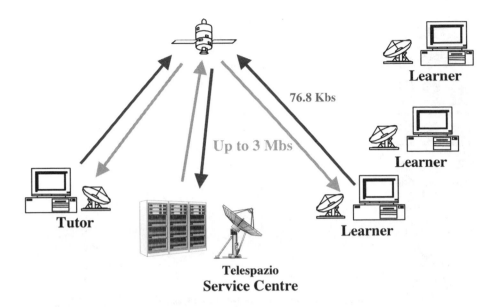

76.8 Kbs

Up to 3 Mbs

Learner

Learner

Learner

Tutor

Telespazio
Service Centre

Figure 5.4   *Trapeze virtual classroom communication*

while in the UK the focus was somewhat younger, with pupils drawn from the 7 to 10 age band.

As indicated in Figure 5.4, the downlink capacity was very high so that substantial amounts of multimedia material, designed and made jointly by the tutors and supporting experts, could be sent regularly to pupils. The uplink capacity enabled exchange and return of resources as well as communication within the groups. Both common and individualized work could be sent, and the satellite system used a mixture of unicast and broadcast modes. (Further technical details can be found in a supplementary project report available from EFECOT (Reynolds, Vanbuel and Marks, 2001).)

For the trials, the young learners were expected to 'attend' the class each weekday morning between 10 am and 12 noon over a period of four weeks. They received new work for each session within a specially designed and transparent learning environment (see Figure 5.5), and could then seek support from their tutor either through an open text-based chat facility, or through individual e-mailing. They could also exchange messages with classmates using either the chat or e-mail facilities. Completed work was automatically returned to the tutors. After 12 noon, the tutors were no longer available in the classroom, but the children could continue to work, return work and communicate with each other.

After some early teething problems, the parents became quite expert in setting up the satellite equipment, and it was significant that tuning a two-way system proved much easier to support than tuning for broadcast (cf. the experience of FLEX). The experiences of the trials are detailed in the supplementary report mentioned above (Reynolds *et al*, 2001).

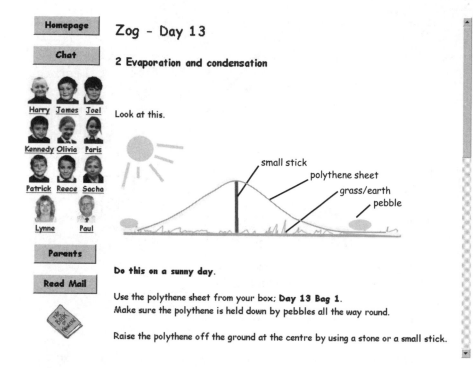

Figure 5.5 *The Trapeze learner interface*

In summary, the evaluation feedback in terms of the teaching/learning process reflected the power of the environment. Parents, children and teachers all felt that the virtual classroom was not just an improvement over previous distance learning approaches they had experienced, but more a revolution in distance schooling. As one parent put it: 'It's like having a classroom in the home.' Motivation and comparative learning gains were high, and some children also reported that they had learnt significantly more than they normally did when they were able to attend local schools.

Trapeze materials were created in a simplified library system to facilitate reuse, and once again teacher-tutors took a supported but lead role in designing and creating materials. The communication system proved much more secure, and the enhanced return link allowed for a significant increase in the capacity to return records and materials to teachers, to allow correction, monitoring and feedback. However, in terms of an evolution of approaches, the most significant aspects of Trapeze were:

- the introduction of a synchronous environment. (The asynchronous option was also still available, with children and teachers able to continue to work outside the virtual classroom sessions.);

- collaborative working could be used to supplement individual tasks, both in the 'classroom' and via projects;
- messaging was extended, and could have included audio as well as text-based chat facilities (the project was unable to locate suitably robust audio software at the time of the trials);
- there was potential access to selected Web sites, although this aspect of the design was not explored during the trials.

Collaborative options also raise interesting questions for EFECOT about the notion of transactional distance; a concept originally conceived for the tutor/ learner relationship. In higher education, collaborative developments have helped to move thinking away from distance as a barrier, and towards a focus on alternative sharing and communication approaches, and styles, within new media. Currently the notion remains useful for EFECOT, because the tutor–learner relationship is still central to thinking about supported school-orientated learning. Perhaps the picture of a 'space between' will now need to be modified by the notion of a 'space around' each individual learner, with a separate sense of space surrounding the tutor. In so far as Moore seeks to highlight the sense of isolation of the learner (and the tutor), the metaphor remains valuable, with mediated collaborative links potentially playing an important part in 'reducing distance' as well as contributing directly to the construction of meanings.

Some issues for the future

The thinking behind the initiatives described in this chapter is not new or startling. It draws together developmental features that are to be found both in work with children in school settings, and distance learning designed for higher education students and adults. What is distinctive is the attempt to develop supported distance learning for children, making good use of the potential of ICT, but within the constraints of a context dependent on non-terrestrial communication. For project participants the involvement with 'leading-edge' communication technology proved both exciting and frustrating, but the signs are that robust and cost-effective systems will become available in the medium term (three to five years). GPRS-based systems[11] are already being explored to support fairground children in the Netherlands. Following FLEX, EFECOT is now experimenting with commercial systems that are Web-based but allow CD ROM alternatives where communication coverage is problematic.[12] Interactive television may well open up new and more secure opportunities linked to one-way satellite transmission, and as the type of two-way satellite communication developed within Trapeze becomes established, this platform can also offer exciting possibilities.

From the distance teaching/learning perspective the experience of the projects has focused attention on a number of issues that are of continuing importance for traveller education, but also have relevance for all those working with children whose schooling is interrupted or outside the normal school environment. These issues cluster around four overlapping themes, and are most readily presented as a series of interrelated questions. It is not possible to do justice to them within the confines of this chapter, and in a sense they are also context-bound. They need to be addressed in terms of the characteristics and situations of particular groupings of children, and of the ICT options realistically available to potential support tutors. However the issues listed here will hopefully resonate with the experience of colleagues working in similar contexts, and could be a useful starting point for others who look to develop distance learning strategies for the schooling years.

The child as learner

The literature of distance education is largely influenced by the ideal of the autonomous, or self-directed, learner. How does this translate into a context of 'required' schooling, and to children with a variety of capabilities and motivations? How can the child be encouraged towards such an active participation? What does this mean in terms of the design of learning packages and the nature of the tutor/learner relationship? Is it realistic to work towards the autonomous ideal, or is a different, partnership approach needed for questions of locus of control? What should be the role of parents and/or significant others in the immediate (face-to-face) environment?

Pedagogical approaches

Michael Moore, who introduced the concept of transactional distance, has more recently discussed the 'death of distance' in the light of improvements to communication technology that have the potential to close the gap between mediated and face-to-face learning (Moore, 1995). Distance education is certainly no longer constrained by the original sense of gap. It need no longer be a matter of materials and activities designed for independent study, supplemented by exchanges with a tutor giving feedback and support. Enhanced tutor/learner discussion and collaborative options already offer something more fluid and potentially closer to the classroom environment. Developments in tactile and other sensory interfaces may further erode distinctions. The new media are also stimulating new and alternative models, which are not simply based on attempts to replicate traditional classroom patterns (see, for example, Jonassen *et al*, 1999). So what are the optimal approaches for particular groupings of children? The cognitive and constructivist perspectives provide some valuable insights, but are there other theoretical positions that should inform the discussion? How do we decide on those patterns of communication and materials exchange that will indeed offer the most effective options for supported learning?

The distant curriculum

At a more pragmatic level it is important to focus attention on the art of the possible. What is a realistic and appropriate curriculum for children as distance learners, and how does this relate to current schooling requirements? Are there parts of the normal school curriculum that are challenging, or even impossible, in the distant setting? How does 'separated' school-orientated learning relate to everyday cultural experience in the more immediate environment of home and community? Are there areas of learning that take on a greater significance for children and families working in the distant setting? How much time, effort and commitment can be expected from the young learners, their parents and others who provide immediate support? How can priorities be decided, and who should decide?

The practical and organizational dimensions

Finally there is a group of issues that are of concern to potential service providers. What are the resource implications of setting up an ICT-based structure to support distance learning for children? Which technical and pedagogical approaches are likely to prove cost-effective in different situations? What are the likely capital and ongoing costs? What technological support is needed? What kind of structure is needed to ensure that tutors have the time and support to carry through their role? Who will train and support parents (or others with a similar supportive role)? Who will create and modify materials and learning activities, what is to be the balance between standardized and individualized materials, and how will the partnership between tutors and design experts be shared? How will staff develop the necessary skills; not just ICT skills but also how best to use mediated learning environments to enable and encourage learning?

These issues and questions are not, of course, exhaustive. However they do reflect the major themes that have arisen from EFECOT initiatives over the five year period 1996–2001. They will continue to be a central focus within the work of EFECOT, and as noted above, may hopefully prove useful for others pursuing similar goals.

Notes

1   Unlike most travelling communities, where the children normally stay with the family, the bargee families of northern Europe have accepted that their children need to be educated in a residential setting, but have formally negotiated 'late entry' into the education system. So the challenge here is restricted to early learning activity, with efforts to provide supported distance learning 'on board' between the ages of four and six.

2   This emphasis is a direct response to parents and representatives of the communities who value aspects of school education and do not want their children to miss out.

3   GSM is an agreed standard for digital mobile telephony which allows inter-operability between European providers.

4   The trials took place in four European countries, and were mainly successful. However, coverage problems in Scotland caused major difficulties, and this part of the trial was effectively abandoned.
5   The technical aspects of the project are described in a detailed project report (Muffler, Panagiotarakis and Marks, 1998).
6   Part of the National Institute for Curriculum Development (SLO).
7   The topic for the discs, Electricity and Business Skills, was selected after community-based surveys aimed at establishing vocational interests and priorities.
8   Further details of the system and platform are available from the project's technical report (Lenaerts and Daems, 1998).
9   The decision of Philips to withdraw from the CD-i market to focus on DVD was also, of course, a constraint to further development of the approach.
10 VSAT stands for 'very small aperture terminal'. This satellite technology was specially developed within the project to allow two-way communication making use of the KU transmission band.
11 GPRS is a technology and standard for mobile telephone networks, but with a higher bandwidth than current GSM-based services.
12 This exploration is within the Qwatra project (2001–03), using the Cohesion/ IMAT platform developed by the Belgian company Advanced Projects and Products nv.

References

Bruner, J (1968) *Towards a Theory of Instruction*, Norton, New York
EFECOT (1999) *Policy Plan: 2000–2007*, EFECOT, Brussels
Elen, J (1996) Didactical aspect of self-study material, in *From Penny Post to Information Superhighway: Open and distance learning in close up*, ed M de Volder, pp 75–77, Uitgeverij Acco, Leuven
Jonassen, D *et al* (1999) *Learning With Technology: A constructivist perspective*, Prentice Hall, New Jersey
Lenaerts, T and Daems, B (1998) *TOPILOT: Description of the communication platform*, EFECOT, Brussels
Marks, K (1999) *Report on E-DSRR 6th Month Trials*, Marac Electronics, Athens
Marks, K (2001) *Final Report: Flexible Learning Environment eXperiment*, EFECOT, Brussels
Marks, K and Pullin, R (1998) *TOPILOT: Overall project evaluation and monitoring report*, EFECOT, Brussels
Moll, L and Greenburg, J (1990) Creating zones of possibilities: combining social contexts for instruction, in *Vygotsky and Education*, ed L Moll, pp 319 *et seq*, Cambridge University Press, Cambridge
Moore, M (1993) Theory of transactional distance, in *Theoretical Principles of Distance Education*, ed D Keegan, pp 22–28, Routledge, London

Moore, M (1995) The death of distance, *American Journal of Distance Education,* **9** (3) pp 2–4

Muffler, K, Panagiotarakis, N and Marks, K (1998) *E-DSRR: User requirements review and state of the art survey,* Marac Electronics, Athens

Reynolds, S, Vanbuel, M and Marks, K (2001) *Trapeze Supplementary Project Report,* EFECOT, Brussels

Utsi, S, Bellens, S and Lowyck, J (1999) *Inventaire of User Requirements in Terms of Learning Processes and Behaviours for Adequately Using FLEX Learning Blocks in a Technological Learning Environment,* EFECOT, Brussels

Relevant Web sites

The EFECOT Web site is at http://www.efecot.net and contains further information about FLEX, TOPILOT and Trapeze, as well as the current Qwatra project.

Further information about Trapeze is also available via the ESA site at http://estec.esa.nl/artes3/projects.

Chapter 6

Open learning and distance education for displaced populations

Michael Brophy

Over the past 20 years we have all grown familiar with television images of refugees: families bundled with their bags onto tractors, gaunt African children with staring eyes walking across barren landscapes. We have seen aircraft parachuting in tents and sacks of food and trucks delivering blankets and medical supplies. But we rarely if ever see or even hear about what happens next. In 1999 there were an estimated 15 million refugees in the world, people who had fled their homes in fear of persecution and crossed into another country for safety. In addition there were between 20 and 50 million internally displaced people (IDPs) who had fled fighting or persecution in their home areas and moved to safer parts of their own country, sometimes trekking on foot for a thousand miles or more (Crisp, Talbot and Cipollone, 2002). No one knows for sure how many refugees and IDPs there are today – 50, 60 or 70 million. But one thing that is certain, a large proportion of those refugees and IDPs are children, probably between 15 and 20 million.

After the planes have dropped the emergency food and water into the camps and the tents and water supplies have been established, there is still the problem of what to do for the children. Should they simply be left to sit with their families, day after day in a tent? Should they be allowed to wander, scavenging for food in the bush or for work in local villages? Or should they be encouraged to settle into some semblance of normality, and restart their education? But how do you provide education and schooling for millions of children in camps in isolated areas of the world, where there is no infrastructure, no schools, few teachers and almost no books, equipment or materials?

Since the 1960s and early 1970s many educationalists have believed that open learning or distance education were the ideal methods for providing 'schooling' for young refugees and IDPs living in camps. The situation in these camps encapsulated the very conditions for which open or distance learning was often advocated. As Thomas (1996) noted, 'distance education and open learning offer a realistic and practical alternative when the facilities and resources of conventional education are unavailable or inaccessible and likely to remain so'.

It is surprising, therefore, that these approaches have not been more widely used. One reason suggested here is that, while distance teaching and open learning have been and can be used successfully to provide education for displaced children, nevertheless there are specific problems with using these methods for displaced people, problems that can negate the other advantages they have. Some of the problems that we shall discuss include the way education is introduced into camps, the transitory nature of life there, and the difficulty of deciding on the purpose of education for refugee and IDP children.

Suitability of distance learning for young children

In most areas where there are displaced populations education is not a priority. Water, food, shelter, sanitation and health are the first considerations; only afterwards is education considered. When it is introduced it is as primary education for children. Even then, the immediate emphasis is not on the teaching of knowledge or skills, but on getting children settled quickly and safely. What is usually advocated is a 'rapid educational response' to quickly bring the children together with teachers in familiar and conventional 'school-like settings' (Crisp *et al*, 2002; Tawil, 1997).

There is also a fairly widely held belief that distance teaching methods do not work well with young children. Thomas (1996), for example, has noted that distance education has rarely made any 'major direct contribution to primary education'. Where distance teaching has been used in primary education for displaced populations it has almost invariably been for training teachers. However, as discussed later, there are a number of more recent projects which are using distance teaching with young children.

The transitory nature of life in camps

A second problem facing those designing distance education programmes for displaced populations is the transitory nature of life in refugee and IDP camps. The people living in these camps do not see them as their long-term homes, but as short-term or temporary solutions.

Distance teaching is not a quick cheap 'fix' which can be dropped in by parachute. The design of good quality distance teaching materials takes time and resources. Just as there is no single school curriculum that can be used in every country, neither is there a single distance teaching 'package' that can be used with all refugees or IDPs.

However, administrators preparing educational programmes for camps are reluctant to plan for any long-term provision. When they design educational provision they are faced with the question, how long is it for? Should they simply provide materials to meet immediate needs or should they plan for the longer term? In what have been termed 'complex emergency situations', refugees and IDPs may be forced to remain in camps for a decade or more. The preferred solution among most UN and international agencies has been not to develop new courses or materials, but to use existing curricula and textbooks, materials designed for use in a conventional and not a distance educational setting.

The problem of choosing education for settlement or return

The choice of curriculum and textbooks raises the questions of what should be the purpose of education for refugees and IDPs. If people have fled or been driven from their homes, should their education be aimed at helping them to return, or should it be focused on helping them to settle in their host country? The governments and authorities in most host countries may be willing to offer refugees sanctuary in emergency situations, but are usually less willing to allow them to integrate and settle permanently.

Choosing the curriculum and textbook

The question of education for return or education for integration has important implications for what is taught. Whose curriculum should be used? Whose cultural and social values taught? What language? Should it be the curriculum, the language and the values of the host country, or of those of the home country that the refugees have fled from? If the curriculum and language of the host country are used, after a few years young refugees are likely to become alienated from their homeland and find it even more difficult to return and settle back. They will read and write, and perhaps even speak, in a foreign language.

There is also the problem that refugees rarely flee to only one country. They go to the first safe place. This means that refugees from one country are likely to be displaced to five or six host countries. Each of these countries will have its own curriculum and its own distinctive cultural and social values. If they do return to their home country the children will have been taught in different languages, used different curricula and textbooks, and may even have been taught to believe in different cultural values and social norms.

The alternative that is often recommended is to use the curriculum, language and values of the country that the refugees have fled from. But they may have fled or been driven out for the very reason that they refused to accept the language and the values of the government in their home country. One of the underlying reasons for the continuing civil war in Sudan has been the rejection by the southern Sudanese of the government's attempts to impose Islamic values, Sharia law and the 'Arabization' of the school curriculum.

Faced with the long-term and political implications of whether a new distance education course should be for return to the home country or settlement in the host country, many administrators avoid making a decision and opt instead for a traditional, conventional approach, using 'safer' existing course materials.

The lack of certification and external examinations

In addition to the difficulty of deciding on 'what' children should learn, there is also the difficulty of assessing and certifying that they have completed a course. Where refugee children from one country attend schools in camps in five or six different host countries, whose standards and certification process should be used? There is no internationally recognized certificate or accreditation for children who have followed the many different courses developed in refugee camps or in the 'autonomous regions' of countries in conflict. When they can, organizations tend to use the certification process of the host country, but these are based on the host country's conventional teaching programmes. Such processes have rarely been designed to assess pupils taught at a distance.

Different names, different approaches

Although the use of distance teaching in camps and conflict situations is less common than might be expected, the approach has been used successfully in a number of places. However, when looking at how it has been used in these situations, it is necessary to ask the perennial question of what exactly we mean by distance teaching.

Thomas (1996) has written that 'The essential difference between conventional and distance education is in the way teachers and learners communicate with each other.' In distance teaching, he suggested, teachers and learners are separated in terms of both time and space, and the teaching and learning materials are centrally produced and then distributed to the learners. He acknowledged, however, that while distance education programmes rely mainly on print and other media, most programmes also include 'at least some' element of face-to-face contact. The question then arises how much of a programme can be delivered through face-to-face teaching before it ceases to be distance teaching. It may even no longer be meaningful to classify programmes as falling neatly into either a distance or a conventional mode; rather we should think of them in terms of a continuum of approaches along a spectrum.

At the 'conventional teaching' end (Case 1 in Figure 6.1) we would find the students and the teacher working together in a classroom. The teacher chooses

Conventional   Distance

Case 1   Case 2   Case 3   Case 4

Figure 6.1 *A conventional distance education continuum*

what is taught. The teacher also chooses the teaching materials. She may have written them or have chosen from a variety of textbooks and resources.

At the 'distance teaching' end of the spectrum (Case 4 in Figure 6.1) we would find an individual student studying self-instructional materials. He would be studying in his own home. The course and the materials would have been prepared by an individual or a team far away, people the student may never have met. There would be no local teacher and no class and no classroom.

However, both of these approaches have become less common than they once were, and there are a range of intermediate approaches. For example, teachers today rarely have the autonomy to choose what they teach, nor can they choose the textbooks and learning materials they intend to use. The curriculum, the teachers' guide and the students' learning materials are all likely to have been produced at a curriculum development centre. The teacher will be told what to teach and even trained how to teach it in the way the central curriculum developers approve. In effect for most modern conventional teaching programmes, teaching and learning materials are produced centrally and then distributed to the teacher and the learners. What was once a characteristic of distance teaching has become a feature common to both conventional and distance teaching.

We can represent this approach as Case 2 in Figure 6.1. Here there is a class of students with a teacher and they are working together in a classroom. The curriculum, the syllabus, the teachers' guides and the students' learning materials have all been produced centrally and then distributed to the schools. Most of the work is conducted during the face-to-face contact with the teacher, but each evening and at weekends the students are expected to do 'home' work or additional study without the presence of a teacher.

A further example (Case 3) is where a number of students in a town or village are studying the same course, one that has been produced at a distance teaching centre. Most of the time the students study by themselves at home, but once or twice a week they meet as a group in a study or resource centre. They do not have a teacher, but a tutor who meets with the group. The tutor helps the students to understand the course materials by explaining and elaborating on the main concepts and ideas.

Most educationalists would regard this approach as being towards the distance teaching end of the continuum. However, we can see that the difference between Case 2 and 3 is not quite so distinct. To some degree it is becoming a matter of vocabulary. One student's classroom is another's study centre. One's teacher is another's tutor. One's homework is another's self study (Figure 6.2). It could be argued that the difference between these two cases may not be so much in the nature of the programmes, but rather in the proportion of the study time spent in the presence of a teacher or tutor.

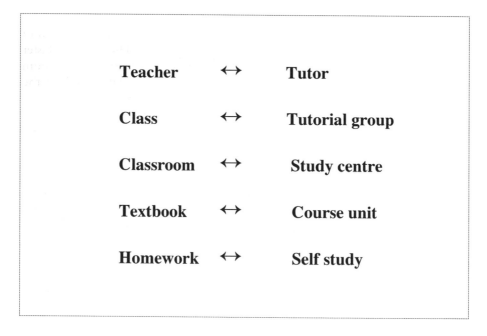

Figure 6.2 *The conventional distance vocabulary*

It has been suggested that programmes could be classified in terms of how they were originally designed, and whether or not they were written and intended to be used for conventional or distance learning. However, simply because a course has been designed to be used for one mode of delivery does not mean that is how it is used in practice. In the 1970s, for example, the modules and materials designed for the then new Open University distance teaching courses in the UK were quickly adopted and used by many traditional universities in their conventional lectures. Other distance teaching projects have also found that students and tutors use distance teaching materials to teach in a conventional classroom. Commenting on just such a change in the SOLO programme for Ethiopian refugees in Sudan, Thomas (1996) noted that there was a move away from distance teaching to traditional teaching methods, which was 'not entirely unwelcome to students and tutors, since it enabled them to go back to methods with which they were more familiar and perhaps more comfortable'.

In refugee and IDP camps it is often difficult to classify a programme as using either a totally conventional or a totally distance teaching approach. What starts out as one thing can metamorphose into another, as students or teachers leave, as the security situation changes, or as equipment or facilities are built or destroyed.

Learning from the 1980s experience in southern Africa

There are two main groups or clusters of programmes that we can draw upon to review the use of distance teaching for displaced populations. The first is a cluster of programmes that were developed in the 1970s and 1980s to assist refugees from southern African states. The 1970s were one of the most brutal periods of the apartheid era. Following the Sharpeville massacre of school children, many thousands of young people fled from South Africa and Namibia into neighbouring countries such as Botswana, Zambia and Tanzania. Many either left to join liberation movements or joined them when in exile. Faced with thousands of young volunteers who had only partly completed their education, the different movements and support organizations set out to provide education for these young people in exile. Distance teaching was one of the most common methods used. A number of distance teaching programmes were developed, including those of the South African Extension Unit (SAEU), the Namibian Extension Unit (NEU) and the Mozambican Open Learning Unit (MOLU).

The programmes in this cluster had a number of features in common:

● the target beneficiaries were living in settlements and camps;
● they were designed initially to provide secondary level schooling;
● there was an emphasis on English, mathematics and science;
● there was usually a link with a liberation or opposition movement.

For example the SAEU programme, which was set up in Tanzania, provided distance education for young South African refugees. Initially it offered secondary-level correspondence courses in English, mathematics and science and a more basic programme in English, mathematics and agriculture. Many of the students were members of South African anti-apartheid movements such as the African National Congress and the Pan African Congress.

Similarly in 1981 the NEU set up a programme in Zambia to provide secondary and remedial education for refugees from Namibia. Its main targets were young refugees who had completed primary education. Most of them were closely associated with the South West Africa Peoples' Organization. Again the focus was on English and mathematics. Around the same time a third programme was set up in Botswana by the Botswana Education Resource Centre (ERC). It too provided a secondary-level distance teaching course for young refugees, and again many of them were members of anti-apartheid and liberation movements. Here also there was an emphasis on English, mathematics and science.

Later (1991) a similar programme was started for refugees who had fled to Malawi from the civil war in Mozambique. This programme by MOLU also set out to provide secondary education. However, here the organizers felt that a purely distance teaching programme would not work, and used a combination of distance and conventional teaching (Boavida, 1994).

Around the same time as the southern African distance teaching programmes, the approach was tried by SOLU to provide education for Ethiopian and Eritrean refugees in Sudan. Again the focus was on secondary-level English, mathematics and science, and here, as elsewhere, the initial level of the course was too high and a lower-level programme was developed. Thomas (1996) has carried out a detailed review of each of these programmes, and there have also been reviews and evaluations of some of them (see Dodds and Mayo, 1990; Dodds and Inquai, 1983). From these we can see that are a number of similarities or common features in the experiences of those involved.

Drop-out and mobility of students

Most of the programmes suffered relatively high drop-out rates. In some cases, as in the MOLU programme, there was an improvement in the later years of the programme, but in others the proportion of people who completed courses or sat for final examinations remained low. Writing about the SOLU programme in Sudan, Dodds and Mayo (1990) reported that the drop-out rate there was due partly to the high mobility of the students. This seems to have been a factor limiting the success of a number of programmes. For example a report on the ERC programme in Botswana noted 'the high degree of mobility amongst students (the students who studied longest often left just before taking their exams; those who took their exams were often comparatively recent arrivals)' (Dodds and Inquai, 1983).

Over-estimation of students' academic level

A second problem found in a number of the 1980s programmes was an initial over-estimation of the academic level of the students. The result was that in a number of programmes the courses were initially set at too high a level.

In the SOLU programme, for example, the secondary course was found to be too difficult for the students. A lower-level remedial course was prepared, but even this was found to be too difficult for some. In Zambia the NEU actually started with a lower-level bridging programme to prepare the students for later entry to secondary level, but even this was found to be too difficult and a lower-level course was developed.

To some extent these difficulties seemed to centre around the problem of obtaining an accurate assessment of the students' previous school background. Since the courses were for refugees in camps, few of the students had any record or proof of their primary school attendance. The organizers were sometimes reduced to asking the students what their level was, and the students tended to exaggerate their attainments.

Delays in production and distribution

While most distance teaching programmes suffer from problems in production and distribution of their courses and materials, a number of the 1980s programmes seemed to have experienced problems that were more severe than usual. A report on the ERC project in Botswana noted that the materials were so scarce that 'the correspondence courses were officially kept in the library as reference materials, but often disappeared with the students and therefore became rapidly incomplete' (Dodds and Inquai, 1983).

Similarly the SOLU programme encountered severe printing problems and 'chronic shortages' of materials and course units. The NEU programme encountered a series of communication and logistical problems with the delivery of materials to the camps. Again the extent of the problems was due in large measure to the difficulty of distributing materials to camps and isolated settlements in rural areas. Refugee and IDP camps are unlikely to have good postal or transport links, and school materials rarely have the same priority as food, clothing and medicines.

The 1990s and the use of radio for children

The second cluster of distance education programmes are aimed more widely at displaced populations, rather than specifically at young people in camps and settlements. They are substantially different in nature from the programmes in the first cluster. They too have a number of common or similar features:

● they place more emphasis on the use of radio;
● they focus on primary and basic education rather than secondary schooling;
● they target children in their own homes as well as those attending classes;
● most of them place relatively little reliance on face-to-face teaching.

The 1980s programmes were aimed mainly at teenagers and young people living in camps, many of which became semi-permanent in nature. Many of the students were actively involved in liberation and rebel movements against apartheid or postcolonial governments. However, although most of the general population may have supported the struggle, the majority did not go into exile but remained in the home country. In contrast the 1990s were a period of mass refugee movements. In Kosovo, Somalia and Afghanistan it was not just the young and active who left. Entire communities and whole populations of children, adults and the elderly fled. The fear was not imprisonment but ethnic cleansing. The projects that started in the late1990s, therefore, were aimed not primarily at teenagers and young people in groups in camps, but at helping children from areas where there had been mass evacuations and disruptions of the whole population.

The late 1980s and early 1990s also saw a wider use of interactive radio instruction (IRI). Here radio broadcasts were used to encourage interaction between the pupils and the teacher, and to emphasize greater pupil activity and participation in learning and teaching. The radio broadcasts carried the bulk of the teaching, and often included questions or exercises for the students to complete and activities for them to carry out during the broadcast. The approach was found to be of particular benefit where there was a shortage of facilities and where there were untrained or poorly trained teachers.

Radio Education for Afghan Children (REACH)

The REACH programme, which started in 2001, is aimed at children aged between 6 and 16. It is not intended for use in schools, but for children who can use the radio to study at home with their parents. The REACH project is managed by the BBC Afghan Education Projects Unit, and uses an interactive radio approach with broadcasts that are 'intended to be entertaining and relevant to children's everyday lives. The programmes will encourage the children listening to become active learners, by giving them tasks to do during and after the programmes that will stimulate learning' (BBC AEP, n.d.).

Programmes are broadcast six days a week in Pashto and Persian. They include stories about everyday life (*Stories for Living*), a science series (*Curtain of Secrets*), a history and geography series (*Faces and Places*) and two magazines: one for 6 to 10-year-olds (*The Pedlar's Bag*) and one for 11 to 16-year-olds (*Castle of a Thousand Windows*).

Although originally intended for out of school children, the broadcasts are also being used in schools in refugee camps to complement conventional classroom teaching.

The Children's Radio Service

This programme was launched by the BBC World Service in 2001. The service aimed at helping children living in refugee camps, and the programmes were broadcast in Persian, Pashto, Nepali, Somali, Portuguese (for Africa) and Azeri. There were 10 15-minute broadcasts in each of the six languages. They were intended for children who were unable to get to school, but were also used as support materials for those attending schools. Although the programmes incorporated suggestions for activities the children could work on after the broadcasts, they were not designed to be interactive, and used a magazine format. One unusual feature was the emphasis placed on using children's voices in the broadcasts.

The Albanian Children's Radio Club (BBC Per Semaye)

This project was similar in nature to the Children's Radio Service, but it had a much greater scope in both time and coverage. Broadcasts started towards the end of 1999 and finished six months later. It was developed to help Albanian refugee children during the transition period between moving back home from the refugee camps in Albania and Macedonia and the opening of schools in Kosovo. The daily 15-minute broadcasts used a magazine format which included educational stories and talks, children's reports about their own lives and events around them, and an interactive game or music section.

Interactive Radio Instruction for Somalis (IRIS)

This is a new project, piloted in 2002, which is being developed by the Washington-based Education Development Centre in collaboration with the Regional Bureau of Education in Ethiopia, with funding from USAID. It is intended for Somali-speakers in Region 5 in Ethiopia, and is designed to meet the immediate needs of 'a multi-aged audience who are at the beginning of the cycle of basic education' (EDC, 2001).

Unlike the BBC programmes, the IRIS project is targeted at children in schools rather than those listening at home. During 2002 the pilot programme will test Grade 1 and 2 basic mathematics and literacy materials, which the planners hope will also address underlying issues about conflict prevention and mediation.

SOMDEL – Somali Distance Education for Literacy

This is another new project which was developed jointly by the Africa Educational Trust and the BBC World Service Trust, with funding from the UK Department for International Development and the Diana, Princess of Wales Memorial Fund. The overall aim is to offer access to basic education for young men and women in areas of Somalia where there are no functioning schools. The project is also open to young people who are not able to attend normal schools, for example, because of disability or because they are over school age. It uses a three-way approach incorporating printed materials, radio broadcasts and face-to-face teaching.

Weekly 30-minute radio programmes are broadcast to the region on the BBC World Service. Workbooks are provided for students, and tutors are expected to conduct an additional two hours of face-to-face teaching each week, using the guidelines and activities in the teachers' guide.

Within the overall aim of promoting functional literacy and numeracy, the project is also attempting to develop life skills related to health, nutrition, the environment and human rights awareness. Through consultations with potential students, teachers, professionals and community organizations across the different parts of the former Somalia, eight main themes were identified. Each broadcast and weekly work module incorporates key words related to at least two of these themes.

The radio broadcasts use a magazine format, which starts with a presentation of new key words or ideas and then moves on to interviews conducted in different parts of Somalia and Somaliland. During the interviews local people are asked to respond to questions that involve the key words and themes. The final section of the programme is a short comedy drama based on one of that week's main themes.

Before receiving training each tutor is required to produce a statement from a village or district committee, showing that he or she has the support of his or her local community. Given the ongoing conflict in many parts of Somalia, the planners felt that it was important to try to build into the programme a way for the students to be able to continue to study, even if the village was cut off or the whole population had to move. The teacher or tutor is from the community, and the broadcasts can be received not only in Somalia but in neighbouring countries throughout the region. To allow for problems with the distribution of the students' and teachers' booklets, the printed materials are available on the Web and can be downloaded by the local offices of UN agencies and non-government organizations (NGOs), and also through the (many) locally owned telephone companies and service providers.

These radio-based programmes in the second cluster are all relatively recent innovations. Some are just starting, while others have been completed but have yet to be evaluated. As might be expected, there have been reports of delays in production and problems with distribution of materials. However, these new programmes do seem to indicate both that a distance teaching approach can be used successfully with young children, and also that it is possible to use this approach as part of a rapid or emergency response for children in conflict areas and in refugee and IDP camps.

Since 1997, increasingly education has been regarded as the fourth component in humanitarian assistance in emergencies, next to food, shelter and medical care. However, there is still a widespread belief among UN agencies, international donors and NGOs that during the first 'rapid response' phase, support for education should be limited simply to the provision of kits and the building of temporary classrooms or shelters (UNHCR, 2000). However, the radio-based programmes that have been developed over the past few years suggest that open learning and distance teaching approaches offer viable alternatives, which can be used to provide education quickly and effectively for children in emergency situations.

Conclusions

Open learning and distance teaching do offer a viable way of increasing access to education for children and young people living in displaced situations. They can be used effectively both as a rapid response in an emergency situation and for the longer-term delivery of education in camps and post-conflict situations.

However, those planning and developing distance courses should be aware of the problems encountered in previous programmes. From past experience it is clear that:

● planners should take care not to overestimate the academic and language ability of their potential students. It is difficult for refugees, IDPs and those living in conflict areas to produce proof of their educational levels, and when asked most young people tend to exaggerate their attainment levels;
● planners should neither rely on nor expect to be able to use an existing course that suits the background and level of their students. They need to allow adequate time in their schedule for either developing a new course or heavily modifying an existing one;
● when planning their schedule for printing and distribution of materials and feedback from students and tutors, planners should allow for logistical delays and communication problems. Refugee and IDP camps and conflict zones are by their very nature likely to have poor communications and transport services;
● students and teachers in camps and conflict zones are more familiar with conventional classroom teaching than with a distance teaching approach. Planners should expect and plan for the tendency of students and teachers to revert to what they feel more familiar with;
● refugees, IDPs and people living in conflict zones are liable to move or be moved. Planners should design their programmes to allow for a high mobility level of students and tutors, so that students will be able to continue with their studies even if they are forced to move.

References

BBC AEP (undated) *Our World Our Future*, Afghan Education Projects, Peshawar, Pakistan

Boavida, J (1994) *The JRS-MOLU Programme: An alternative approach to refugee education – the Malawi experience*, Jesuit Refugee Service, Mozambique–Malawi

Crisp, J, Talbot, C and Cipollone, D (2002) *Learning for a Future: Refugee education in developing countries*, United Nations High Commissioner for Refugees, Geneva

Dodds, T and Inquai, S (1983) *Education in Exile: The educational needs of refugees*, International Extension College, Cambridge

Dodds, T and Mayo, J (1990) *Distance Education for Development: Promise and performance*, International Extension College, Cambridge

EDC (2001) *IRI for Somalis*, Education Development Centre, Washington

Tawil, S (1997) *Educational Destruction and Reconstruction in Disrupted Societies*, International Bureau of Education, Geneva

Thomas, J (1996) *Distance Education for Refugees*, International Extension College, Cambridge

UNHCR (2000) *Consultation Report: Inter-agency consultation on education in situations of emergency and crisis*, United Nations High Commissioner for Refugees, Geneva

Part 3

Methods

Chapter 7

Distance learning in India with open schools

Santosh Panda and Suresh Garg

Introduction

The Jomtien World Conference on Education for All (EFA) in 1990 called for massive initiatives by both government and non-government organizations to accelerate the pace of implementation of basic education for all, and adopt open and distance learning (ODL) and non-formal education strategies to achieve the goal of functional literacy by all. Even before 1990, India had hosted many international meetings/conferences/round tables on EFA, and several policy initiatives emanated as a result of these efforts. India is also signatory to the E-9 Summit resolution of 1993, with its resolve to launch joint initiatives to take education to the marginalized and the disadvantaged. Though the goal of universal elementary education for the age group 6–14 years has been enshrined in the constitution, it has not been realized so far. Further, legislation enacted in 2001 by the Indian Parliament made free universal elementary education a fundamental right. This chapter is presented against this background, and examines the contribution of ODL to EFA and at the primary, secondary and post-secondary levels in the largest democracy in the world.

Context

With 29 states and six union territories, India is the second most populous country in the world, with 64 per cent literacy in 2001. The governments (central and state) have been the major sources of funding for education: on an average they spend about 3.9 per cent of the GNP and 22 per cent of the state budget respectively on education (Panda, 1999). The conventional education system comprises 12 years of schooling, three years of first degree education, and two years of postgraduate education. However professional courses, such as nursing, medicine, engineering and PhD at the tertiary level, have variable systems.

Education is in the concurrent list, which means that responsibility is shared between union and state governments; the state governments are free to implement the 10 + 2 + 3 pattern of education with scope for flexibility. Education is transacted through government (fully funded and partially aided), as well as private schools at primary (grade 5), elementary (grade 8), secondary (grade 10), and senior secondary (grade 12) levels. The curriculum is framed by the National Council of Educational Research and Training (NCERT) by pooling national expertise, but the states have authority to make changes to allow for local requirements. The assessment and accreditation is done by the state boards of education, or the Central Board of Secondary Education (CBSE). Only a few schools are affiliated to the All India School Certificate Examinations (AISCE) board.

For 1998–99, out of a total child population of 190.54 million (120.45 million aged 6–10 and 70.09 million 11–14 years), which comprised about 19 per cent of the total population, the enrolment ratios in grades 1–5 (6–11 years) and in grades 6–8 (12–14 years) were 96.89 per cent and 46.03 per cent respectively. The drop-out rates were 39.74 per cent and 56.82 per cent respectively in 1998–99 (GOI, 2000). For secondary schooling (in which about 35 per cent of the relevant age group participate), not more than six out of 100 enrolled in grade 7 pass out from grade 10 (Mukhopadhyay, 1994). The formal and non-formal schooling sectors had the capacity to enrol about 150 million children, leaving about 40 million outside provision. As a rough estimate, with all drop-outs put together, nearly 70 million children need to be provided with schooling and about 360 million of the population need to be made functionally literate. Open schooling, therefore, has become a compulsion, rather than being an option where wide variations exist in perception and practices of quality schooling.

Open schooling

In India open education at the school level, as at the tertiary level, had its beginning in the correspondence model. Its growth has been truly phenomenal, and for the sake of discussion we can classify it into three phases.

Early years

Correspondence education at the secondary level was first introduced in 1965 by the board of secondary education in the state of Madhya Pradesh, primarily to improve the academic standards of out-of-school students appearing as private candidates. The concept attracted the attention of many, and today several state boards of secondary education allow students to appear as private candidates. In the state of Kerala, such students at times outnumber the regular schoolgoers.

Expansion phase

By 1968, two more correspondence schooling centres/boards – Patrachar Vidyalaya (Correspondence School) of Delhi and the Board of Secondary Education of Rajasthan state – were established. Subsequently the states of Uttar Pradesh and Orissa also began to offer secondary education through correspondence courses. The objective was to provide another opportunity to those who could not attend formal schooling (working adults, homemakers), or who failed in the secondary school examinations. The same curriculum was followed for formal and corre-spondence students, except that the latter were supported with some kind of learning materials and occasional personal contact programmes.

It was in all likelihood the pressure of prospective students for matriculation, rather than any defined policy of providing quality learning through ODL, that led state governments to initiate correspondence schooling. As pointed out by Dewal (1994), correspondence education provided the students with only the freedom of location. However, the felt needs for freedom of eligibility, duration, curriculum choice and evaluation procedures in existing correspondence courses culminated in the establishment of an open school for the country.

The open era

The establishment of an open school for those above 14 years of age was strongly recommended by the NCERT's 1974 Working Group, and in 1979 the central government established the Open School (OS) as a project of CBSE. This was certainly a bold step, since openness of schooling for any age group was seen as a mechanism leading to continuing and lifelong education. The OS proposed to cover the entire spectrum of schooling and extension education through:

- preparatory (bridge) courses to enable learners to be eligible to enter grade 10;
- secondary and senior secondary education;
- life enrichment and vocational courses.

In the first phase of its operation (until 1989 when the Open School took the shape of the National Open School), only preparatory and secondary courses were offered. Unfortunately, contemporary thinking about offering open basic education for neo-literates was marginalized by the affiliating board. Since CBSE was the certification body for OS graduates, curricular innovations for open schooling were a hard bargain; logistics, rather than academic considerations, occupied centre stage, and conduct of examinations and certification gained higher priority over pedagogy in the early years of the OS. This was obviously not a good beginning, and has influenced all subsequent developments.

The idea of open schooling attracted two southern Indian states: Andhra Pradesh and Tamil Nadu established open schools, respectively as a registered society and as part of a Directorate of Teacher Education, Research and Training. These efforts for open schooling were commensurate with the national initiative of taking distance education to the school sector, in spite of initial resistance and scepticism.

New beginning

In 1989 the Government of India upgraded the Open School of CBSE to a National Open School (NOS) as an autonomous institution (National Open School Society) under the Union Ministry of Human Resource Development (MHRD), in pursuance of the National Policy on Education 1986 (see NOS structure in Figure 7.1). NOS was empowered to:

- offer open school programmes;
- act as a certificate awarding institution;
- expand open schooling systems in the country by facilitating the establishment of open schools in different states;
- coordinate and maintain standards of open schooling in the country.

In 1997 NOS was authorized by the union government to offer its courses overseas. In recent years, various national policies on education have eulogized the lead role that open schooling and the National Open School should play in providing basic education to all. However, a lack of comprehensive government policy, planning and declarations on open schooling has limited its spread as well as acceptability.

In pursuance of its role as a national body, NOS has provided support to the establishment of seven state open schools: Haryana (1994), Rajasthan (1994), Madhya Pradesh (1995), Karnataka (1996), Punjab (1997), West Bengal (1997) and Kerala (1999) (Table 7.1), and three state centres of open schooling. Currently, 17 institutions (including one national open school and eight state open schools) are offering distance/correspondence education at the school level, catering to about 3 per cent of total secondary and senior secondary students. (At the tertiary level, the open learning system caters to about 20 per cent of learners.) Low student enrolment in state open schools reflects ignorance about open schooling and its subsidiary status in Indian society.

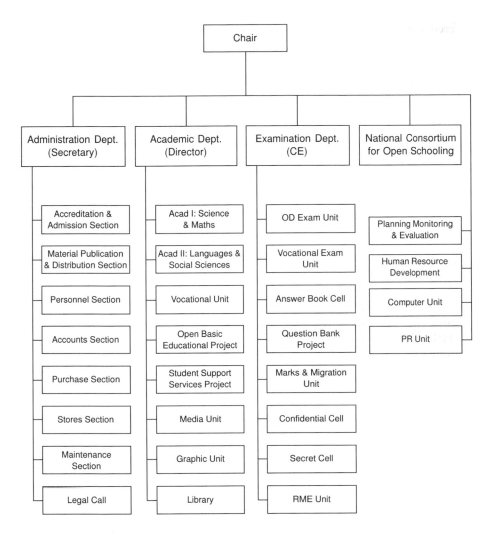

Figure 7.1 *Organizational structure of NOS*

It is important to point out that although correspondence/open schooling was initiated in India about five decades after such developments internationally, the system has expanded fast with the establishment of the NOS. The CABE has recommended that every state in the country should have an open school. Subsequently, the union government proposed to establish 15 open schools in the country during the Ninth Five Year Plan period 1998–2002. However, this target has been only half met. In its earnest desire to achieve the target of EFA, the MHRD has asked open universities to offer school-level programmes in states where open schools are not operating. In the long run, however, this option may not prove beneficial to the growth of open schooling, and it therefore needs more careful consideration.

Table 7.1 *Information on open schools*

	NOS (1999)	APOS (1992)	TNOS (1997)	HOS (1997)	ROS (1997)	MPSOS (1997)	KOS (1997)	POS (1997)	WBOS (1997)
Year of establishment	1989 (1979 as Open School)	1982	1982	1994	1994	1995	1996	1997	1997
Status	Autonomous	Regd society	DTERT	Board	Board	Regd. society	Regd. society	Board	Regd. society
Courses	Bridge/ Sc/Sr Sc/ OBE/LE/Vo	Bridge/ Sc/Vo	Sc/Sr Sc/Vo	Sc/Sr Sc	Sc/Sr Sc	Sc/Sr Sc/Aw	Sc	–	Sc/Sr Sc/OBE
Students registered	122,726	7,601	2,500	12,451	25,952	7,028	–	–	–
Students on rolls	400,000	–	–	40,000	–	–	–	–	–
Students awarded	249,547	–	–	6,249	–	–	–	–	–
Regional centres	10**	–	–	–	–	–	–	–	–
Study centres/AIs	1030	–	–	30/DCCs	500 FOs	210	8	–	APs
Audio/video	Audio/ video	Audio/ video	Radio/TV	–	–	–	–	–	–
Rural/urban (%)	–	–	28:72	66:34	43:57 ★ (Sr. Sc)	–	–	–	–
Male/female (%)	68:32	30:70	54:46	74:26	62:38★	74:26	–	–	–
General/disadvantaged (%)	76:24	30:70	–	80:20	82:18★	36:64	–	–	–
Funding sources	Student fees; central govt.	–	Student fees	Student fees	Student fees	Student fees; NOS; state govt.	Student fees; trust funds	–	–

NOS = National Open School; APOS = Andhra Pradesh Open School; TNOS = Tamil Nadu Open School; HOS = Haryana Open School; ROS = Rajasthan Open School; MPSOS = Madhya Pradesh State Open School; KOS = Karnataka Open School; POS = Punjab Open School; WBOS = West Bengal Open School.

DCCs = district coordination centres; SC = secondary (10+); Sr Sc = senior secondary (12+); Aw = awareness programmes; OBE = open basic education; LE = life enrichment; FOs = forwarding officers (school principals); DIET = district institute of education and training; APs = accredited persons; AIs = accredited institutions; DTERT = Directorate of Teacher Education Research and Training

Figures in parentheses in column headings refer to the year of availability of data.

★ data for 1993

** includes two state centres for open schooling

Source: NOS (1997);Virmani (1994); NOS (2000).

The efforts of NOS, both for itself and for the state open schools, have primarily been to reach the unreached: women, scheduled castes and scheduled tribes, disabled people, and those from rural, slum, tribal and isolated areas. Recently it has also been working to provide open basic education and functional literacy to neo-literates, and bring those in the relevant age group into the fold of (open) schooling. Perraton (2000) has pointed out that there have also been twin pressures from governments (central and state) and society to meet the educational needs of the ever-growing mass of people. This is largely because of the growing realization that education is the most reliable vehicle for socio-economic empowerment and creation of informed citizens for the development of the country. However, the enthusiasm of the leaderships (largely political and to some extent educational) about the potential of open learning, as a panacea for the limitations of the conventional system and the growing demand for schooling, is obviously misplaced.

Student enrolment

After the establishment of NOS, the expansion of open schooling has been reasonable in terms of enrolment, programme offerings and target groups (see Table 7.1). All the open schools put together have on their roll about half a million students. Some – such as NOS, Andra Pradesh Open School (APOS), Punjab Open School (POS), Tamil Nadu Open School (TNOS), Madhya Pradesh State Open School (MPSOS) and West Bengal Open School (WBOS) – have expanded into offering vocational, awareness and open basic education courses, besides the conventional secondary and senior secondary level programmes.

At NOS, student enrolment (Table 7.2) has registered an annual growth rate of about 28 per cent (NOS, 1997); the enrolment of scheduled tribe students has increased over the past years, and female enrolment (about 32 per cent) is significantly higher than that of the conventional schools. TNOS has female enrolment of 46 per cent, while at APOS it is as high as 70 per cent. For all disadvantaged groups, APOS and MPSOS have shown tremendous achievements, while NOS compares favourably with the national average. Even in Haryana, which provides the second largest enrolment to NOS, enrolment from rural areas at its own open school is 66 per cent.

Available data for NOS indicate that student ages range from 14 to 89, with most students falling within the 18–24 years age group. During 1996–99, enrolment in the 14–16 age range increased from 1 out of 10 to 1 out of 4. However, enrolment at 19 years and above has registered a decline (Table 7.3). TNOS shows a different profile: 15–19 years 22 per cent, 20–24 years 20 per cent, 25–39 years 48 per cent, 40 years and above 10 per cent. This, along with the fact that 76 per cent of students are employed, is a healthy trend, since a significant proportion of students are mature enough to take up open schooling. It contrasts with the trend observed at NOS, where about 60 per cent of learners are below 18 years of age.

The distribution of NOS enrolments across the country is uneven; it is skewed in favour of the northern region (66 per cent). Within this region, the states of

Table 7.2 *Enrolment trends at NOS*

Category	1990–91	1991–92	1992–93	1993–94	1994–95	1995–96	1996–97	1997–98	1998–99
General	32,862 (80.37)	28,461 (81.82)	42,962 (80.20)	45,343 (72.76)	54,322 (85.25)	53,949 (75.71)	68,965 (76.11)	81,730 (76.77)	92,879 (75.68)
Scheduled caste	5,923 (14.48)	4,103 (11.79)	7,017 (13.09)	10,120 (16.23)	6,779 (10.51)	9,354 (13.12)	11,861 (13.09)	14,241 (13.38)	17,173 (14.00)
Scheduled tribe	1,697 (4.15)	1,941 (5.58)	3,044 (5.70)	6,142 (9.87)	2,548 (3.95)	7,283 (10.22)	8,934 (9.86)	9,499 (8.92)	11,633 (9.48)
Handicapped	284 (0.69)	214 (0.64)	337 (0.63)	446 (0.77)	503 (0.78)	409 (0.59)	607 (0.67)	726 (0.68)	794 (0.64)
Ex-servicemen	118 (0.30)	62 (0.17)	207 (0.40)	232 (0.37)	324 (0.50)	258 (0.36)	245 (0.27)	264 (0.25)	247 (0.20)
Total	40,884 (100.00)	34,781 (100.00)	53,567 (100.00)	62,283 (100.00)	64,476 (100.00)	71,253 (100.00)	90,612 (100.00)	106,460 (100.00)	122,726 (100.00)
Male	26,166 (64.00)	20,645 (59.35)	33,593 (62.71)	40,945 (65.74)	41,945 (65.16)	48,126 (67.54)	59,061 (65.18)	71,478 (67.14)	83,225 (67.81)
Female	14,718 (36.00)	14,136 (40.65)	19,974 (37.29)	21,338 (34.26)	22,531 (34.84)	23,127 (32.46)	31,551 (34.82)	34,982 (32.86)	39,501 (32.19)

Note: Figures in parentheses are percentages. Enrolment percentages up to 1995–96 exclude students in vocational and regional medium courses.
Sources: Menon (1998); NOS (1997a, 1998, 1999)

Table 7.3   *Age profile of NOS students 1996–97 to 1998–99 (with %)*

Age	1996–97	1997–98	1998–99
14–16	9,478 (10.46)	27,404 (25.74)	33,294 (27.12)
17–18	30,010 (33.12)	34,688 (32.58)	40,323 (32.86)
> 18	51,124 (56.45)	44,368 (41.68)	49,109* (40.02)

*Age group 18–19 constitutes 50 per cent of this

Delhi (47,510), Haryana (20,089) and Uttar Pradesh (6,652) have the largest share. The southern states account for only about 9 per cent. Courses in the regional medium of instruction account for only 1.4 per cent of students. NOS is proposing to transfer the regional medium courses to the respective state open schools, so that the concentration in its programmes will be in English, Hindi and Urdu. Further, the bridge courses (leading to secondary course enrolment) cover only 0.7 per cent of students, an issue of concern if open basic education and open elementary education are to be pursued seriously. In fact, enrolment in bridge courses has been declining, from 1,020 in 1991–92 to 855 in 1998–99. The annual growth rate in the overall enrolment in vocational courses has also shown a steady decrease, from 59 per cent in 1995–96 to 23 per cent in 1998–99. This suggests that hands-on experience is either not appropriate or not relevant, and that these have failed to provide the students with an edge in the job market.

Course offerings

A wide range of choices is offered for secondary, senior secondary and vocational courses at NOS. While a student has to opt for five courses at the foundation (bridge) level to be eligible for grade 8 equivalence, no certificate is offered. For a secondary certificate, five subjects, with a minimum of one and a maximum of two languages, have to be studied. A student is free to take any combination of languages, maths, science, business studies and word processing courses. Still wider choices are offered at senior secondary level; five subjects including one language course is the minimum course requirement, with a wide choice of vocational subjects.

In addition, open basic education courses are offered by the national and state open schools, in collaboration with the National Literacy Mission, to neo-literates at three levels: A, B and C, equivalent to grades 3, 5 and 8. A learner at NOS can combine vocational courses (24 stand-alone and 17 others) with secondary or senior secondary courses, or take up vocational certification separately. NOS proposes to start open elementary education for non-schoolgoing children soon.

All courses are available in both English and Hindi (the national language). The secondary courses are also available in the regional languages Urdu, Telugu, Gujarati, Marathi and Bengali. MPSOS and Haryana Open School (HOS) use only

NOS course materials; and the NOS courses and certificates are recognized by 118 state boards and universities, including the Association of Indian Universities, and the Council of Boards of Secondary Education.

The entire course offering at NOS is modular, and has linkages at various levels; a learner can opt for open basic education A, B and C step-wise, and go for secondary, senior secondary or open secondary education. Similarly, a learner can enter secondary education through the foundation course or vocational courses. And all those learners who go from open basic education to senior secondary, as also the general public, can take life enrichment courses: Science For All and Environmental Science. Besides modularity and flexibility, a student can accumulate credits over five years to clear all courses for final certification. (NOS does not currently use a credit system, and a learner has to accumulate exam passes for senior-level courses.) At present, NOS allows transfer of credits (ie subject passes) for a maximum of two subjects for unsuccessful ex-CBSE secondary and senior secondary students to help them to continue their education and obtain an NOS certificate. This is good practice, and a bold step towards convergence of the conventional and the open systems to realize the goal of seamless education.

Course design and development

In course design and development, NOS follows a top-down model for curricular choices (Biswas and Priyadarshini, 1999). The head of the institution and/or the academic division decides on the programmes/courses to be initiated, and the academics are constrained to work in a given area and perspective. Subsequent in-house meetings lead to finalization of course structure, study scheme, implementation strategy, and the like. Some programmes can be developed to meet the customized needs of various sponsoring agencies, but the institution needs to be more flexible and allow academic freedom to its in-house faculty for programme design and development, so that the pool of wisdom becomes bigger.

It has been observed that a course travels for about three years from conception to launch. For instance, the senior secondary courses were planned as early as 1986 and were offered in 1989. Similarly, the revision of secondary courses began with a brainstorming in 1990 and course modules were offered in 1993.

The process of curriculum development follows the following steps:

- development of approach papers for the subject committees;
- constitution and orientation of subject committees;
- development of curricular framework;
- discussion in subject committees regarding content, density (spread and depth), approach, treatment and weighting;
- vetting of syllabus by expert practitioners and feedback thereon;
- formulation of learning outcome for each domain;
- final approval by curriculum committee and executive board (Biswas and Priyadarshini, 1999).

Approval of the curriculum is followed by the orientation of course writers from outside NOS. The process of material production goes more or less as follows:

- orientation of course writers and preliminary meetings;
- receipt of first draft and first review meeting with outside experts;
- receipt of revised draft, conduct of final review meeting, and preparation of graphics;
- receipt of final draft and first editing by in-house academic and outside editor;
- editing of test items and language editing;
- final editing (and simultaneous translation to other languages and editing thereof);
- preparation of camera ready copy for press.

A slightly different model of course development is used by TNOS. Staff of the district institutes of education and training located within the state develop all study materials. Subject committees are formed and oriented for two to three days for each subject/course. The course units are reviewed by outside reviewers, and assignment response sheets are also prepared. Though in both NOS and TNOS in-house staff work as course/programme coordinators, other models of course production have somehow not been tried. The team approach of NOS, with subject experts and head of the team from the conventional system, has been generally successful. The course lessons, which are invariably modular and self-instructional, have been widely appreciated by other open as well as conventional schools. It may be more reasonable to involve academics working in open universities/schools/correspondence course institutions, and try the model of in-house editor with individual writers. Such alternatives are crucial since the course design, development, implementation and administrative support necessary to cater to the educational needs of about 123,000 students (plus a backlog of students) is carried out with a staff of only 186, of whom only 30 are academics.

Print has been the mainstay of academic delivery so far, with audio and video as add-ons at the periphery, although NOS is likely to get its recording studio readied soon and should be able to produce its own programmes. To partly offset this disadvantage, NOS has since August 1998 had a regular Friday half-hour slot on the national TV channel Doordarshan. It also uses the teleconferencing facility of the Indira Gandhi National Open University (IGNOU) to orient academic facilitators for student support. It would be worthwhile to share the 24-hour educational channel Gyan Darshan and radio cooperative Gyan Vani of IGNOU to reach out to learners in all parts of the country. Even if all students do not have access to either study centres or audio/video cassette players and television, these media could be usefully harnessed.

Course delivery

Learner support is a crucial area in the operational effectiveness of open learning. Every open school has a network of study centres to accommodate the academic needs of its students. MPSOS has 210 study centres and NOS has 1030: 812 accredited institutions, 204 accredited vocational institutions, and 14 special accredited institutions for education of the disadvantaged. On the other hand, ROS has engaged about 500 distance learning facilitators as forwarding officers (who are invariably school principals), to take care of individual academic needs and personal problems of students. The NOS service network is operated through eight regional centres, two state centres of open schooling, and a student support services unit at the headquarters.

The learner support service models have evolved with time. In the initial years, with student enrolment of less than 2,000, the OS conducted personal contact programmes (PCPs) for 8–10 days in a year at different PCP centres; the tutors were responsible for admission, distribution of materials and counselling. This model was upgraded to regulate resource-cum-study centres (RCSCs) in 1984 and all services, other than the teaching provided by the tutor, were transferred to the RCSCs. In 1989, support services were decentralized to designated institutions called accredited institutions (AIs) and later on to accredited vocational institutions (AVIs). AIs and AVIs were required to sell admission forms, distribute learning materials, collect exam fees and distribute certificates, besides offering regular (weekly) tutoring and counselling (Priyadarshini, 1992). At present, the learner support model includes regional centres, study centres (AIs, AVIs and SAIED), and distance learning facilitators (DLFs), besides the tutor. The DLFs are senior academics or social workers. They supplement the work of regional centres by promoting open and distance learning, and by supervising and monitoring the work of study centres (tutorials, supply of study materials to students, evaluation of assignments) in areas where learner enrolment is low and establishing a RC/SC is not a viable option. During 1998–99, about 100 facilitators provided expert guidance and assistance to NOS on a part-time basis, and supervised about 400 study centres.

A study of NOS shows that attendance at PCPs had a positive correlation with the chances of success and the exam scores of the students (Sharma, 1997). It has therefore been suggested that at least 50 per cent of PCPs/tutoring should be made compulsory. In our view, this may not be advisable unless NOS is able to arrange PCP in the vicinity of learners. Failing this, mandatory provision would limit flexibility. Instead, the assignment system needs to be seriously pursued. In the early days at NOS, computer marked assignments were compulsory; these were discarded for a long period, and were then reintroduced in the form of tutor marked assignments with some weighting of scoring. Designing 'customized' assignments, which is a challenging task for the academics, would be desirable. Activity-based assignments, drawn from the context/environment of the learner, would probably serve the purpose better, since these provide an opportunity to tackle new situations.

Learner satisfaction is an important indicator of the quality of materials and services. Regular feedback and monitoring, and programme evaluation surveys, coupled with a strong management information system, are prerequisites for quality services. Moreover, institutional as well as personal research on open schooling now needs higher priority. Such mechanisms help raise the level of confidence about quality of processes and provisions among parents and the public, and also the institutional planners responsible for informed decision making.

Funding and unit cost

The initial funding, rather expenditure, for OS came from the CBSE. The income generated by NOS itself increased tenfold in the 1990s: from Rs 17.77 million in 1990–91 to Rs 181.99 million in 1998–99. Also, the non-plan expenditure during this period increased from Rs 17.86 to Rs 154.33 million. A comparison of income and expenditure for the year 1996–97 is given in Table 7.4. As may be noted, NOS is able to generate the funds needed to meet its non-plan expenditure. If this trend continues, NOS may soon be a self-sufficient organization. In the corresponding period the contribution by the union government for plan expenditure increased from Rs 8.5 million to Rs 35 million; for non-plan it decreased from Rs 7.78 million to Rs 1.5 million. At present the non-plan grant from the government is nil. The total government contribution was about 22 per cent in 1998–99. If only recurring expenditure is considered, the government's contribution stands at less than 5 per cent. It is likely to decrease further in the coming years, but it is hoped that quality will not be a casualty.

Table 7.4 *Sources of income and expenditure at NOS (non-plan) (1996–97)*

Income		Expenditure (non-plan)	
Head	% contribution	Head	% contribution
Tuition fees	51	Printing	58
Exam fees	35	Misc	13
Others	12	PCP	11
Government	02	Salary	8
		Exams	8
		Media	2

The cost per student (recurring and non-recurring) in the period 1989–90 to 1996–97 increased from Rs 471 to Rs 1,050, because of increases in printing costs, exam costs and staff costs, and the expansion of student support services. The senior secondary unit cost for production of learning materials for 1996–97 was made up as follows: paper and printing 75.6 per cent, academic staff salaries 12.2 per cent, expert committee meetings 4.0 per cent, typists 2.2 per cent, artists 2.1 per cent, course writers 1.4 per cent, editors 1.3 per cent, miscellaneous 0.9 per cent and proof readers 0.3 per cent. It may be noted that this cost structure may vary and show economies of scale if alternative methods of materials production are explored.

In 1998–99 NOS offered concessions in admission fees to 59,109 students belonging to the weaker sections of society (scheduled castes, scheduled tribes, ex-servicemen, disabled people and women), worth Rs 13.56 million, from funds generated on its own. Though this has increased the unit cost, it is a sensible step to further strengthen the concerns of equity and social justice.

Fees for overseas secondary and senior secondary students are US $600 and US $700 respectively (as compared to about $20 and $30 for students in India). This suggests that NOS could easily offset the costs incurred on in-country provision of equity and access by increasing overseas enrolment (only 81 in 1998–99) and income. Even in the case of Indian students, it may be desirable to charge differential fees: the employed, and higher-income-group learners could be asked to pay more to subsidize the education of those who cannot afford to pay.

New initiatives

In the last few years, the National Open School has taken several bold steps and initiated reforms that have far reaching implications for open schooling in the country. These include the following:

- **Pursuance of open basic education and open elementary education**. This provides a continuum to lifelong learning, in networking with the National Literacy Mission, state resource centres for adult education, other schools, and non-government organizations. With provision for combining higher schooling with vocational and life enrichment courses in later years, the learners will be competent for immediate employment as well as for higher studies. Further expansion of life enrichment and vocational courses will facilitate a wide variety of skills for self, private or state employment.
- **The setting up of Special Accredited Institutions for Education of Disadvantaged (SAIED)** has enhanced access to open learning for special groups, and provides all possible learning support to them according to their needs. The priority target groups comprise people with orthopaedic disabilities, hearing impairment, visual impairment, mental retardation, learning disabilities and multiple disabilities (Table 7.5). NOS has established study centres in a few special education institutions. Moreover, its programmes for jail inmates have been a great success.
- The **National Consortium for Open Schooling** (NOS, 1997) is a bold and much awaited initiative. With its establishment, the state open schools can be strengthened by capacity building through exchange of learning materials, resource (human and financial) sharing and networking. NOS has a strong information technology local area network at its headquarters, giving all

Table 7.5 *Learners with special needs enrolled with NOS in various programmes*

Year	Cerebral palsy	Orthopaedic handicap	Visual impair- ment	Hearing impair- ment	Learning disabled	Mentally retarded	Multiple handi- caps	Total
1999– 2000	16	406	81	277	343	103	78	1,304
2000–01	26	402	85	267	228	85	26	1,119

Source: NOS (2002)

academics and officers access to independent PCs and the Internet. Such facilities are also available at some regional centres. This needs to be strengthened in a networking environment, so that all open schools and correspondence institutions are included in a wide area network.

- The initiative of the **Indian Open Schooling Network (IOSN)**, linking the Internet-based open and conventional schools, aims at developing a broader canvas (and facilitating convergence) for easy mutual access to information and archives, supporting teachers and students, offering career counselling and courses through the Internet, and the like.
- NOS has introduced **on-demand examinations and walk-in admissions** at primary and elementary levels under OBE and OEE. A proposal has been initiated to introduce a National Testing Service to support this, as well as facilitating certification to those learners who study in unrecognized schools.
- In 2002 an **International Centre for Training in Open Schooling (ICTOS)** was established, and certificate and diploma programmes are under preparation. These will facilitate pre-service and in-service training in open schooling and open basic education all over the world. The launch of the *OSAC Journal of Open Schooling* in 2001 supports this initiative.

Conclusion

Open schooling in India has shown phenomenal growth since the establishment of the National Open School, despite the pressures of unexpected expansion, and the monolithic cultural (social and institutional) dynamics. The system displays extra wings capable of emulation internationally. There are, however, some areas which need introspection and improvement. A few are suggested for immediate attention:

- Staff development, systemic research and training need to be built into organizational and individual work ethics.
- Quality assurance, especially in learner support, and the skills of learning to learn, need to be strengthened to meet the challenges of access and equity in a globalized economy.

- There is a need for qualitative provision of interactive and accessible ICTs.
- The existing consortium working towards further networking, collaboration and sharing, including convergence with the formal and non-formal systems, needs to be expanded.

NOS has now transcended national boundaries with a view to taking Indian education abroad, and to meet the aspirations of the Indian diaspora which would like to keep contact with the indigenous culture and maintain its ethnic identity. Four study centres have been opened in the Middle East and two in Nepal to extend educational facilities internationally. In keeping with emerging trends in the globalized era, it may be appropriate to use the Internet, teleconferencing and videoconferencing to enhance coverage and facilitate learning. With access to KU band technology and the Internet, it is possible to cater to learners around the globe. This could be expanded in future as a strategy to support innovations in-house.

Note

While this chapter has been in the press, NOS has been further upgraded and renamed by the Government of India. It is now the National Institute of Open Schooling.

Acknowledgement

The authors gratefully acknowledge the help of Dr Ashok Gaba, Senior Research Officer, STRIDE, IGNOU, in facilitating acquisition of relevant data. Further detailed information on NOS is available at http://www.nos.org.

References

Biswas, G and Priyadarshini, A (1999) Distance education at school level: National Open School, in *Open and Distance Education: Policies, practices and quality concerns*, ed S Panda, ABI, New Delhi

Dewal, O (1994) Open learning in Indian school education, in *Open Schooling: Selected experiences*, ed M Mukhopadhyay and S Phillips, Commonwealth of Learning, Vancouver

GOI (2000) *Selected Educational Statistics*, Government of India, Ministry of Human Resource Development, Department of Secondary and Higher Education, New Delhi

Menon, M (1998) Open learning and distance education, *Indian Journal of Open Learning*, **7** (3)

Mukhopadhyay, M (1994) The unfolding of an open learning institution: the National Open School of India, in *Open Schooling: Selected Experiences*, ed M Mukhopadhyay and S Phillips, Commonwealth of Learning, Vancouver

NOS (1997) *Launching of National Consortium of Open Schooling: Report,* National Open School, New Delhi

NOS (1997a) *Annual Report 1996–97*, National Open School, New Delhi

NOS (1998) *Annual Report 1997–98*, National Open School, New Delhi

NOS (1999) *Annual Report 1998–99*, National Open School, New Delhi

NOS (2000) *National Open School – a profile*, National Open School, New Delhi

NOS (2002) *Annual Report 2001*, National Open School, New Delhi

Panda, S (1999) Developments, networking and convergence in India, in *Higher Education Through Open and Distance Learning*, ed K Harry, pp 199–212, Routledge, London

Perraton, H (2000) *Open and Distance Learning in the Developing World*, Routledge, London

Priyadarshini, A (1992) *Reducing the Distance: A study of the Personal Contact Programme of National Open School,* Diploma in Distance Education Project, IGNOU, New Delhi

Sharma, O (1997) Attendance in personal contact programmes and performance of open learners, *Indian Journal of Open Learning*, **6** (1&2), pp 71–75

Virmani, M (ed) (1994) Education for All, *National Open School*, New Delhi

Chapter 8

Reflections on open schooling and national policy in South Africa

Neil Butcher

Background to the policy debate on open schooling in South Africa

Since its first democratic elections in 1994, South Africa has been a hive of activity in the development of educational policies of various kinds. In the short span of eight years, almost every aspect of the country's education system has come up for intensive research and review, as part of a process of trying to restore equity and build quality of delivery of education to all of the country's people. In mid-1999, this process turned its attention to the issue of open schooling.

South Africa has a long history of distance education delivery in public education, although this history is predominantly located in the country's higher education systems. The University of South Africa, for example, launched distance education programmes in 1946, awarded 180,578 degrees between 1967 and 1999, enrolled 115, 856 students in qualifications in 2000, and is regarded as one of 11 'mega' distance education universities in the world. Distance education delivery has grown throughout the public higher education system, through two other dedicated providers – Technikon Southern Africa and Vista University's Distance

Education Campus – and increasingly through the launch of distance education programmes by historically 'contact' higher education institutions. In recent years, this growth has also spread into private sector provision of higher education.

At the general and further education and training (GET and FET) levels – the levels at which South Africa's schooling system operates – distance education has, however, had a much more limited history. There has been one dedicated public distance education provider in operation since 1984, the Technical College of South Africa, but this institution focuses on providing vocational training in a variety of learning areas, such as engineering, business studies, communication and social services. There are also some private providers offering secondary schooling at a distance. These courses are, in general, aimed at adults who were unable to finish their secondary school careers through the formal education system, although they are also available to people of schoolgoing age unable or unwilling to attend a contact secondary school.

Within this context, awareness grew in South Africa that many countries around the world, when faced with problems of learner access to conventional schooling systems, have implemented some or other form of open school as a response. While the reasons for establishing such systems internationally are many and varied, depending on the context in which they are implemented, South African policy makers were aware that, very often, establishment of open schools has been motivated by intrinsic weaknesses in the mainstream, 'contact' schooling system. Consequently, the Centre for Educational Technology and Distance Education (CETDE) of the South African Department of Education commissioned policy research on open learning in the GET and FET sectors. This research project, which was completed in early 2000, had its origins in various informal policy discussions that took place around the policy of establishing an open school in South Africa. This chapter reviews the results of that policy research – which were released in a report entitled *Opening Learning in South African General and Further Education and Training* (SAIDE, 2002) – and its implications for open schooling in South Africa.

How open learning has been defined in South African policy

The starting point of South Africa's policy research into open schooling was to re-examine the concept of open learning itself, in order to flesh out what implications it might have for policy formulation. The term 'open learning' does not invite easy definition. As Mackenzie *et al* (1975: 15) pointed out, 'Open Learning is an imprecise phrase to which a range of meanings can be, and is, attached. It eludes definition. But as an inscription to be carried in procession on a banner, gathering adherents and enthusiasms, it has great potential.' Thus, open learning describes a concept that is complex and yet invigorating educationally. This problem is compounded by growing use of the term internationally – as well as the emergence of hybrid terms such as open and distance learning – which is leading to further divergence in definitions of the term.

The research process chose not to debate the relative merits of different inter-pretations of the concept. Instead, it constructed its own, drawing on international literature, analysis of national educational policy, and practical experience of education and training in South Africa. From these sources, it extrapolated what seemed to be the most relevant working definition of open learning to the South African education and training context. In doing this, the report grappled with a conceptual challenge that has become critical in South African policy thinking, and that ultimately significantly influenced the country's policy directions on open schooling.

Differentiating open learning and distance education

Internationally, there has been a growing tendency to conflate open learning and distance education. Derek Rowntree points out that 'for most people, open learn-ing implies that the learner's work is based around self-study materials' (Rowntree, 1992: 16). For example Hilary Temple, when describing a training programme that was introduced at British Telecom, observes that 'it is now company policy for distance learning to be the first choice for delivery unless the cost-effectiveness of alternative forms can be demonstrated'. She then goes on to describe this as a 'victory for open learning' (Temple, 1991: 86), thus equating distance education with open learning. In this example, though, there is nothing to suggest that the application of distance education had any intrinsic link to efforts to increase open-ness; rather it was simply a tactical switch of teaching methods by the company concerned for financial purposes. This conflation of terms becomes most apparent in discussions on the costs of 'open learning'. David Bosworth, for example, makes the following comment: 'costing open learning is complicated, since a number of savings can be made, but initial costs of packages, equipment, software and so on can be high' (Bosworth, 1991: 29). It is clear that he is actually describing a costing process for distance education, as do many other people (for example, Rowntree) when considering cost factors for 'open learning'.

Opening Learning in South African General and Further Education and Training argued that this is a distortion. As it noted, the term 'distance education' describes a collection of methods for the provision of structured learning. Its object is to avoid the necessity for learners to discover the curriculum by attending classes frequently and for very long periods in order to listen to it being spoken about. This does not mean that there is no face-to-face contact, but that most communication between learners and educators is not face-to-face. Instead, it makes use of different media as necessary. Distance education, therefore, provides techniques of educational design and provision that – under certain circumstances – can bring better chances of educational success to vastly more people at greatly reduced costs.

Nevertheless, the provision of distance education does not automatically equate with openness in education. As Rumble points out, for example, 'the technological basis of distance education may . . . lead to a closed system if undue emphasis is placed on 'programmed' media such as texts, broadcasts, audio- and video-cassettes, computer-based instruction, etc, where the content is pre-determined and communication is one way (from the teacher to the student) (Rumble, 1989: 31).

Both in South Africa and internationally, a vast amount of distance education provision is closed in many respects. Consequently, although distance education is a collection of educational practices that has demonstrated great potential for increasing openness in learning, the report argued that these terms should not be confused.

Unfortunately, this confusion has been taken to great lengths in some circles, leading, in its most explicit manifestation, to growing use of the conflated term 'open and distance learning'. The conceptual integration of open learning and distance education in the United Kingdom and Australia into 'open and distance learning' has created a real misperception that distance education is intrinsically 'open', and regretfully the term has a growing currency in South Africa. This is a problem, not only because poor distance education practice can easily close off opportunities of actual learning, but equally because it contains an implicit assumption that only those educational strategies clustered under the banner of distance education have the potential to create openness in educational systems. This is a fundamental distortion of the conditions necessary to create more open education systems. It appears as often as not to have had its origins in attempts by distance educators to market their offerings.

Critically, then, *Opening Learning in South African General and Further Education and Training* took a position that open learning has no conceptual value as a synonym for distance education. As will be seen, this apparently pedantic semantic consideration has had important consequences for the future of open schooling in the country.

In addition to confusing the terms 'open learning' and 'distance education', the report noted a further tendency to regard open learning as something that can find final expression through individual projects, initiatives, institutions or other educational systems. This is expressed quite clearly in the names of several organizations: for example, the Open Learning Agency in Canada, the Open Learning Institute of Hong Kong (now also renamed as an Open University) or the Open University in the United Kingdom.[1] The idea is also contained in opinions such as 'A sensible use of educational technology theories and technological devices can provide a truly open system' (Bosworth, 1991: 8). This notion is, however, misleading, as Rumble makes clear:

There is, I believe, an attempt to highjack [sic] the descriptive adjective 'open' and apply it to learning systems to form a compound noun 'open-learning-systems', which is then used in sentences such as 'the [institution's name] is an open learning system'. Such sentences are then used to define the particular system in a way which is attractive politically, given the political and financial advantages which may accrue from claiming status as an open learning-system. In practice the systems so described may be anything but open.

(Rumble, 1989: 33)

There is a great danger in labelling individual initiatives in this way, because it implies the creation of a separate 'open learning' system alongside conventional education and training, running parallel to it through various 'open learning projects'. Such thinking, for example, led to a proposal in the African National Congress's[2] *Policy Framework for Education and Training* that a National Open Learning Agency should 'conduct an analysis of the capacity of existing institutions which might form part of the national open learning system' (ANC, 1995: 74). Such a tendency robs open learning of its strengths as a concept. This is because it suggests that open learning is a perceptible method of educational provision that is to be offered alongside conventional education. Such educational provision will inevitably be regarded as inferior and marginal to mainstream education, as the history of distance education has clearly demonstrated. In addition, this conceptualization can be used by existing educational providers as an excuse for doing nothing to open their own mainstream provision.

Redefining open learning

Using the above as a framework, *Opening Learning in South African General and Further Education and Training* noted that open learning is not something that can be contained in individual educational projects, initiatives, institutions, or indeed any educational system, each of which is subject to too many constraints to offer truly 'open' learning. It argued that attempts to describe systems or institutions as 'open' are contradictory and unhelpful. All systems and institutions depend on sets of rules of operation that necessarily create closure at different points within them. These points of closure are not intrinsically problematic, as all social systems require understood and agreed rules of operation to function effectively and within the boundaries of financial constraints. Indeed, any educational system or institution that strives for complete openness sets itself a final goal of anarchy, in which all learning will become impossible.

Rather, then, the report interpreted open learning as an approach to education whose principles can continually inform all educational practices with the aim of improving them, a position that is now common in several policy instruments in South Africa. It saw this most easily expressed in a simple grammatical switch, from understanding 'open' not as an adjective – which then describes a particular kind of learning – but rather as a verb, creating an impetus for action. Thus, it argued that the strength of the concept lies in its capacity to lead to action focused on systematically opening learning. This it is able to do because open learning brings together key educational principles, all of which focus in one form or another on opening learning. These principles do not amount to a coherent doctrine or philosophy; indeed, often they exist in tension with one another. This tension is important, because it can help educational planners to understand where closure in their educational systems is required and where it is unhelpful. Thus, the principles of open learning provide a set of benchmarks against which all aspects of any educational system (international, national, provincial, or institutional) can be measured. This process can lead to improvements in the underlying design of such a system, because it can remove unnecessary closure and consolidate closure where it is important to the efficient and financially viable functioning of the system.

For the purpose of its analysis, the report began developing a locally relevant definition of open learning by offering a definition taken from government policy:

> Open learning is an approach which combines the principles of learner centredness, lifelong learning, flexibility of learning provision, the removal of barriers to access learning, the recognition for credit of prior learning experience, the provision of learner support, the construction of learning programmes in the expectation that learners can succeed, and the maintenance of rigorous quality assurance over the design of learning materials and support systems. South Africa is able to gain from world-wide experience over several decades in the development of innovative methods of education, including the use of guided self-study, and the appropriate use of a variety of media, which give practical expression to open learning principles.

> (DoE, 1995)

This definition effectively helps to sort through differing international interpretations of the concept in moving towards a locally relevant understanding. The report went on to identify the following as key principles of open learning, drawing on definitions of open learning provided in the country's *White Paper on Education and Training* (EM, 1995):

1. **Learner-centredness.** The notion of learner-centredness is the primary prerequisite of openness. The principle of learner-centredness, in essence, acknowledges that the learner should be the focus of the educational process and an active decision maker in an interactive process. To be successful, education should build on learners' own experiences, using these as the starting point and basis for any learning process. This, in combination with efforts to encourage independent and critical thinking, empowers learners to be able to interact confidently and effectively with society and to construct their own lifelong career of learning.
2. **Lifelong learning.** This concept is central to the notion of open learning. It argues that learning should continue throughout life (rather than being limited to childhood) and should be of direct relevance to the needs and life experience of learners. This, in essence, acknowledges that an understanding of education as an end-on preparation for life is no longer feasible.
3. **Flexibility in learning.** The concept of open learning entails increasing the flexibility of learning provision to cater for the needs of learners, allowing them flexibility in choosing what they want to learn, how they want to learn, when they want to learn, and the pace at which they wish to learn.
4. **The removal of all unnecessary barriers to access.** Such barriers would include geographical isolation, discrimination on the basis of race, gender, age,

or physical disability, the inability to take time off work for a course, lack of 'appropriate' qualifications, and the use of pedagogical approaches that restrict accessibility to learning and expertise.

5. **Recognition of prior learning experiences.** In opening access to learning opportunities, it is important that relevant prior learning experiences of learners are recognized and credited where applicable. In so doing, open learning extends the definition of terms such as 'learnt', 'knowledgeable' and 'competent', and insists that institutions be transparent about their requirements for admission to, and successful completion of, programmes of study. As part of increasing openness in education and training, learners should be able to accumulate credits, earned in the same or different learning contexts, which can lead to the achievement of national qualifications.

6. **Learner support.** Increasing the amount and flexibility of learning opportunity is not effective unless it is accompanied by adequate learner support by educational providers. Learner support is multi-faceted, and includes pre- and in-programme counselling, support given by tutors and facilitators, the encouragement of interaction between learners, support built into course materials, and provision of access to the necessary facilities.

7. **Expectations of success.** Offering learners a reasonable chance of success involves not only offering opportunities to complete learning programmes successfully, but also ensuring that the qualifications earned have value in the occupational marketplace.

8. **Cost-effectiveness.** Cost-effective education is not simply education offered as cheaply as possible; it is education that uses the full range of resources available, in the most appropriate and effective educational combinations for different contexts, in order to offer the highest quality education to as many people as possible. The principle of achieving cost-effectiveness in education is the driving force behind an education and training system committed to open learning approaches. This is particularly important because inefficiencies are most heavily borne by institutions providing education for the poor and marginalized.

9. **Working with legacy systems.** Linked to the issue of cost-effectiveness is commitment to working with legacy systems. The whole concept of open learning is significantly devalued, if it is not located within the practical context of systems that have already been established and are currently providing access to educational opportunities in South Africa. Commitment to understanding and improving legacy systems is implied in many of the discussions above, but requires foregrounding as a separate principle if efforts to open learning are to be taken seriously. This commitment should not be confused with efforts to maintain the status quo. The central thrust of open learning is to effect ongoing changes and improvements to educational systems – based on clear guiding principles – not to entrench current systems. Nor should this be taken to mean that new systems cannot be considered as a possible strategy to open learning. Decisions to implement new systems, however, need to be taken with direct reference to their impact on existing

systems (particularly where they might create space for existing systems to avoid processes of opening learning).

In order to become effective in South Africa, the report argued that these principles need to suffuse the schooling system as a whole in order to allow for its effective transformation. Openness in education can only start to be translated into practice when large numbers of projects, initiatives and institutions use the principles of open learning to rethink and redesign all aspects of their educational systems on an ongoing basis, and coordinate their efforts to offer as wide a range of learning opportunities and methodologies to individual learners as possible. It argued that it is necessary to debunk the myth that open learning is an absolute goal which can achieve full practical expression in individual initiatives. This can be regarded as both positive and challenging for educationists: positive because it does away with simplistic distinctions between 'correct' and 'incorrect' educational practices, moving instead towards a more relative approach when judging the merit of educational initiatives; challenging because it demands an ongoing process whereby educational aims and goals lead to actions that are evaluated and consequent feedback which contributes to the continual revision of the goals and amendment and improvement of educational practices.

Open schooling and mainstream school policies

Why is any of the above relevant to open schooling? In South Africa, simply because it provided the conceptual framework that has, to date, guided policy choices in this area. As has been noted, the policy research process in South Africa had, as one of its goals, consideration of the appropriateness of establishing an open school in the country. Using this framework, the process defined an open school as 'an educational institution operating in the spheres of primary and/or secondary education, providing courses and programmes predominantly through use of distance education methods'.

The report noted that most schools of this nature have been established for some time. The Correspondence School in New Zealand, for example, was established in 1922, while the Open School in India is over 20 years old. Reasons for establishing such schools have tended to revolve around accessibility to traditional schooling. In the two examples mentioned above, part of the motivation to establish the school was to provide access to students in remote farming communities (New Zealand) and access to large numbers of students whom the mainstream schooling system could not absorb (India).

The report observed that establishment of open schools has often been motivated by intrinsic weaknesses in the mainstream, 'contact' schooling system, which policy makers have seen requiring years of structural change before large-scale improvements will become noticeable. Thus, open schools provide handy, reasonably quick institutional solutions to problems of educational delivery, which can operate largely outside of the mainstream schooling system and hence not be slowed down by the pace of these structural changes. On the face of it, these appeared to be structures of particular interest and relevance to South Africa. The country faces severe problems in the area of schooling, and there have been concerns that changes to this massive system will seriously delay meaningful educational delivery to many South Africans.

Under these circumstances, it certainly is tempting to consider establishing a new educational institution outside the mainstream system. The report argued, however, that there is a very real danger implicit in this, namely that such expediency further retards the pace of change in mainstream systems. Recent educational developments compound this problem, suggesting that, while open schools may have provided some sensible, 'easy' solutions to policy makers of yesteryear, they no longer remain a viable educational intervention.

Open schooling and distance education

Emerging from its research work, *Opening Learning in South African General and Further Education and Training* argued that open schools are based on a historical distinction that has existed in educational systems between 'distance' and 'contact' education. This distinction has been very useful for many years, particularly as it allowed for the establishment of innovative responses to educational problems – such as open schools   that could be set up and run without waiting for changes in mainstream educational systems. Such flexibility was important to the success of many distance education institutions around the world, but has also had the unfortunate consequence of establishing two distinct educational systems, which have historically operated in parallel and created long-term policy problems. This problem has been compounded recently, as there has been an explosion of educational delivery options, around which it has become increasingly difficult to establish meaningful policy and regulatory frameworks.

The experience of distance education in South Africa suggests that it is becoming increasingly difficult to maintain neat categorizations, as these increasingly contain too divergent a range of educational practices to remain relevant. This has become particularly problematic in the area of distance education. For example, distributed lecturing systems using videoconferencing equipment, and systems using instructionally designed study guides and decentralized tutorial support, find themselves located within the same category, although they bear almost no resemblance in terms of their pedagogical approach, technologies used, and financial implications. This is not to suggest that one is intrinsically better than the other. It simply points to the inadequacy of planning approaches that assume the planning requirements of both will be adequately met by a single framework called 'distance education'. The report argued that this conceptual problem lies at the heart of any concept of an 'open school'.

The research project therefore came to the conclusion that the traditional dichotomy of 'distance' and 'contact' education has outlived its usefulness. The growth of distance education methods of delivery has been a key feature of education in the 20th century, a feature that has marked South African education as much as education in any other country in the world. Initially, these methods were developed as distinctly different from contact education, resulting in the establishment of dedicated distance education institutions such as the University of South Africa (UNISA) and the Technical College of South Africa. To most people, distance education came to be seen as provision for those people denied access to contact education (either because they cannot afford the latter or because circumstances demand that they study on a part-time basis), and distance education was regarded as a separate educational 'mode' operating through systems that ran parallel to contact education systems.

The examples and case studies researched in this and other research exercises (eg DEC, 1999; SAIDE, 2000a), however, reflect an ever-growing diversity of educational practices being clustered under this 'catch-all' phrase of distance education. Further, many educational practices using what might historically have been described as distance education methods are not labelled overtly as distance education by their protagonists. This may be because it has simply not occurred to them to do so, because they are conscious of the threat of seeing government subsidy reduced (a problem in South Africa mostly restricted to higher education), or because of concerns about student perceptions. These practices are also being integrated into contact education, as their growth at traditionally contact higher education institutions demonstrates.

Awareness is now growing that elements of distance education have almost always existed in face-to-face programmes, while educators involved in good quality distance education increasingly recognize the importance of different types of face-to-face education as structured elements of their programmes. This trend has rendered rigid policy distinctions between the two modes of delivery meaningless. Compounding this problem, the growth of new information and communications technologies (ICTs) has begun to make the notion of distance difficult to interpret, while creating a number of educationally and financially viable new means of providing education. Many educational providers in general and further education are busy with processes of developing strategies to harness ICTs effectively.

Consequently, the report suggested that an appropriate solution to this problem is the conceptual introduction of a planning continuum of educational provision. This continuum has, as two imaginary poles, provision only at a distance and provision that is solely face-to-face. The reality is that all educational provision exists somewhere on this continuum, but cannot be placed strictly at either pole. A major advantage of this blurring is that educational planners can turn from meaningless hypothetical debates about the relative virtues of particular methods of educational provision, to consideration of the nature of learning and the educational value of a course's structure and content. Educators often end up equating particular methods of education with good quality education, even when these methods are being poorly implemented. The notion of this continuum is free of such premature and unnecessary judgements about quality. The report argued that it should form the basis of any strategic planning processes undertaken to harness the potential of distance education methods in South Africa, rather than somewhat anachronistic efforts to set up 'single mode' distance education institutions such as open schools.

Such an approach is interesting in this context precisely because it can enable planners to remove the baggage of educational models developed for fundamentally different contexts, while allowing them to draw on the lessons contained in the implementation of these models. This conceptual shift is vital in changing the structure of GET and FET systems in South Africa. In particular, it allows for greater flexibility and opens possibilities of collaboration, both of which are vital to improvements in educational quality and cost-effectiveness of educational provision, issues of particular relevance to South African policy makers currently.

Based on the above discussion, the report concluded that an open school was neither a viable nor a desirable intervention at this stage for South African schooling. It argued that such an institution would be based on a dichotomy that is losing relevance in educational planning, and would also be likely to draw additional scarce resources away from solving fundamental problems dogging the mainstream schooling system.

The international consultants participating in this research exercise[3] agreed that, politically, it would probably not be possible in their countries to establish a separate, open school under current circumstances. Most also agreed that, given the kinds of changes described above, it would also not be particularly desirable. Interestingly, the international case studies completed for the report also reflected a growing trend for these 'open schools' to be providing support services to the educational system as a whole. This trend seemed to be significantly more interesting and relevant to South Africa. Thus, the report argued that efforts should rather be made to integrate the best and most relevant practices emerging from such interventions around the world into the mainstream GET and FET systems in South Africa, a policy position that currently remains intact in the country today.

Emerging policy recommendations

Having reached the conclusions outlined above, the Policy Research Report went on to make a range of proposals aimed at opening learning throughout South Africa's schooling system. The following are some relevant examples.

Learning from distance education and resource-based learning

In an effort to encourage the development of increasingly flexible educational provision, the report argued that it was necessary to, first, work systematically through every national policy implementation framework – starting with the systems of gathering national data on GET and FET – to remove unnecessary inflexibilities that may be constraining the growth and development of innovative educational strategies and more flexible institutional systems. It proposed that the time frame for completing this work in its entirety could be set at five years.

Second, it was necessary to develop a plan of action to make small strategic investments in increasing the capacity of GET and FET providers – including schools – to redesign their administrative and logistical systems to accommodate increasing levels of flexibility in educational provision where appropriate.

Generating and disseminating curriculum resources

The report proposed that, in re-emphasizing the importance of appropriate content and supply of suitable learning materials at GET and FET level, government should take practical measures to break down an unhealthy dichotomy that has been established between content-based and outcomes-based education. This should be done through establishment of a national Curriculum Resource Coordination Agency. The mission of this agency should be to implement strategies to provide educators in GET and FET with the content they require to bring developing curriculum frameworks alive from an educational perspective. Its work should not be prescriptive, but should focus on providing support to educators and – over time – an increasing range of choices for them as they seek to implement learning programmes. It was envisaged that the agency would have the following features:

- It was to be funded nationally, but would establish regional hubs to ensure that it focuses on providing extensive support to provincial departments of education. It would actively seek a range of income streams in addition to government funding, including advertising revenue, sale of resources, regional agreements with other southern African governments, sponsorship and money from funding agencies.
- Its work was to be based on establishing partnerships with a range of key agencies, in government, parastatal, commercial and non-profit sectors.
- It was to focus on ensuring that curriculum resources recognize, enhance and support indigenous cultural values and educational principles. Thus, the agency would have funds available to support development of curriculum content and resources to redress imbalances in the content that currently permeate GET and FET education systems.
- It was to focus on ensuring that resources are made available in various languages, to accommodate the different learning requirements of South Africa's learners.

Roles for information technology

The report went on to propose that a Curriculum Resource Coordination Agency should make strategic investments in online curriculum management systems. These would capture detailed information on curricula for GET and FET educators and learners, allowing for easy printout of or online access to all relevant curriculum materials, statements of outcome, assessment strategies and criteria, descriptions of learner support strategies and other pertinent curriculum information. It would also contain integrated feedback mechanisms, thus leading to systematized quality assurance strategies and real-time improvement of curricular frameworks.

Conclusion: developments since 2000

As this chapter has outlined, there are currently no serious open schooling institutions in South Africa. This is, however, not simply a historical fact; it is also the consequence of a series of policy deliberations undertaken in the country since independence in 1994. South Africa has a provincially organized schooling system, which comprises over 27,000 schools. In reviewing the history of open schooling, policy research in that country concluded that the urgent priority in South Africa is not to create alternative schooling systems, but rather to integrate alternatives, greater flexibility and increased efficiency into the mainstream schooling system. This hopefully will come to represent not a reactionary move against educational innovation, but rather a considered effort to integrate the principles of open learning into mainstream education systems, as this is where the bulk of national educational investments are currently made.

In this regard, there have been ongoing attempts to reform schooling in South Africa, both before and since the release of *Opening Learning in South African General and Further Education and Training*. The challenges are many and the barriers to creating an effective schooling system significant. Much attention has focused – and continues to focus – on restructuring curricula, both to remove the legacy of apartheid education and to integrate best educational practices that developed around the world during South Africa's isolation from the international community. Although the concept of a Curriculum Resource Coordination Agency never came to fruition, the functions proposed for it are starting to be implemented in some quarters. Most notably, the national Department of Education has begun a process of coordinating the development of a Web-based portal for curriculum resources to support the school system as a whole.

Recently, processes focusing on deployment of ICTs at school have led to the establishment of a national ICT Forum, which was jointly launched by the Departments of Education and Communications early in 2001 as a first step towards achieving the vision described above. This forum is intended to bring together private and public sector players to support implementation of the vision of a dedicated national education network. It met for the first time in February 2001, with a view to soliciting active support from the private sector in supporting rollout of ICTs throughout the country's education system. This has been supported by development of ICT rollout plans in at least four of the country's nine provinces.

Furthermore, significant attention has gone towards reform of the country's management information systems, as these are often critical pillars in improvement of the quality of schooling. For example, in the Northern Cape province, the provincial government is working with USAID to develop prototype management information systems for one of its four districts (which are then being rolled out to pilot districts in three other provinces in the country). The logic behind this is that accurate, up-to-date management information is critical to successful operation of the schooling system, and that a well-designed administrative system harnessing computer networking to replicate data from school to district to provincial levels provides such information.

Thus, strategically, South Africa has decided to focus its attention on tackling key barriers within the mainstream schooling system, rather than setting up parallel systemic capacity to bypass those systems. This may not be an appropriate solution for all parts of the world, but it appeared to be the most logical way forward in South Africa, particularly because relatively very large percentages of government spending are directed at the mainstream system. Time will tell if this was the most appropriate solution.

Notes

1   Temple (1991) contains a number of case studies of training projects in British companies which are described as 'open learning projects' despite the fact that none of them are even close to being fully 'open'.
2   The African National Congress is the ruling political party in South Africa.
3   Although case studies from several countries were reviewed, consultants were brought out from New Zealand, India, Canada's British Columbia and Sweden.

References

ANC (1995) *A Policy Framework for Education and Training*, Education Department, African National Congress, Macmillan, Manzini
Bosworth, D (1991) *Open Learning*, Cassell, London
DoE (1995) *White Paper on Education and Training*, Notice 196 of 1995, Department of Education, Pretoria [Online] http://www.polity.org.za/govdocs/white_papers/educ2.html
DEC (1999) *The Feasibility of Establishing a Dedicated Educational Broadcasting Service in South Africa*, Departments of Education and Communication, Pretoria
EM (1995) *White Paper on Education and Training*, Government Gazette No. 16312 of 1995, Education Ministry, Pretoria
Mackenzie, N *et al* (1975) *Open Learning: Systems and problems in post-secondary education*, UNESCO Press, Paris
Rowntree, D (1992) *Exploring Open and Distance Learning*, Kogan Page, London
Rumble, G (1989) 'Open learning', 'distance learning' and the misuse of language, *Open Learning*, **2** (28), p 31
SAIDE (2000) *Open Learning in South African General and Further Education and Training*, unpublished policy research paper prepared for the South African Department of Education, South African Institute of Distance Education, Johannesburg
SAIDE (2000a) *Distance Education in Traditionally Contact Public Higher Education*, report prepared for the Council for Higher Education, South African Institute of Distance Education, Johannesburg
Temple, H (1991) *Open Learning in Industry: Developing flexibility and competence in the workforce*, Longman, Harlow

Chapter 9

Education by television: Telecurso 2000

João Batista de Araujo e Oliveira, Claudio de Moura Castro and Aimee Verdisco

Why education by television is not dead

In all but the poorest countries, television sets are commonplace. They have permeated far down into our social strata and have become a conventional and ubiquitous means of communication. By being everywhere and accessible to almost everyone, television has proved to be a convenient and cost-effective means for promoting and delivering education. *Sesame Street*, for instance, was launched in 1969 as an innovative way to supplement educational opportunities for children in the United States; the series is currently aired in 144 countries. And over the 30-plus years of its existence, there has been a proliferation of other educational programmes and projects. Kentucky's Educational Television, for example, features a lively classroom linked by closed circuit television to other schools that lack teachers in the subject at hand. South Korea supports a programme for high school drop-outs.

With technology creeping into all walks of life, these types of programmes appear to be strictly conventional uses of television. They are not particularly innovative by current standards, nor do they reach the masses. Indeed, in the United States, South Korea and many places in between, conventional schools deliver an adequate quality education to the masses of children and youth. *Sesame*

Street may still be popular but, increasingly, Big Bird and the Cookie Monster appear as digital images on computer – not television – screens. This is where the action and interaction are. It is also where the hype and the money are. Education may be 'returning to the basics', but it is doing so with CD ROMs, the Internet, expensive private tutoring and the like. Innovation and individual attention are the name of the game, and the slicker and more personalized the production, the better. Seen in this light, television seems all but passé, even for education, a field notoriously behind the curve when it comes to sophisticated technologies.

Has television lost its edge in education – if it ever had one? Is it but one more educational technology on the way into the trashcan of history? And since just about all innovation in technology comes from or via the United States, are other countries following in its footsteps?

This chapter argues that television is neither a dead nor worn-out medium for education. Taking the example of Telecurso 2000 in Brazil, it finds that television in education is alive, well, and doing a lot of good. Brazilians' love of television is no secret. The country's soap operas are internationally known, even exported to all continents. Nor is the country's dismal education performance any secret: a scarcity of good teachers and repetition and drop-out rates among the highest in the region. Putting the two together, Brazil has been able to make great strides in the area of educational television. It (like Mexico) is one of the few countries in the world sufficiently poor to have plenty of students out of regular schools and sufficiently rich to be endowed with a world-class television industry.

Simply put, Brazil has applied the costs, scales and approaches of commercial television to education. In combining innovation with slick production and good content, Telecurso 2000 has become an all but direct means for reaching populations of young adults, already beyond the reach of regular schools, and of doing so with a level of support rarely given to educational initiatives. Results have not only been impressive: they recast the potential and promise of television in education in a new light.

Telecurso 2000: past and present

The first generation

Telecurso 2000 traces its roots to the education programmes launched by the Roberto Marinho Foundation (RMF) in the late 1970s. Building on its strengths and previous experience with awareness-raising programmes (eg in environment and citizenship), the RMF created a tele-course – Telecurso – for fifth to eight grades and another programme for secondary school. Its results were promising. Targeting drop-outs, Telecurso (secondary level) boasted more than 600,000 viewers by the end of the 1970s. The grades these viewers obtained on equivalency exams paralleled those received by students in more mainstream preparatory courses, albeit at a lower cost: costs per Telecurso student were about a third of those for more traditionally delivered courses. This programme as well as its successor (Telecurso 2000) is open education, preparing its students to pass official examinations granting either a primary school or a secondary school diploma.

Just as Telecurso was a product of its time, so too were many of its weaknesses. The use of multimedia was limited, as were tracking mechanisms to gauge programme impact and evaluate student progress. Although its students tended to perform adequately in subjects such as geography and Portuguese (where traditional materials would often suffice), performance plummeted in 'more difficult' subjects – eg maths and science – that, even when taught face-to-face in traditional classrooms, often required additional supports, materials and time on task to produce the desired results. The absence of tracking mechanisms further complicated matters, in that there was little empirical evidence on how to adjust course content and create incentives to keep interest piqued and participation ongoing. Indeed, the number of written booklets purchased at the beginning of each cycle far outpaced those bought for the third phase (100,000 and 18,000 respectively), indicating a steep drop-out rate. Technology, in turn, limited the ways in which the courses were delivered. For the most part, Telecurso operated as broadcast television. Although organized learning did take place and students routinely attended classes in tele-classrooms, the programme and its courses of study were neither as structured nor as facilitated as they are today.

Telecurso 2000: the new generation

Telecurso 2000 mitigates many of the weaknesses of its first version. Initiated in 1993 and launched two years later in partnership with the State Federation of Industries in São Paulo (FIESP), it benefits from advances in technology, pedagogy and a greater awareness in society of the need for education. Industrialists from São Paulo were becoming painfully aware of the inadequacy of the education levels of workers, and started giving financial support as an incentive to get them to return to school. But what they found was very low quality education. The creation of Telecurso 2000 was an initiative to bring workers back to a better quality school, this time via television. But as it turned out, this clientele was being – and remains – overshadowed by a younger group of students still in public schools that increasingly use Telecurso 2000 as mainstream education.

The production of the programme brought the best of commercial television to bear, mobilizing the staff and resources more commonly associated with the production of soap operas and other shows that tend to draw far more viewers and advertisers than educational programming. A permanent staff of between 18 and 25 coordinates Telecurso from within the RMF. These professionals define the pedagogic approach of the courses and their alignment with official curricula, define the content of videos and booklets and tests, and come up with broadcast and social marketing strategies. But all production, of video, written materials and tests, is outsourced to private film makers, schools, foundations and universities. FIESP provided full financial support and coordination with the industries that were to offer the course to employees. RMF provided intellectual leadership and production supervision. Globo TV provided free airtime for advertising and content delivery on a national scale (depending on the programme, the Globo audience may reach 50 million or more viewers). The end result is edutainment: fast-paced and slick television that is not only entertaining but very serious education.

Two features of Telecurso 2000 are worth mentioning. For one, it is and has been an initiative of a private institution. The Roberto Marinho Foundation is part of the Globo Network, the fourth largest television network in the world. It is 100 per cent private. The funding for the programme came from FIESP; development and launching of the programme are also private. In this major respect, Telecurso 2000 thus differs from the vast majority of educational television around the globe. In fact, seen in this light, Telecurso 2000 epitomizes the whole notion of new public–private partnerships: private financing for a good that is eminently public in nature.

Second, Telecurso has been targeted and marketed as a second-chance programme. After all, it is an equivalency programme. Its targets are basic and high school drop-outs 15 years of age or older. Being targeted to older students means that the entire focus and learning strategies are tuned to this clientele. But perhaps more important, it is open education, not subject to any government control or regulation. Students take the public equivalency exams and their results are all that matter. The freedom to organize programmes without constraints imposed by state regulations is a major explanation for its success.

Who tunes in

There is no typical Telecurso student per se. Rather, based on recent statistics, two broadly defined groups can be identified. The first is defined by the sphere of influence of the Brazilian training system. As this system is sponsored by employer associations (and funded by a payroll levy), viewers tend to be workers, particularly industrial workers. Men between the ages of 20 and 40 dominate. Most dropped out of school more than 15 years ago and did so for reasons related to financial or family circumstance. Particularly in São Paulo, most of these students work in industry and attend tele-classes at their place of employment.

The second group attends tele-classes offered by non-government organizations, philanthropic institutions and local governments. As a result, it is less homogeneous. Identified through a sampling of participants in Rio de Janeiro, São Paulo and Amazonas, students are split equally between men and women. In general, these viewers tend to be younger than those identified in samples where the influence of FIESP is strong. And a considerable percentage (44 per cent) is unemployed. In many respects, these viewers represent those for whom the first Telecurso was created. Telecurso 2000 comes to them, either through their television sets at home or in tele-classrooms located within their communities, schools or other 'open' venues.

The surprising migration of Telecurso 2000 to regular classrooms and beyond

Very clearly, there has been a drift in clienteles. From a programme designed and paid for by industrialists to educate their workers, it has been migrating – quite spontaneously – to a broader clientele of poorer and younger people. This is a welcome development, but not one foreseen by anybody involved in the creation of the programme, some of the present authors included.

Yet there has been a new and perhaps even more dramatic and spontaneous shift in clienteles. Regular schools, particularly those catering to poorer areas, tend to have many overage students – a dramatic and chronic feature of Brazilian education. Many of these students are at an age threshold: although still in the formal education system, they are old enough, or almost old enough, to take the equivalency exam. While the statistics are not clear, regular schools catering to these students seem to be adopting Telecurso materials and methods. In other instances, Telecurso 2000 has migrated *en force* to, and become all but mainstream in, regular schools; that is, implemented in existing schools as part of the regular curriculum. For example, Telecurso has functioned as an alternative to regular academic education in the state of Rio Grande do Norte since 1993. Similar set-ups have been in operation in Maranhão since 1995. The inputs – the tapes and print resources – come from Telecurso; the school provides the classroom and teachers, usually trained and supervised under arrangements through contract with the RMF.

The migration of Telecurso to schools and other organizations has brought the programme into territories and areas well beyond anything originally intended. Tele-classrooms are no longer the monopoly of the FIESP and the industrial training system. Indeed the door has been opened to many programmes supported by individual businesses, as originally planned. Yet unions, too, have established tele-classrooms. This is probably one of the few examples of a programme initiated by employers' organizations that has been massively co-opted by workers' unions – creating a neutral territory where a long truce has prevailed. NGOs and civil society organizations have also taken up the programme in earnest, and now boast a large share of enrolment.

How Telecurso delivers its goods

Telecurso comes to viewers primarily through two mechanisms: organized and open broadcasts. Organized viewing takes place in tele-classrooms, monitored and facilitated by trained staff; it is not distance learning in the pure sense of the term. Open broadcasting more closely approximates the distance learning ideal, although, as will be discussed below, not all viewers tune in for strictly education-related purposes.

Organized viewing

When Telecurso is delivered as organized broadcasting, teachers/facilitators are on hand to encourage students and to track their performance and progress. Although the specific criteria used to hire teaching staff vary by Telecurso sponsor,[1] they are generally required to have at least some secondary education to direct the tele-classrooms at the basic level, and some higher education to work at secondary level. There is no requirement that they have a university degree or be licensed to teach. In fact, the Telecurso method all but guarantees that any facilitator passing the minimum standards can be 'successful' in the tele-classroom.

Classroom activities are detailed in manuals produced by the RMF and, although not obligatory, most teaching staff receive some training (24 to 40 hours) prior to stepping into the tele-classroom. Their primary task is to make explicit the link between students and the educational material presented on the television screen and to encourage students 'to learn to learn'. They plan and initiate complementary activities to help students grasp key concepts, evaluate student progress towards content and other learning goals, and prepare weekly lessons in such a way that they are flexible and appropriate to the audience at hand. In some cases, the sponsoring agency provides on-site supervision of these activities.

Two additional notes on these teachers/facilitators merit mention. First, no strict guidelines for payment exist. Some staff are paid by the hour. Others receive additional payment for tutoring or preparatory activities. In all issues that are related to pay, there is a clear dividing line between levels of education. Although the same teacher may work with basic and secondary education, accounts are kept separate. Hours spent with basic education are charged as such and remain separate from those accrued to secondary education.

Second, during the planning stage of Telecurso, it was feared that regular teachers and teacher unions would protest. After all, this was the quintessence of capitalism, creating an education programme that can operate without certified teachers, and with all the attractions of commercial television. In addition, there is a high degree of structure to the classes, something that left-wing pedagogy does not like. Much to the surprise of many, this did not happen. Teachers reacted only by demanding that the facilitators be regular teachers. And, as mentioned, Telecurso is insidiously migrating into regular schools. Even more surprising, a very well-known leader of one of the two national unions, a former metal worker, studied with Telecurso 2000, passed the examination and subsequently became a law student. He has praised the programme in front of Globo cameras on prime time television.

Most tele-classrooms are as well equipped as regular classrooms – if not better. At first glance, the Telecurso classroom appears much like a regular classroom. Tele-classrooms are equipped with the basics (such as sufficient desks and chairs for all students, bookshelves, a blackboard) as well as an array of pedagogical supports, including a complete series of Telecurso tapes, textbooks, additional reading and educational materials, such as maps and dictionaries. What serve to differentiate them are the television and video cassette recorder, an absolute must in the tele-classrooms; a luxury in regular classrooms. Differences can also be noted in time on task. There is no fixed schedule for the operation of tele-classrooms. Although the RMF recommends a minimum of two hours a day (15 minutes for the presentation of the video, 45 minutes for individual study, and 60 minutes for activities coordinated by the teacher/facilitator), some offer as many as four hours of service a day. Students take on average one or two subjects at a time; more ambitious students may venture to take three. Again, this situation stands in contrast to that generally found in regular classrooms. Notice, however, as will be discussed below, that Telecurso curricula are shorter and more focused than those of regular academic schools.

Open broadcasting

Open transmissions are not targeted. Rather, they are broadcast over different channels at different times of day, to an audience potentially as large as the sum total of all viewers in all catchment areas. The end product is a public good in the broadest sense of the word. A survey conducted by Globo in 1999, for example, found that an estimated five per cent of those interviewed had tuned in to Telecurso 2000 during the previous week – a figure that translates into around seven million viewers. Not all watch Telecurso 2000 in an effort to prepare for equivalency exams. In fact very few do, since those who want to take the exam attend classes where Telecurso videos and books are the means of instruction, with the support of a live teacher or instructor. Given the fact that no formal registration process exists for these viewers, there is no record of how many do actually take the exam. Many tune in for entertainment value, others because they like educational and cultural programmes. This in itself is an extraordinary result. Seven million people choose a programme that has to remain faithful to primary and secondary school curricula, instead of watching the fast-paced and highly entertaining staples of Brazilian television.

What sets Telecurso apart from other similar programmes

Telecurso consists of much more than just open and/or organized broadcasting. An entire series of support materials (including lessons, videotapes, printed texts, guides for teachers/monitors) and information networks exists. The inventory is impressive (Table 9.1).

Table 9.1   *Compilation of resources: Telecurso 2000*

	Lessons*	Videos	Books
Basic education	396	52	17
Secondary education	456	60	18
Technical training: mechanics	360	52	18

* Includes printed materials and videos
Source: RMF

These resources include several innovative features. Although curricula are closely related to the official curricula for the primary and secondary levels, they are not one and the same. Telecurso concentrates on selected or core areas of the official curricula, and presents its content in a manner appropriate to its target population, which is older. At the design stage, there was a decision to condense the official curricula. For a number of reasons – one being the low status of equivalency programmes – the public authorities in charge of formulating the open tests did not object. Ironically, the contents of Telecurso 2000 anticipated the new and much abbreviated curricula approved several years later.

Content is heavily contextualized. It takes the realities of everyday life of a young adult and uses them to illustrate key concepts and build core competencies. No classrooms, students, teachers or chalkboards appear on the screen. Rather, lessons revolve around what takes place on the street, in offices, factories, small enterprises, newspaper stands and so on. Such contextualization is taken seriously. For instance, English language classes take place in a simulated travel agency catering to English speaking tourists or in the simulated apartment of an imaginary American family living in São Paulo which hires a Brazilian maid.

Embedded in this approach is an emphasis on basic skills. Lessons focus on those skills that are important in life, leaving aside much of the theoretical content of official curricula. Presentations, in turn, are done modularly. Subjects are addressed as student demand warrants.

Lastly, production reaches the quality level of Globo – on a par with the soap operas it exports to all continents. Just as there are no classrooms, students or teachers depicted on the screen, there are no teachers or students acting the parts. All participants are professional actors – some of them known to viewers for their roles in soap operas or commercial advertising. No real teacher can match the resources of television or approach the refinement, structure, variety of images and humour conveyed on the screen. Nor can computers or the Internet do it, being media constrained to little more than the printed word. These media may be interactive, but their styles of presentation remain poor and primitive when compared to the shine and punch of television. And, of course, interaction is given by the live facilitators in the tele-classrooms.

The visual quality and the humour have been keys – if not *the* keys – to Telecurso's success. It is world class, high quality and entertaining television that is – at the same time – serious education, linked to and in line with regular curricula at junior high school level.

The numbers: a big programme in a big country

Students and viewers

Telecurso's targeting and distribution mechanisms have proved effective, in both attracting students and preparing them to take equivalency exams. Indeed, accounting for 15 per cent of all enrolments in equivalency classes, Telecurso has become the country's largest educational institution. Official data from the

Ministry of Education indicate that *supletivo* (equivalency) courses currently enrol a population of over 2.2 million, of whom 445,963 attend class in one of the 13,187 tele-classrooms located throughout the country.

The price tag

Telecurso 2000 is not cheap. Produced for a television-aware population with high expectations, the price of its development was steep. RMF estimates that more than US $30 million has been invested in production of materials and programmes. Globo, in turn, estimates an opportunity cost of more than US $50 million forgone income in spots and transmission of classes of Telecurso 2000, between 1995 and 2001. If calculated in dollar terms – at the exchange rate of the time it was produced – costs for production alone hover around US $2,000 a minute. But, given the scale of operation and the number of viewers, cost-effectiveness is high, even if calculated only for those who officially register. Assuming a (officially enrolled) student body of almost 450,000 and a shelf life of 10 years for the programme and its materials, per student costs per year would not exceed US $25. In other words, spending heavily on television production translates into modest per student costs, considering the huge numbers involved.

These per student costs also are comparable with that of the regular school system. Average cost per student at the basic level is around 450 reais, a figure that increases to 600 reais at the secondary level.[2]

There are data to indicate that drop-out rates in Telecurso hover around 17.5 per cent.[3] This figure is considerably lower than that found in regular schools offering preparation for equivalency exams where, on average, for every four students enrolled in the first year of secondary education, only one will complete the entire course of study. Although no hard data are available on other equivalency programmes, most estimates put drop-out rates in these programmes at around 20 to 50 per cent – on a par with rates in the regular secondary schools – with variations due to venue and provider (eg drop-out in community-based tele-classrooms tends to be higher than in tele-classrooms in firms).

Where the private meets the public: the tests and diplomas

While Telecurso 2000 is open education, operating independently from government oversight, in the end, students have to pass a public examination to obtain school certificates that are legally equivalent to a primary or secondary school diploma. This is where the private meets the public.

True to its objective, between 400–800,000 viewers use Telecurso 2000 to prepare for equivalency exams at either the basic or secondary level. As mentioned, to facilitate such preparation, content and learning objectives are linked to official curricula. Taking this underlying logic a step further, it would only seem natural

for each cycle of Telecurso to end with an equivalency exam. Yet this is not always
the case, nor is the equivalency exam itself a particularly convincing control of
quality. Passing or failing an equivalency exam often says more about the exam
itself than the form of preparation, particularly for those students tuning in to open
broadcasts of Telecurso. This is because exams are prepared on a state-by-state basis,
and the technical competency of some state departments of education is sorely
inadequate. In addition, this is the lowest status education within such departments,
and ends up in the hands of the weakest staff.

In an attempt to mitigate this situation somewhat and ensure a close fit between
the preparation delivered through Telecurso and performance in exams, the Carlos
Chagas Foundation, under agreement with the RMF, has produced a database of
test questions. At present, this contains enough questions for the elaboration of
more than 12 rounds of equivalency exams. These exams, in turn, are administered
by the (state) Secretariat of Education in São Paulo. In other states, exams are
elaborated and administered by the respective secretariats. In much the same vein,
exams set by the Serviço Nacional de Aprendizajem Industrial (SENAI) are
prepared by SENAI.

The results: does it make a difference?

With regular television, viewer numbers and revenues generated through advert-
isements would tell the difference between success and failure. In educational
television, the burden of proof is higher. Viewers also have to show some concrete
results on the education side of the equation. That is, Telecurso has to do more than
simply attract viewers; it has to prepare those viewers to pass equivalency exams,
reinforcing basic skills and creating new ones.

Seen in this light, the question arises whether Telecurso improves the odds of
passing the *supletivo*. Unfortunately, there is no straightforward answer. The lack of
standardized testing complicates any analysis of results, as do the variations in
delivery mechanisms.

Some of the large providers of Telecurso opt for an internal evaluation. In these
instances, they are responsible for both monitoring student progress and student
certification. Tests are designed for use in individual tele-classrooms and are applied
in some cases by individual teachers and in others centrally by the supervisors of
the provider. Comparability is therefore difficult, if not impossible. Methodological
caveats aside, however, existing data indicate that pass rates are high. For example,
data collected from ISAE/FGV reveal that of the 2,802 enrolled in Telecurso in
early 1999, 2,450 took the equivalency exam (given in each tele-classroom,
prepared by the State Secretariat of Education in Amazonas). Of these, 2,300 – or
94 per cent – passed.

Similarly, data from Viva Rio find that of the 5,643 students sitting for the
supletivo in 1999, 4,254 – or 75 per cent – passed. In this case, a single exam was
prepared centrally and administered in all tele-classrooms.

Open-access exams

Differences in scores obtained on equivalency exams stem from a multitude of factors, including variations in the level of difficulty of exams prepared by different institutions, the lack of 'fit' between the test and its target population, differences in student profile, and different preparation methods. Indeed, neither screening processes nor formal requirements exist for preparing for or taking such an exam. Those wishing to take one, regardless of level, simply register and sit for it. Telecurso 2000 is thus one of many avenues of preparation. Others include self-learning and preparation, and tele-classes sponsored by the (federal) Secretariat of Education, firms or other vendors. Indeed, Telecurso also appears to be an effective means for preparation for those taking open-access exams. Data collected by the FIESP and RMF for São Paulo indicate that 34.1 per cent and 42.7 per cent of Telecurso viewers pass subject exams (open-access) at the basic and secondary level, respectively.

The determining factors: still a mystery

Just as there is no typical Telecurso student, there is no student profile for which Telecurso appears to be most effective. Data compiled by SENAI find the impact of age on performance to be insignificant, regardless of the level at which exams are taken. Nor does prior learning (as measured in years of schooling completed) seem to influence success. In fact, at the basic level, additional years of schooling above and beyond first grade have a negligible impact on test scores: there is little difference between those who have completed grades 2–4 and those who have completed grades 5–8. At the secondary level, some relation between prior schooling and performance does appear. Although a more detailed analysis is necessary, it thus appears that the value added of the programme is greater at the secondary than at the primary level. That is, skills and knowledge acquired at the secondary level seem to be associated with better performance on and with Telecurso (secondary level).

It is worth noting that there appears to be a greater differential in performance in those tele-classrooms that are located in firms and receive technical assistance and support from SENAI or SESI. In these cases, better scores are likely to be related to more regular attendance, and a more homogeneous and motivated student population. These factors relate more to the nature of the firm and its structure of control than to the Telecurso provider. They also differ from the demographics and realities of community-based tele-classrooms (where attendance is less regulated and structured than in a firm, and the student body is more diverse), although the data from Viva Rio show the unemployed to have both the time and the motivation to attend community-based tele-classrooms regularly.

Lessons learnt

Telecurso is education for the masses. At the secondary level alone, it reaches about four per cent (250,000) of all students, in more than 13,000 tele-classrooms throughout the country. An additional 200,000 tune in to open broadcasts. Telecurso attracts a study body that is diverse in every sense of the word: in prior education attainment, socioeconomic status, and learning goals and objectives. And it is able to retain a good proportion of these students, graduating them at rates equal to, if not above, those of other equivalency programmes.

Telecurso focuses on the student. Those seeking a second chance find it an easily accessible means of obtaining equivalency diplomas and, in turn, of improving mobility in the workforce. For some it may be the only alternative, in that the only basic inputs needed are time, motivation and a television set. Telecurso's curricula and scheduling are flexible. Students can attend classes in tele-classrooms or study on their own. Course materials are geared towards these students, a fair number of whom have been out of school for as many as 15 years. For them, Telecurso provides a new approach to education: relevance to everyday life. This, as has been discussed above, stems from the contextualization of key ideas and sophisticated presentation.

In many ways, then, Telecurso can be seen as a laboratory for educational innovations. With condensed and contextualized curricula, it parts company with the watered down and run-of-the mill contents found in most programmes of this type. It focuses on relevant basic skills, not abstract theory, and weaves core concepts around and through what otherwise would be – and often is – entertaining television. Its supporting materials (video and printed) are of high quality, so high, in fact, that some state secretariats of education have chosen to use them through-out their respective systems. They also serve multiple populations, guiding self-learners as well as students in tele-classrooms. And to add further appeal, regardless of the quantity of viewers, the level of quality remains constant for the simple reason that classes are captured on videos and do not depend on the inspiration or prior preparation of teachers – a definite constraint for the kind of teachers who otherwise tend to reach such modest clienteles.

Following much the same logic, Telecurso introduces a new type of teacher – a facilitator. This teacher is not responsible for 'giving content' or 'covering curricula', as is often expected and demanded of teaching staff in the regular academic system. Rather, Telecurso teaching staff are facilitators, motivators, counsellors and organizers of individual and group opportunities for learning. They are focused on their students at all times. They help students to learn, rather than deliver conventional lectures.

In terms of education policy, Telecurso provides an interesting study in deregulation. Conceived as an open broadcast distance education programme, it provides ample and convincing evidence that education need not be the monopoly of the state to be effective. Indeed, Telecurso students perform at levels comparable with those of their peers in the formal system.[4]

Telecurso is by no means perfect. For a start, it sorely needs a more systematic and rigorous means of data collection and analysis of internal and external efficiencies. As evidenced by this chapter, it lacks basic statistics and a more reliable means to evaluate results. The activities and efforts of its major players – such as RMF and FIESP – could be better coordinated, with each respective institution concentrating its efforts in areas where it has comparative advantages. Such considerations are particularly important if Telecurso is to maintain and fine-tune its market segmentation, or eventually to franchise its name.

Telecurso 2000 is not a panacea. It is not a silver bullet solution for long-standing and structural problems within the Brazilian education system. At most, it offers a partial solution to complex issues, serving an estimated 200–300,000 out of a universe of 80 million Brazilians who have not completed basic or secondary education.

Notes

1   Although the RMF deals with some of the programmes, signing contracts with enterprises, municipalities and state governments, more students attend programmes run by other institutions. These include the employer-run training system, and large philanthropic foundations such as Bradesco and Viva Rio.
2   If reliable and comparable data were available, better comparisons could be made. For example, given the condensed nature of Telecurso's curriculum, comparison with the regular system should be based on 18 months (Telecurso) versus three academic years (regular system) – a comparison that would probably put Telecurso's costs per graduating student far below those found in the regular system. A better comparison still would be costs per approved graduate, a figure that would be telling of the levels of internal inefficiencies in both systems.
3   Drop-out rates for Telecurso cannot be evaluated by the same criteria used elsewhere, in that there is little emphasis given to timeframes or continuous study. Once students are enrolled, they can successfully complete their coursework either by returning to tele-classes, even after lapses, or by taking an equivalency exam offered by the relevant state secretariat of education or other qualified provider (eg SENAI).
4   Proficiency in English is a notable and worrisome exception. Research conducted by the Carlos Chagas Foundation found that no Telecurso student has any reason – professional or otherwise – to use, let alone become proficient in, the English language.

Part 4

The future

Chapter 10

E-learning and the development of open classes for rural students in Atlantic Canada

Ken Stevens

In urbanized societies like Canada, with economies that depend on the development of resources located in rural and remote areas, there is a direct economic relationship between the viability of schools in rural communities and national prosperity. It is difficult to maintain viable rural community infrastructures without schools that are perceived by parents and students to be at least as good as those in urban areas. However, it is often difficult for educational administrators to justify the provision of full-time, on-site teachers for small senior classes in rural schools. Economies of scale have in the past encouraged senior students from rural communities, particularly those intending to enrol in tertiary educational institutions, to complete their education in larger, usually urban, high schools, or in boarding schools (Stevens, 1997).

The introduction of e-learning in rural communities in Atlantic Canada has provided a new way of delivering educational opportunities to those who live beyond major centres of population, by using the Internet to interface schools academically and administratively. Within the new electronic structure that is created by linking schools as sites within teaching and learning networks (school district digital Intranets), open (virtual), classes have been organized.

The open classroom has a special role to play in the provision of education for rural people. In the Atlantic Canadian province of Newfoundland and Labrador, most schools are located in small, rural communities. In school district 8, the Vista school district of Newfoundland and Labrador, open classes in selected areas of the curriculum have been organized within a new electronic structure known as the Vista School District Digital Intranet. The development of open classes within a school district digital Intranet has created new learning, and indirectly career, possibilities for many senior students in small rural schools in this remote part of Canada. It has also encouraged new ways of organizing teaching and learning.

Education in Newfoundland and Labrador

Newfoundland and Labrador is characterized by its predominantly rural social structure, its distinctive history and its unique culture. Approximately two-thirds of schools in this province are located in rural communities. Thirty-one per cent of schools in Newfoundland and Labrador are designated 'small rural schools' (N = 122), and 75 of these have fewer than 100 students. Seventy of these small rural schools are all-grade (K–12), which means that they must offer a senior high school programme.

The reorganization of primary, elementary and secondary education in Newfoundland and Labrador into 10 school districts provided an opportunity to develop the first digital Intranet in the province. The Vista School District contains 18 schools ranging in student enrolment from 40 to 650. The region in which it is located extends from Bonavista in the north (the place where John Cabot landed in North America in 1497) to the Burin Peninsula in the south. It is a large geographic area, covering about 7,000 square kilometres. The region has a population of about 35,000 and an economy supported by a diverse infrastructure, including fishing, forestry, farming, mining, aquaculture and tourism. The Vista School District was formed in 1996 and became a legal entity in January 1997. There were 5,165 students enrolled in the 18 schools in the district, who were taught by 366 teachers. The district is approximately two hours by road from the capital city, St Johns, which is the location of the Memorial University of Newfoundland. Eight schools within the district, together with the TeleLearning and Rural Education Centre of the Memorial University of Newfoundland, formed a digital Intranet within which senior science courses were taught in open classes. By including this research and development centre (which is located within the Faculty of Education of the only university in the province) in the new rural school structure, collaborative research between academics and teachers was encouraged. The synergy of professional development between schools and a professional faculty addressed a concern recently raised by Thompson, Bakken and Clark (2001), that 'seldom are classroom teachers required to become involved in research/scholarly inquiry'. As schools and academics were involved in the organization of teaching and learning in the new electronic structure, collaboration quickly followed. Collaboration between participating schools and the Centre for TeleLearning and Rural Education at the Memorial University of Newfoundland led to the development of Web-based courses.

The development of Web-based science courses

The development of Advanced Placement Web-based courses in biology, chemistry, mathematics and physics took place within a development team in each subject area. A lead science teacher in each discipline was paired with a recent graduate in the same discipline who possessed advanced computer skills including Web page design, Java and HTML. The lead teacher and the graduate assistant were advised from time to time by Faculty of Education specialists in each curriculum area, and where possible, scientists from the Faculty of Science. The extent to which each Web-based course was developed by a team of four people varied. Most course development took place through interaction between lead teachers and the recent graduates.

This model of course development encouraged interaction between schools, graduate students and professors in the Faculties of Education and Science. Although at times professors had different opinions as to the most appropriate approach to the design of the courses, this model enabled the four courses to be developed over a 16-week summer recess period in time for the new school year.

Minimum specifications were adopted for computer hardware and network connectivity. All schools involved in the project had DirecPC satellite dishes installed to provide a high speed down-link. In most rural communities in this part of Canada, digital telecommunications infrastructures do not enable schools to have a high speed up-link to the Internet. Appropriate software had to be identified and evaluated for both the development of the resources and the delivery of instruction within the Intranet. Front Page 98 was selected as the software package. Additional software was used for the development of images, animated gifs and other dimensions of course development. These included Snagit32, Gif Construction Set, Real Video and similar packages.

Many software packages were evaluated and finally WebCT was selected. This package enabled the instructor to track student progress, it contained online testing and evaluation, private e-mail, a calendar feature, public bulletin board for use by both instructor and student, a link to lessons and chat rooms for communication between teacher and student. For real-time instruction, Meeting Point and Microsoft NetMeeting were selected. This combination of software enabled a teacher to present real-time interactive instruction to multiple sites. An orientation session was provided for students prior to the implementation of this project. They had to learn how to communicate with each other and with their instructor using these new technologies before classes could begin.

Teaching senior science in open classes

In eight schools within the district, students were enrolled in Advanced Placement (AP) biology, chemistry, mathematics and physics courses (N = 55). Such courses enable students to gain credit towards first-year university programmes while still at school, depending on the level of pass they achieve. AP courses are of post-secondary level, and designed to provide students intending to enrol in universities with the opportunity to begin their tertiary studies in their final year at high school. While these courses are a well-established feature of senior secondary education in the United States and Canada, it is unusual for students to be able to enrol for instruction at this level in small schools in remote communities. This initiative challenged the usual practice of senior students in small rural schools leaving home to complete their education at larger schools in urban areas.

By participating in open classes in real (synchronous) time, combined with a measure of independent (asynchronous) learning, senior students were able to interact with one another through audio, video and electronic whiteboards. From time to time they met for social occasions and to spend some time with their science teachers in person.

The electronic linking of eight sites within the Vista School District to collaborate in the teaching of these courses created a series of open classes in rural Newfoundland. The creation of the Vista School District Digital Intranet was an attempt to use information and communication technologies to provide geographically isolated students with extended educational, and indirectly vocational, opportunities. This has been part of a broader pan-Canadian initiative to prepare people in Canada for the information age (Information Highway Advisory Council, 1995, 1997). It is rare to find high school students in small and remote communities anywhere in the world who are provided with instruction in university-level studies. In Iceland (Stefansdottir, 1993), New Zealand (Stevens, 1995a, 1995b) and Finland (Tella, 1995) there have been attempts to provide alternative models for the delivery of education to rural students. The development of the Vista School District Digital Intranet involved the introduction of an open teaching and learning structure to a previously closed one. Accordingly, adjustments had to be made in each participating site so that administratively and academically, AP classes could be taught.

Research into the organization of senior students who were independent learners in a networked environment in New Zealand (Stevens, 1994, 1995b) preceded the formation of the Vista Digital Intranet in Canada. Independent learners in New Zealand were found to learn effectively and were able to obtain very satisfactory results in national examinations within an electronic network of small rural schools. In the New Zealand situation though, students usually had at least one teacher on site to assist with questions of academic nature. In the Canadian Intranet, this was not always possible. A question in the minds of teachers and researchers in the initial stage of the Vista Digital Intranet was whether students who were not used to being unsupervised could cope with new freedom and accept increased responsibility for their learning. Students were unanimous at the conclusion of the school year, that to be successful in an AP online course it was necessary to be able to learn independently, cope with a high volume of work and be willing to ask teachers and other learners questions as they arose (Stevens, 1999).

It was recognized early in the school year that a common schedule had to be adopted throughout the school district to allow students to interact with their instructors in the new Intranet. Unfortunately, this was not fully realized until after classes commenced, with the result that some instructors had to repeat classes for small numbers of students. It is anticipated that in future there will be asynchronous as well as synchronous teaching and learning within the Intranet. The initial plan was to allow for five online sessions and five offline sessions. This schedule was not followed in all schools. Online sessions were scheduled in the morning when network traffic was at its lowest point. Offline sessions were scheduled in the afternoon.

The shift from closed to open teaching and learning

The move from a closed to an open environment in the teaching and learning of science was based upon a transition from an analogue to a digital environment. The province of Newfoundland and Labrador has a high rate of use of satellite dishes per capita, and there are many schools in this province with local area networks (LANs). As a province, Newfoundland and Labrador provided excellent opportunities for the development of these technologies.

The linking of eight rural schools into a Digital Intranet has policy implications for the teaching profession, for the management of learning, for the organization of participating sites and for the future direction of education in this part of Canada. For the teaching profession there are three major policy implications.

First, teaching within a Digital Intranet is much more public than teaching face-to-face in traditional classrooms. One's colleagues can, and frequently do, observe one's online classes and one's teaching methods. This leads to new considerations of how one communicates as a teacher in a virtual class (Tiffin and Rajasingham, 1995).

Second, teaching in a Digital Intranet involves the application of a range of information and communication technologies to pedagogy, a process that at present has few guidelines. Those who are currently teaching AP subjects in the Vista Digital Intranet in Newfoundland are very conscious of being pioneers.

Third, the implementation of teleteaching within the open classroom environment of a Digital Intranet requires the integration of traditional (face-to-face) and virtual classes. With the appointment of lead science teachers for subjects in Intranets, assisted by on-site colleagues at participating sites, new professional relationships may emerge to support lead teachers.

Students in the Vista School District Digital Intranet were frequently subject to scrutiny by their peers as they responded through chat rooms, audio, video and with their AP online teacher. The Digital Intranet provided students with access to multiple sites simultaneously, as well as with the opportunity to work independently of a teacher for part of the day. The need to prepare for classes before going online became increasingly apparent to both teachers and students, if the open, synchronous science classes were to succeed. The advent of the Digital Intranet had implications for students, who had to interact with teachers and their peers in a variety of new ways. The teaching of each of the four AP science disciplines took place within classes that were open between participating sites. Many students experienced difficulty expressing themselves, and in particular asking questions, in open electronic classes, when they did not know their peers from other small communities. The organization of social occasions for students learning science in open classes in the Intranet helped overcome these problems. As students became more comfortable with one another, inhibitions such as those about asking questions online were overcome. In future, interaction in the Vista Digital Intranet will be both synchronous and asynchronous.

The major change for the students, however, has been the opportunity provided to study advanced science subjects, as members of open classes, from their small, remote communities. A Digital Intranet has many implications for the management of education, based on the need to ensure all sites collaborate both academically and administratively. The most important administrative issue in the first year of the Vista Digital Intranet has been the coordination of timetables across participating sites.

The need for increased technological support for this new, open structure has become increasingly urgent for teachers and students, who are using information and communication technologies to teach and learn across dispersed sites. Both have to be provided with expert advice and instruction in the use of new applications. A particular problem has been the difficulty in securing and maintaining instructional design expertise in the preparation and upgrading of courses delivered through the Intranet.

A new model of rural education

Schools as we have known them are autonomous institutions with their own teachers, their own students, their own classrooms and even their own cultures. Traditionally, schools have been established to serve geographically defined communities, and in rural areas the school–community relationship is often a particularly close one. Schools in any community to a considerable extent duplicate what schools are doing in other communities, with students being taught by teachers assigned to them to teach whole classes face-to-face, or in small groups, and in some cases individually. There is nothing remarkable about this model of the school, and it is an accepted part of the global educational landscape. Perhaps the most remarkable thing about it is that it remains largely unchallenged at a time when educational structures are being reshaped by new information and communication technologies. This traditional model can be considered to be a closed model of the school.

The open model challenges the closed model. It is based on schools academically and administratively integrating with one another for at least part of a school day. Information and communication technologies facilitate the linking of classes in schools to share teaching, learning and resources. In Newfoundland and Labrador virtual classes have been a feature of the province's education system since 1988, when audiographic technology was installed to establish an analogue learning network. The transition from an analogue network to a digital network is a critical part of the development of the Vista Digital Intranet.

The open model challenges the closed model of the school by questioning the need for appointing all teachers to schools, rather than, in appropriate cases, some teachers being appointed to networks of schools. It questions the appropriateness of learners engaging solely with their peers within their own, physical classrooms, and it questions the very notion of a school itself. The open model is grounded in the application of information and communication technologies to teaching and learning, and the construction and deconstruction of virtual, open classes.

The Vista Digital Intranet also provides a framework for the provision of open science classes for rural students. There will hopefully be future opportunities to take this development to other areas of the curriculum, to other school districts and to other than AP students in schools. Through the application and coordination of a range of information and communication technologies, selected Advanced Placement science students in Newfoundland and Labrador have made the initial shift from closed to open learning environments.

The potential of the development of open classes for rural students is not limited to the provision of extended learning opportunities. Biesta and Miedema (2002) argue for a transformative conception of education, in which the pedagogical task of the school is the education of the whole person of the student, not just the provision of his or her instruction. The development of open classes between schools in rural Newfoundland has enabled students to participate in online classes synchronously and asynchronously. The delivery of Advanced Placement courses to students in small schools in rural communities has extended even the most academically able students and provided pathways to post-secondary education. For all the Advanced Placement students in the Vista School District Digital Intranet, courses in biology, chemistry, mathematics and physics were intellectually challenging. They were transformative in the sense that there was an explicit understanding that these were post-secondary level courses, intended to enable them to begin university degrees before they left school. Students were therefore participating in a new dimension of education in which there was a collective understanding that enrolment in university courses would probably follow. The delivery of these courses involved participation in the development of an understanding of what post-secondary education is all about. Biesta and Miedema noted that:

Participation, to take part in a shared activity, requires that one's approach to and understanding of the activity is sufficiently coordinated with the activities of the other participants. Therefore, the success of collective action depends on the extent to which the approaches and interpretations of those taking part are sufficiently coordinated.

(Biesta and Miedema, 2002: 180)

The broader educational and sociological implications of the move from closed to open classes have yet to be considered. Collis (1996) notes that telelearning is the future of distance education. This research suggests that there is considerable potential in this new educational structure for rural communities in Canada in the 21st century.

References

Biesta, G and Miedema, S (2002) Instruction or pedagogy? The need for a transformative conception of education, *Teaching and Teacher Education*, **18**, pp 173–81

Collis, B (1996) *Telelearning in a Digital World: The future of distance learning*, Thompson Computer Press, London and Boston

Information Highway Advisory Council (1995) *The Challenge of the Information Highway*, Industry Canada, Ottawa

Information Highway Advisory Council (1997) *Preparing Canada for a Digital World*, Industry Canada, Ottawa

Stefansdottir, L (1993) The Icelandic Educational Network – Ismennt, in *Tele-teaching: Proceedings of the IFIP TC3 Third Teleteaching Conference*, ed G Davies and B Samways, pp 829–35, Elsevier Science, Amsterdam

Stevens, K (1994) Some applications of distance education technologies and pedagogies in rural schools in New Zealand, *Distance Education*, **15** (4), pp 318–26

Stevens, K (1995a) Geographic isolation and technological change: a new vision of teaching and learning in rural schools in New Zealand, *Journal of Distance Learning*, **1** (1), pp 32–38

Stevens, K (1995b) The technological challenge to the notion of rurality in New Zealand education: repositioning the small school, in *New Zealand Annual Review of Education*, ed I Livingstone, **5**, pp 93–102

Stevens, K (1997) Three approaches to the provision of education in small, rural schools in Australia and New Zealand – assisted out-migration, distance education and telelearning, in *Perspectives of Distance Education in the School*, ed J Salminen, University of Helsinki Press, Helsinki

Stevens, K (1999) *The Vista Digital Intranet: The development of a new structure for teaching Advanced Placement science*, presented to the Vista School District Administrative Council Clarenville, Newfoundland, Canada, June

Tella, S (1995) *Virtual School in a Networking Learning Environment,* University of Helsinki, Department of Teacher Education, Helsinki

Thompson, J, Bakken, L and Clark, F (2001) Creating synergy: collaborative research within a professional development school partnership, *Teacher Educator,* **37** (1), pp 49–57

Tiffin, J and Rajasingham, L (1995) *In Search of the Virtual Class: Education in an information society*, Routledge, London

Chapter 11

Virtual high schools in the United States: current views, future visions

M D Roblyer

Introduction

As microcomputers began to enter American schools and classrooms in the 1970s, an increased interest in distance learning accompanied them. Until the Internet became so popular in the mid-1990s, distance learning in schools usually took the form of supplementary and enrichment lessons (Roblyer, 2003). Except for the occasional satellite delivery or instructional television initiative for schools (US Congress, 1991; Kirby and Roblyer, 1999), the practice of offering complete courses by distance learning was primarily the province of higher education.

However, as the popularity of the Internet spiralled upward in the 1990s, online course delivery migrated steadily downward from colleges and universities to pre-secondary schools. Currently, there is a thriving 'virtual high school' (VHS) movement in which high school credit courses are taught largely or wholly via various resources on the Internet (Berman and Tinker, 1997; Elbaum, 1998; Carr and Young, 1999; Clark, 2001; Loupe, 2001). This chapter describes some of the characteristics of this rapidly-growing phenomenon, as well as some implementation issues and concerns, recent research findings, example virtual high schools, and visions for the future.

Background on virtual high schools

The virtual high school movement began to appear early in 1996, shortly after the Internet went graphic with browser software. VHSs quickly captured the attention of educators, parents, and students and added fuel to the engines of school reform across the United States (Berman and Tinker, 1997; Roblyer and Elbaum, 2000). The vision that led to the birth of virtual high schools and still drives the movement today is one of increased access to additional education opportunities for more students, especially those who currently lack such opportunities. Increased access to education has broad, pervasive implications for the economic growth of countries and political involvement by their citizens; thus, many legislators and school policy makers have high hopes for the success of this movement. Virtual high schools described in this chapter offer various approaches to realizing this shared vision.

A keyword search using any Internet search engine reveals hundreds of hits on the phrase 'virtual high school'. Actual sites offering courses are substantially fewer, and most may be found in the United States; currently 14 of the 50 states are sponsoring at least one such project, and about two-thirds are involved in one sponsored elsewhere in the United States. However, there are VHS sites originating in other countries, including Israel and Canada, and more planned in still other locations. In the United States, approximately 40–50,000 school students currently are taking credit courses on the Internet, and the number promises to grow exponentially in the next five years (Clark, 2001).

Current characteristics of virtual high schools

Since the number of virtual high schools expands each year, the description given here will be a 'snapshot in time', capturing a current image of a rapidly changing and evolving educational innovation. Over the next few years, advances in technologies and findings from current VHS experiences seem likely to bring about widespread changes to this picture.

VHSs may be classified in two different ways: (1) by their administrative structure and (2) by the curriculum approach they use to teach courses.

Administrative structures

Most VHSs are organized around one of two common administrative structures that may be called the 'school coordination model' and the 'school replacement model'.

School coordination model

This is the most common arrangement. It calls for individual schools to be part of a central organization such as the Concord Consortium (described in the examples section below). In this model, the consortium central office trains VHS instructors, organizes advertising and registration, and maintains a course Web site. However, course credit comes from the individual schools, each of which is housed in a physical school building and employs full-time teachers who offer regular, face-to-face courses in addition to virtual ones. This model offers several advantages. Since students in any VHS member school may take any VHS course offered in the consortium, one school need not shoulder the whole curriculum, and students in participating schools have a wide variety of courses to choose from.

School replacement model

This model also has centralized administration, but in a different way. In this model, all courses are offered by an organization that is purely virtual, like the Florida Virtual High School (also described below). The organization obtains credit-granting authority from the county, state or country and offers all courses through its full-time staff of teachers or facilitators. This structure has the advantage of uniformity and simplicity where course credit is concerned, since students have only one credit-granting agency to deal with. However, it can be more expensive, since it must employ full-time staff. The vision for this latter model is that eventually we will be able to cut down on the number of physical school buildings, since students will not need to attend face-to-face classes.

Curriculum approach

VHSs vary much more by the instructional model they use to teach courses than they do by administrative structure. There are several common approaches, and a VHS may use two or more of them, depending on the course topic and kinds and levels of students involved. Some of the most common current instructional approaches are described here.

Online 'cyberbooks'

These are either Web pages of texts or self-led tutorials in which students read information, visit Web links related to the content, and do exercises and tests which they usually send to the instructor by e-mail. Except for their use of Web links and e-mail exchanges with instructors, these courses vary little from the old fashioned correspondence courses of the pre-Internet era. However, to self-motivated learners such as college and adult students, they offer the benefit of easy access to course materials.

Interactive courses

Most VHS courses offer (and require) more interactivity between student and instructor and, less often, among students in the class. Frequently, this interaction is made possible by placing the course on a delivery system developed by a proprietary group, such as WebCT or BlackBoard. The VHS subscribes to the service, pays a per-student fee, and places the course system software on its own server. Instructors develop their courses using the options available from the system. These include features such as spaces for instructors to post readings and assignments; bulletin boards where students may post copies of their work, make comments on a discussion topic, or leave critiques of each other's postings; an e-mail system for class members; and a chat room for class members. Other companies such as Apex Learning and JonesKnowledge.com offer both these delivery system components and starter courses or course design templates.

Most learning activities are primarily asynchronous; that is, students need not be online with the instructor. They access materials and do work at any time. Threaded discussions on a bulletin board are one of the most popular activities. However, some instructors require students to gather for real-time 'chats' in a course chat room. For example, chats can be debates where groups defend various positions on an issue. Others assume a Socratic dialogue between students and instructor.

'Live' interactive, synchronous learning

While cyberbook and interactive courses are primarily asynchronous, another less common model is synchronous: the instructor and students 'gather together' in a virtual space to work with each other in real time. The Babbage Net School in Long Island, New York (http://www.babbagenetschool.com), bills itself as 'the only school offering live, interactive teacher-led classes over the Internet'. If it is, it probably will not be the last. As videoconferencing becomes more available over the Internet, more VHS courses are likely to take advantage of it to support synchronous learning experiences for courses that seem to lend themselves to this approach.

Implementation issues: observations and research findings

Although there is little doubt that VHSs are becoming more popular each year, they have their share of issues and controversies. Researchers and policy makers are looking closely at the performance of VHSs in light of the implications for answers to the following questions.

Do VHS courses work?

Studies of distance learning courses have a long history of results indicating that students can achieve equally well in virtual courses or face-to-face ones, and VHS results are consistent with this finding. Most studies agree that achievement in either environment depends greatly upon similar factors: student readiness, course quality, instructor competence. Course drop-out rate is another matter. In higher education, distance courses continue to reflect a much higher drop-out rate than face-to-face courses (Carr, 2000; Loupe, 2001; Roblyer and Marshall, 2002). While there is little formal documentation to this effect with VHS courses, available evidence suggests that from 40 to 60 per cent of VHS students drop out before completing a course.

What makes a VHS course successful?

As one might expect, VHS courses vary considerably in quality, as perceived by students. In a study of schools in the Concord Consortium (Kosma, Zucker and Espinoza, 1998), factors that predicted students' satisfaction with a course included: perceived quality of course content, interaction through discussion and teacher communication, the number of resource materials perceived as useful, and availability of a site coordinator. The most important of these, consistently reported in the literature on distance courses, seems to be the degree of interactivity during learning (Fulford and Zhang, 1993; Klesius, Homan and Thompson, 1997; Roblyer and Wiencke, 2003). One VHS observer found that courses with higher retention rates are often those which have some face-to-face component, which is one way of increasing interaction (Loupe, 2001). Other factors that contribute to course success are logistical. Technical problems are often mentioned: for example Internet access is interrupted at key times, students have difficulty sending or receiving files, or a system does not work as expected. Successful courses are those that have technical support to resolve these problems quickly.

What motivates students to sign up for VHS courses?

Not all students seem to want the access and flexibility VHS courses offer. Roblyer (1999) did a study to determine the cognitive characteristics of students who volunteer to learn in online environments. She found that students who chose distance formats were more likely to value most highly having control over the timing and pace of course assignments, while those who selected traditional formats were more likely to place highest value on interaction with students and instructors. Many VHS teachers believe that students are drawn to VHS courses by the false assumption that, since it does not meet in a physical sense, the course will be easier for them. However, once they find that this is not true, whether they drop out or do well depends on their perceived locus of control and ability to organize and regulate their time.

What kinds of students succeed in VHS courses?

Teachers who work with VHS students find that students who are self-motivated and organized and have good, consistent access to computers are likely to be successful (Clark, 2001; Loupe, 2001; McLester, 2002). Studies on what kinds of students succeed in online courses confirm that demographic characteristics do not predict success. However, Wang and Newlin (2000) found that college students who had higher degrees of success in Internet courses had higher 'intellectual striving and motivation' and higher internal locus of control. Locus of control reflects a person's perception of who controls his/her destiny. Those with external locus of control believe that even their best efforts are secondary in importance to luck and outside factors over which they have no control. Those with internal locus of control believe that their success or failure is largely a matter of their own effort. Osborn (2001) found similar results to those of Wang and Newlin. In their study to validate an instrument to predict success of virtual high school students, Roblyer and Marshall (2002) found that a combination of four characteristics predicted success in online learning: achievement beliefs, responsibility, self-organization ability, and technology skill/access.

Are VHS courses reaching those who most need them?

There is some evidence from current studies that VHSs have not yet realized their vision of better access to educational opportunities for students who need them most. Some educators fear this is a symptom of the digital divide syndrome (Roblyer, 2000), which has been found to be based primarily in economic disparities. To take advantage of VHS courses, students usually need a computer at home. However, studies have shown that less affluent students are not as likely to have this resource. As a result, more affluent students are showing up in much greater numbers in VHS enrolments. Roblyer and Marshall (2002) found that nearly 70 per cent of VHS students in their survey were Caucasian. This may be due to the current high correlation between race and economic level. While some VHS projects make a point of offering courses in schools with lower socioeconomic populations (Kosma, Zucker and Espinoza, 1998), this may not yet be sufficient to erase the negative effects of the digital divide on VHS participation.

Can VHSs offer whole programmes, as well as courses?

If VHS courses are as successful as they seem to be, the big question that remains is whether or not whole high school programmes can – or should – be offered the same way. Some policy makers believe the VHS movement will be successful only if it helps decrease the costs of providing high-quality educational opportunities. However, since teachers are still so important to success in online courses, costs would come down only if physical school buildings were no longer needed. That is, VHSs will be cost-effective only if they take the place of face-to-face schools. As one might expect, this is a highly controversial issue. As VHS popularity continues to grow, this issue seems likely to dominate discussions about its future.

An introduction to five VHS projects

There are far more VHS programmes than can be reviewed in this chapter. The ones described here are a selection of those that are noteworthy for being among the first and/or the largest.

The Concord Consortium VHS Project (http://vhs.concord.org/home.htm)

The first, and still the largest, of the VHS programmes, this consortium set the standard (if not the administrative structure) for all those that followed. Funded in 1996 by a US Department of Education initiative called the Technology Innovation Challenge Grants Program, the VHS project is currently nearing the end of its government-funded cycle. It is a collaboration among high schools from around the country, each of which offers students 'NetCourses ranging from advanced academic courses to technical and specialized courses' (see Web site). Each school also provides a VHS site coordinator who is responsible for project management and support of teachers and students at his/her local school. The VHS grant provides training, software and technical and administrative support. Each school can enrol up to 20 students for each course a teacher from the school contributes. As of the beginning of 1999, the Concord VHS offered 33 courses in 11 states (Rutkowski, 1999). However, the number reported on its Web site now stands at 156 courses in 200 schools across the United States, as well as 15 international sites (http://vhs.concord.org/Pages/About+Us-Statistics). Courses range from elective, enrichment types of courses such as mythology, astronomy, and investing in the stock market, to core courses such as biology and calculus for business.

The Florida High School (FHS) Project (http://www.flvs.net/)

This was one of the first of the VHSs set up by an individual state department of education in the United States. Funded by special legislative allocation from the State of Florida, the FHS project began in August 1997, as a collaboration between two Florida school districts (Orange County in Orlando and Alachua County in Kissimmee). Its original offering of Scholastic Achievement Test (SAT) preparation and computer programming courses for students in two counties has expanded to 60 courses ranging from Latin to algebra and serving hundreds of students in all of Florida's 67 county school districts, as well as some private schools in Florida. Its stated mission was to place a complete high school curriculum online by the year 2001.

The Virginia Internet High School (http://www.internet-high.com)

According to its Web site, this state VHS 'was founded in 1996 with the goal of eliminating time, distance, and location as factors in the delivery of quality education'. Like the Florida VHS, it was established by the state to serve its own students. Unlike other VHSs that offer mostly elective courses, the VIHS offers all courses required for graduation from a Virginia high school. Most courses are three months long, although some remedial courses are offered in a 45-day period (Rutkowski, 1999). The VIHS was established to provide a high-quality alternative to traditional high school courses, especially for those students who are unmotivated by or do not succeed in traditional settings. Students are given a variety of online resources and must log in to courses every day, Monday through Friday, but have wide latitude as to how and when they complete their work within the course period. Technically, students could complete their whole high school education in the VIHS, but they are limited to three courses at a time, must have the permission of their own school, and must pay $500 per course.

CyberSchool (http://CyberSchool.4j.lane.edu/)

This site seems to have been the first to propose the idea of offering online high school courses when it published a concept proposal in 1995. It was founded primarily to serve Oregon students but currently has a consortium consisting of California, Idaho, Kansas, Michigan, Ohio, Oregon, Pennsylvania and Wisconsin, and offers courses to students in these states and countries around the world. Course credit was originally awarded by one school in the Eugene (Oregon) Public School District, but now credit is offered by one school in each of the participating states.

E-school (http://www.eschool.k12.hi.us)

Like the Concord Consortium, Hawaii's E-school was started with a US Department of Education Technology Innovation Challenge Grant. Since its beginning in 1996, its courses have expanded to its current offering of 30 courses to about 200 students located throughout the islands of Hawaii. The hallmark of E-school's VHS seems to be a focus on the state's cultural heritage. Through E-School, Hawaii is not only able to provide its students access to elective courses, such as journalistic writing and advanced placement for computer science, but can also offer courses such as history of the Pacific and environmental studies of Hawaii. Thus E-school shows how a VHS can help local areas serve students' unique curriculum needs.

In addition to consortium and state efforts, VHS courses are also beginning to be offered by higher education institutions (Carr, 1999a and 1999b; Clark, 2001). The University of Nebraska (http://www.uneb.edu) was the first such enterprise with a vision of merging the curricula of pre-secondary and post-secondary levels. Clark lists eight other US higher education institutions that have followed suit.

A complete listing of VHSs in the United States as of November 2001 may be seen in Clark's report at: http://www.dlrn.org/trends.html. See other links to VHSs outside the United States at:

Israel: http://aviv.k12.il/
Ontario: http://www.virtualhighschool.com/

In summary: the possible futures of virtual high schools

The experiences and models described here show that virtual learning at the high school level is potentially a viable concept, at least for some types of students and for some curriculum. Teachers can teach and students can learn in virtual environments, but several issues remain to be resolved before the VHS movement achieves the momentum to drive it forward into the foreseeable future.

Oversight and funding issues

Guerard (2002) describes several issues of paramount concern to school district superintendents, who met twice in 2001 at a Superintendents' Technology Summit and discussed who should oversee and fund VHS schools in the future. Superintendents were asked to identify items of concern to them and then surveyed to gauge their position on each of them.

- **Curriculum alignment.** When asked whether or not VHS curriculum standards should be aligned to state and local standards where the students reside, about 90 per cent agreed. However, the superintendents apparently did not discuss the logistics of aligning standards when students from a given VHS come from more than one state.
- **Teacher certification.** Most superintendents disagreed with the idea of allowing VHSs to have the authority to certify their teachers. About 38 per cent felt that the state should certify teachers, and 29 per cent said this authority should reside with the district.
- **Accreditation.** The superintendents were split on the issue of whether course credit should be granted by the VHS or the school district. This was also the issue with most variability in survey responses.
- **Funding.** There was substantial agreement on who should fund the operation costs of VHSs. About 67 per cent of the superintendents felt that VHSs should be funded by the states, rather than local taxpayers, voucher programmes or the federal government. This seems to be the issue with most potential for dissension. Guerard (2002) reports that the Pennsylvania School Boards

Association, after submitting a report highly critical of the state's cyber-schools movement, filed a lawsuit with the state to prevent their authorization with public funds.

- **Negative consequences.** Finally, 77 per cent of the superintendents agreed that VHSs offered potential for negative socialization effects on students. A similar number (75 per cent) felt there should be an accreditation process for all virtual schools.

Economic survival issues

A concern that remains central to the success of these schools is true of many educational enterprises in our time. In order to be sustainable, VHSs must offer enough courses that are perceived as needed and of high quality to enough students to justify the administrative costs of running the school. In some cases, sustainability has not yet become a critical issue, since some schools still survive on specially allocated external funding. However, this issue will become increasingly important in the next few years, as initial funding sources dry up. One possible future is to aim for the vision of the Florida High School and the Virginia High School: offering entire high school programmes online, thus eliminating the need for students to attend a physical school building. Another possibility is for a central agency to offer courses on a more widespread basis, subsuming other such schools and offering a more economical service to more students.

One major misconception must be corrected before the VHS concept can step forward with answers that are economically sound. This misconception is reflected in one author's observation that VHS courses are not subject to overcrowding, since learning occurs in an asynchronous environment. In fact, virtual courses, like face-to-face ones, are usually highly dependent on competent, caring teachers to make them successful and responsive to students' needs. It may actually be easier to 'overcrowd' a virtual class than a face-to-face one, since most distance teachers agree that virtual courses take much more time to organize and teach than traditional ones. The teacher-to-student ratio may need to be lower, rather than higher.

Access and equity issues

It is clear that we have a long way to go to fulfil the vision on which the VHS concept was founded: increased access to learning opportunities to those who may be able to profit most from them – students from diverse backgrounds with limited resources. While the digital divide persists, this could also be the greatest potential challenge – and possibly the greatest benefit – of this new format.

Some schools that offer VHS courses are not waiting for students to obtain Internet access in their homes. Instead, they provide special time periods during the school day and increased access to Internet-ready computers before and after school, so students can take VHS courses whenever they want. These and other innovative approaches are needed to make sure that VHSs take advantage of their potential to help erase the digital divide, rather than becoming a victim of it.

Possible futures

What virtual high schools will become in the next decade is one aspect of larger questions that pervade every area of our information age society. What will we do with our technology? What will we become as a result of using technology? At this point, there are several possible futures but no clear answers. As our technology capabilities and resources develop, and as we come to terms with what we want to become as a society, we may evolve an expanded vision for this concept, or we may find that virtual learning can fulfil a much more limited role than we originally thought. But however uncertain its final form, the 'school that technology built' seems likely to remain a permanent part of the education landscape.

References

Berman, S and Tinker, R (1997) The world's the limit in the virtual high school, *Educational Leadership*, **55** (3), pp 52–54

Carr, S (1999a) University of Nebraska will supply online high-school courses in Kentucky, *Chronicle of Higher Education*, 8 October [Online] http://chronicle.com

Carr, S (1999b) Two more universities start diploma-granting virtual high schools, *Chronicle of Higher Education*, 10 December [Online] http://chronicle.com

Carr, S (2000) As distance education comes of age, the challenge is keeping the students, *Chronicle of Higher Education*, 11 February [Online] http://chronicle.com

Carr, S and Young, J (1999) As distance learning boom spreads, colleges help set up virtual high schools, *Chronicle of Higher Education*, 22 October [Online] http://chronicle.com

Clark, T (2001) *Virtual Schools: Trends and Issues*, report commissioned by the Distance Learning Resource Network, a WestEd Project; co-sponsored by the Centre for the Application of Information Technologies at Western Illinois University, October [Online] http://www.dlrn.org/trends.html

Elbaum, B (1998) Is the virtual high school 'educational reform'? *@Concord.Org: Newsletter of the Concord Consortium, Concord*, MA, Winter, pp 10–11

Fulford, C and Zhang, S (1993) Perceptions of interaction: the critical predictor in distance education, *American Journal of Distance Education*, **7** (3), pp 8–21

Guerard, E (2002) Superintendents' opinions evolving rapidly on virtual schools, *eSchool News*, **5** (1), pp 16–17

Kirby, E and Roblyer, M (1999) A glimpse at the past, an eye to the future, *Learning and Leading With Technology*, **27** (2), pp 46–52

Klesius, J, Homan, S and Thompson, T (1997) Distance education compared to traditional instruction: the students' view, *International Journal of Instructional Media*, **24** (3), pp 207–20

Kosma, R, Zucker, A and Espinoza, C (1998) *An Evaluation of the Virtual High School after One Year of Operation*, SRI International, Arlington, VA, October [Online] http://vhs.concord.org/Pages/About+Us-Project+Evaluation

Loupe, D (2001) Virtual schooling: a new dimension to learning brings new challenges for educators, *eSchool News*, **4** (6), pp 41–47

McLester, S (2002) Virtual learning takes a front row seat, *Technology and Learning*, **22** (8), pp 24–36

Osborn,V (2001) Identifying at-risk students in videoconferencing and Web-based distance education, *American Journal of Distance Education*, **15** (1), pp 41–54

Roblyer, M (1999) Is choice important in distance learning? A study of students' motives for taking Internet-based courses at community college and high school levels, *Journal of Research on Computing in Education*, **32** (1/2), pp 157–71

Roblyer, M (2000) Digital desperation: research reports on a growing technology and equity crisis, *Learning and Leading with Technology*, **27** (8), pp 50–53, 61

Roblyer, M (2003) *Integrating Educational Technology into Teaching*, 3rd edn, Pearson Education, Upper Saddle River, NJ

Roblyer, M and Elbaum, B (2000) Virtual learning? Research on virtual high schools, *Learning and Leading with Technology*, **27** (4), pp 58–61

Roblyer, M and Marshall, J (2002) Predicting success of virtual high school distance learners: preliminary results from an educational success prediction instrument, *Journal of Research on Technology in Education*, in press

Roblyer, M and Wiencke, W (2003) Design and use of a rubric to assess and encourage interactive qualities in distance courses, *American Journal of Distance Education*, **17** (2), accepted for publication

Rutkowski, K (1999) Virtual schools: charting new frontiers, *Multimedia Schools*, **6** (1), pp 74–79

US Congress (1991) *Star Schools for all our Students: Examining the status of the Star Schools Program*, Senate Committee on Labour and Human Resources, Washington, DC, April (ERIC Document Reproduction no. ED344570)

Wang, A and Newlin, M (2000) Characteristics of students who enrol and succeed in Web-based classes, *Journal of Educational Psychology*, **92** (1), pp 137–43

Chapter 12

From distance education to e-learning: the organization of open classes at local, regional and national levels

Ken Stevens and Carol Moffatt

Distance has a special meaning for New Zealanders, who live in a small and isolated country at the bottom of the globe. Primary production has always been prominent in the New Zealand economy, so it is not surprising that rural and distance education have been, and remain, important dimensions of the national social and economic infrastructure. A feature of distance education during the last decade in New Zealand has been growing reference to open learning. A decade ago Renwick (1993) suggested that 'The differences between open and distance education are matters for debate but both are usually defined in contrast with conventional face-to-face teaching. This conceptual distinction has become a settled feature of policy discourse in education.'

Just as the New Zealand economy is very open – the country trades in many areas of the Pacific basin, North America, Asia, the Middle East and Europe – so openness is a growing feature of the national education system.

This chapter outlines three areas of open learning in the New Zealand education system. At the local level, many schools have developed relationships with the New Zealand Correspondence School in the capital, Wellington, while at the tertiary level the Open Polytechnic of New Zealand and Massey University have for decades provided vocational and academic courses respectively throughout the country. At the regional level, in several parts of the country, rural schools formed electronic Intranets in the early 1990s, within which they shared resources. By doing so, they provided a new dimension to open learning in New Zealand schools. At the national level, the Ministry of Education's current initiatives encourage schools to consider the teaching and learning possibilities of the Internet.

In 1993 Ormond Tate, as Principal of the New Zealand Correspondence School, summarized distance education in New Zealand in positive terms (Tate, 1993):

- It is comprehensive and extends from early childhood through special and school education to the tertiary level;
- It is experienced, from many years of teaching, student support and course development;
- It has common curricula with on-campus face-to-face institutions, and cross-crediting of courses is possible;
- It has creditable standards and student achievement resulting in fairly general acceptance within the country.

Until the 1980s, distance education was a specialized area of education in New Zealand, provided by designated institutions. Since then, the rapidly increasing use of computers in schools and universities, an expanding range of educational software, and in particular a growing realization of the teaching and learning possibilities of the Internet, have made off-campus teaching and open learning possible for teachers and students at all levels of the New Zealand education system. Prebble (1993) observed that 'The government has withdrawn its protection of the monopolies the major institutions enjoyed over distance education. Virtually all the New Zealand universities are now involved, albeit in a small way, with distance education teaching of various kinds.'

Three dimensions of open learning in New Zealand

Open learning in New Zealand has evolved over many years, and today there are three discernable dimensions to be found at the school and tertiary levels: national open learning institutions; regional networks of rural schools (Intranets), and the recent development of open interactive education.

The New Zealand Correspondence School and the Open Polytechnic of New Zealand – the provision of local access to learning opportunities

The New Zealand Correspondence School (NZCS) is the largest school in the country. This institution has several functions in New Zealand society, including the provision of education for rural and remote students as well as for a diverse range of adult and second-chance learners. The school provides courses in early childhood education and in a range of specialized areas including English for second language learners. It is a unique, multi-purpose national educational institution with a very diverse enrolment.

An important role of the NZCS has been the provision of extended curriculum options for students, largely at the secondary level, who attend local schools but for whom access to specialized subjects in traditional, face-to-face classrooms is not possible. Many students of the NZCS maintain daily attendance at their community schools while they are concurrently enrolled with this national institution. The school has become an integral part of the academic life of many schools throughout the country through this open relationship. It provides distance education for students in a very wide variety of educational settings, including schools, homes, hospitals and prisons. It also enables New Zealanders living or travelling overseas to continue to receive a New Zealand education.

A feature of the NZCS has been the provision of local learning opportunities from a central location. Print has been the basis of most courses, supplemented for many years by a range of audio and video technologies. The Internet now offers it new ways of providing learning opportunities throughout the country, although its name reflects its origins that predate the cyber world. The Correspondence School is moving many of its courses online, which will further extend its educational base both within New Zealand and beyond.

The Open Polytechnic of New Zealand is also a unique educational institution. As its name suggests, it provides a large range of post-secondary courses for New Zealanders, primarily, but not exclusively, of an applied, technological nature. The Open Polytechnic has for many years provided access to courses as diverse as agriculture, business, technology and applied science, while also preparing students for such occupations as real estate, tourism, quantity surveying and many others. Like the Correspondence School, it provides open access across a wide range of courses for students who are in employment and who wish to study part-time to enhance their careers. During 1999 the Open Polytechnic piloted the delivery of selected courses in an online 'virtual campus' while continuing to offer courses from certificate to degree level. As with the NZCS, the Open Polytechnic is moving many of its courses online.

The New Zealand Correspondence School and the Open Polytechnic of New Zealand together provide open learning opportunities from the pre-school to degree level. Massey University has had, and continues to have, a pre-eminent role in the provision of distance education degrees in New Zealand. However, the growth of information and communication technologies, an expanding range of educational software, and the increasing prominence of the Internet in education, have encouraged other New Zealand universities to consider the possibilities and the institutional advantages of open learning. Open learning is now an established dimension of academic life in most New Zealand universities.

Regional Intranets – increasing access to learning opportunities

Many senior students in rural New Zealand communities have in the past been assisted to migrate to larger, urban schools for part, or in some cases all, of their secondary education. Enrolment in boarding schools has long been favoured by farming families. In boarding schools rural people are likely to find a broader range of curriculum options for their sons and daughters than those available in their small,[1] local schools, some of which are located in remote[2] parts of New Zealand. Boarding schools have had, and continue to have, an important role in the provision of education for rural New Zealanders, but developments in information and communication technologies have enabled educators to consider other ways of providing extended curriculum options for students who live beyond major centres of population.

During the last decade several new educational structures were created in rural New Zealand, based on opportunities provided by the convergence of information and communication technologies. During the 1990s it became possible and increasingly common to link schools electronically within defined areas of the country to form regional Intranets (Stevens, 1995). Within regional Intranets virtual classes were organized for the delivery of specialized secondary school subjects.

Small schools in rural New Zealand that were linked with one another by audio-graphic technology during the last decade usually had very few full-time teachers in specialist areas of the curriculum (such as economics, agriculture and Japanese). All small rural schools had teachers who could provide instruction in subjects of the core curriculum (such as English, mathematics and science), while many had at least one member of staff who could also teach a specialized subject. In many cases they had too few students to justify the inclusion of specialist subjects in the curriculum. However, by linking with one another through audio-graphic technology to share specialist teaching resources, regional school networks were formed which were able to provide many rural students with considerably increased options in the senior curriculum. The electronic interfacing of schools in several regions to create Intranets provided a new dimension to open learning. Through the creation of regional Intranets, these schools were able to share scarce specialized resources for students beyond the communities in which teachers were located. The development of these new, open structures enabled students in rural communities to access many subjects that previously were not locally available. The argument for government assistance for the migration of rural New Zealand students to urban boarding schools could no longer be made solely on academic grounds.

An example of a regional Intranet was the Cantatech network in the Canterbury region, which enabled students in small schools throughout this part of the South Island of New Zealand to learn together, online, from specialist teachers located in various participating schools. The sharing of resources between sites enabled all schools in this region to provide their students with extended learning opportunities.

Interactive education – the provision of national access to learning opportunities

Government and the Ministry of Education encourage the development of e-learning in schools and support it through national initiatives such as the development of online curriculum resources, the provision of professional development programmes for teachers and principals, and the growth and spread of national infrastructures.

In 1998 a national *Information and Communications Technology Strategy* for schools (Ministry of Education, 1998) was developed. It was implemented throughout New Zealand during the years 1999–2000. There were four objectives in the strategy.

The first objective was to improve learning outcomes through the use of ICT in schools in teaching and learning. The second objective was to increase the effectiveness and efficiency of teachers and schools by helping them to use ICT. The third objective was to improve the quality of teaching and leadership in schools by helping teachers and principals to identify their ICT needs and to develop the skills necessary to meet them. The final objective was to increase opportunities for schools, businesses and government to work together in developing an information-technology-literate workforce.

The national strategy had two focus areas: the development of infrastructure and improvement of schools' technological capabilities. Four initiatives have recently been developed to promote online learning opportunities for New Zealanders.

An online resource centre (Te Kete Ipurangi)

Te Kete Ipurangi – the Online Resource Centre – (a bilingual portal) is providing teachers and schools with a mechanism for the delivery of multimedia resources, including curriculum and administration resources, using the Internet. This online centre is intended to support curriculum materials and to provide links to curriculum experts, databases, multimedia and a variety of other sites. It contains search engines for teachers.

In addition to these supports for New Zealand teachers, the online resource centre contains private areas for e-mail, online chats, discussions and shared resources for teachers and students to use.

Infrastructure support

The computer recycling scheme: the aim of this scheme is to enable more schools to obtain more computers for student and teacher use, at low cost. The government has initiated a publicity campaign to promote the donation of computers by industry for 'recycling and up-grading in schools' (Ministry of Education, 1998). The programme also informs schools throughout New Zealand about the availability of recycled computers that they can access.

ICT grant: a one-off $25 million ICT grant for schools. The grant can be accessed by all state and integrated schools when they complete an ICT plan. It is up to each school to make its own purchasing decisions. While some may elect to purchase additional hardware and software, others may choose professional development.

Professional capability

ICT leadership: one-day seminars for principals have been devoted to planning for the use of ICT in their schools and included practical advice about the purchase and maintenance of computers, together with an introduction to their applications in teaching, learning and administration.

ICT integration: clusters of schools are strategically selected from throughout New Zealand to implement locally developed and coordinated three-year programmes of ICT professional development. Each cluster is headed by a lead school. The purpose of the lead schools is to assist the development of ICT in the other schools within their cluster. Each lead school must have proven achievements in the use of ICT. The role of the 23 professional development schools has been to promote good practice, through direct assistance, in the use of ICT in teaching and learning in the localities for which they are responsible. Indirect assistance is provided through the online resource centre in Wellington.

The three-year contracts the schools signed with the Ministry of Education require each lead school to provide professional development for teachers in participating schools in the use of ICT for teaching, learning and administration. The lead schools are also expected to develop activities that integrate ICT into the teaching–learning process to promote the learning outcomes of the New Zealand curriculum. They are expected to explore innovative ways of using ICT in educational activities for students, teachers and their communities, and to develop printed and digital resources for dissemination that reflect good practice in the use of ICT in teaching and learning. The lead schools are expected to utilize information and communication technologies to meet a variety of administrative needs in New Zealand schools, and to develop systems and strategies for their technical support and sustained ICT development.

Piloting new solutions

In addition to the programmes initiated through the national strategy, the government has also instigated a number of important pilot programmes that are seeking to investigate and evaluate e-learning options. These include the Digital Opportunities Programme and the Kaupapa Ara Whakawhiti Matauranga (KAWM) project.

The Digital Opportunities Programme

Four pilot projects began in early 2001, based on partnerships between government and information and communication technology businesses. These include:

- **FarNet:** a community of 10 schools in the far north of the country using ICT to collaborate and enhance teaching and learning.
- **Generation XP:** A group of eight schools in West Auckland and in the Gisborne district of the north-east coast of the North Island, offering Microsoft certification courses to senior secondary students.
- **Notebook Valley:** A group of four secondary schools in the Wellington region using laptops to collaborate and enhance teaching and learning in senior maths and science.
- **WickED:** A group of four study support centres in the South Island using ICT to provide online self-study activities.

The Kaupapa Ara Whakawhiti Matauranga (KAWM) project

This initiative began in 2000 and is focused on using information and communication technologies to strengthen curriculum delivery and broaden options for Maori learners in schools, including boarding schools. It addresses the shortage of Maori-medium subject specialist teachers at the secondary level through the provision of 'expert teachers' to provide lessons via video conferencing across a number of Wharekura sites. The implementation of KAWM has three component areas, each supported by technology solutions and technical and professional support:

- online learning through a video-conferencing network;
- ICT professional development programme for teachers;
- building appropriate ICT infrastructure in schools.

A problem for the continued expansion of e-learning is bandwidth. In New Zealand the provision of broadband services beyond major centres of population is not seen as commercially viable. In the Otago region in the south of New Zealand's South Island, many rural schools are benefiting from a community trust which recognizes that upgrading connectivity for secondary schools outside cities is not just an educational need, but is linked to economic development. The outcome has been the signing of a contract for the delivery of e-learning services by Telecom New Zealand and the trust. This commercial framework provides a structure with potential for collaborative work between schools and other educational institutions, including the University of Otago. The collaborative dimension of e-learning has mutual benefits for teachers and academic researchers, a situation described by Thompson, Bakken and Clark (2001) as 'creating synergy'. By bringing teachers in small schools in rural New Zealand into new professional relationships with academic researchers, there is potential for the emergence of new synergies.

From the beginning of 2001 a further 28 ICT professional development clusters were added to the programme, bringing the total up to 51, which are currently serving 612 schools. At the beginning of 2002 an ICT helpdesk was set up for all schools and the government supported a free Microsoft software package for all state and integrated schools. In addition to the provision of free laptops, a dedicated portal called Leadspace was made available for all school principals (www.leadspace.govt.nz).

The shift from distance education to e-learning

Learning at a distance in New Zealand is in a state of transition. The correspond-ence model has served the country well for many years and has provided New Zealanders in many parts of the country with learning opportunities that were not otherwise locally available. As new technologies became available, particularly audio and video, they were used to supplement printed materials. The New Zealand Correspondence School has made extensive use of radio broadcasts to supplement teaching and learning, while television has been used by tertiary educators to add an extra dimension to open learning for those who wish to undertake degree studies part-time.

The advent of personal computers in schools, polytechnics and universities has added a new element to teaching and learning in New Zealand and, at the same time, inherently challenged the dominance of traditional distance education providers and their methods. The Internet has added a new dimension to open learning, in New Zealand education as in other developed countries. The Internet, together with recent initiatives by the New Zealand Ministry of Education, provides a new basis for national educational networking with extensive global links (Stevens and Moffatt, 1996).

The introduction of new technologies in education has been continuous in New Zealand and schools, particularly small secondary schools, have had to make many changes to survive. In a study of organizational change in Ontario secondary schools, Hannay and Ross (2001) observed that the development of 'alternative organizational models required that individuals become conscious of their implicit understanding of a secondary school in order to question its organizational structure'. As schools in New Zealand increasingly adopt e-learning, and as more small educational institutions academically and administratively integrate with one another across widely separated sites, the organizational change may see the emergence of new electronic teaching and learning structures.

At present there are competing models of open learning in New Zealand, indicating a move from centralized distance education to computer and Internet facilitated e-learning. Students in some parts of rural New Zealand have a choice between enrolling in courses from the Correspondence School or in courses within a local Intranet, from which they may enter a class electronically within a particular region. However, this is changing, as schools work together and with distance education providers to offer courses in a much more collaborative environment.

The provision of open learning opportunities has for generations helped New Zealanders to form relationships with teachers and peers located well beyond their homes and local schools. As open learning enters a new dimension through current government initiatives, New Zealand education can be expected to become increasingly open as local communities connect to global changes.

Notes

1   The Ministry of Education has classified small schools as those schools having a roll of 150 or under as at 1 July.
2   Remote schools have been defined by the Ministry of Education as being at least 30 km from a centre with the most recent census-determined population of at least 2000.

References

Hannay, L and Ross, J (2001) Internalizing change capacity in secondary schools through organizational change, *Alberta Journal of Educational Research*, **47** (4), pp 325–40

Ministry of Education (1998) *Interactive Education – An Information and Communication Technologies Strategy for Schools*, New Zealand Ministry of Education, Wellington

Ministry of Education (2002) *ICT Draft Strategy for Schools – 2002–2004*, New Zealand Ministry of Education, Wellington

Prebble, T (1993) New Zealand, in *Distance Education in Asia and the Pacific: Country reports*, National Institute of Multi-media Education, Chiba, Japan

Renwick, W (1993) The future of face-to-face and distance teaching in post secondary education, in *The Impact of Information and Communication Technologies on Post-Secondary Education*, CERI/OECD, Paris

Stevens, K (1995) Geographic isolation and technological change: a new vision of teaching and learning in rural schools in New Zealand, *Journal of Distance Learning*, **1** (1), pp 32–38

Stevens, K and Moffatt, C (1996) TeleLearning and New Zealand secondary schools: some pedagogical and management issues in the development of courses for flexible delivery, *Technology for Flexible Delivery Conference*, Massey University, Palmerston North, New Zealand

Tate, O (1993) *A Vision of Distance Education in New Zealand*, Inaugural Conference of Distance Education and Information and Communications Technology Providers, National Library of New Zealand, Wellington

Thompson, J, Bakken, L and Clark, F (2001) Creating synergy: collaborative research within a professional development school partnership, *The Teacher Educator*, **37** (1), pp 49–57

Part 5

Conclusion

Chapter 13

Open classrooms and globalization: connections and reflections

Barbara Spronk

Introduction and aims

The contributions to this volume are connected in at least two ways. First, each of them deals with 'openness' and the application of distance methodologies to primary and secondary education, levels that have been only infrequently treated in the distance education literature. Second, the various open classrooms they describe all reflect in some significant way the impact that globalization and its associated neoliberal agenda are having on education, at all levels. This concluding chapter looks at this impact, by considering three questions:

- What do these contributions tell us about the impact globalization is having on primary and secondary education?
- What do we learn about the realities of this impact in the face of promises of increased efficiencies, cost effectiveness and equity?
- What alternatives to 'traditional' schooling are being created in the political and financial spaces that can be found within the neoliberal agenda for education?

Globalization and the neoliberal agenda for education

Before addressing these three questions, it is important to define our operative terms, 'globalization' and 'the neoliberal agenda'.

In this discussion, following Hoogvelt (2001), I use globalization to mean the growing interdependence and interconnectedness of the contemporary world, in particular the thickening of relationships between the players at the centre of that world. The increased ease of movement of capital, goods and services – including information and education – and to some extent people, is rapidly creating a single global economy. Globalization is more than internationalization, however. The world political economy has been international since the voyages of exploration and conquest of the 15th century. What we are now witnessing, with increasing rapidity since the end of the cold war, is global restructuring.

The process of this global restructuring receives powerful assistance from what is widely labelled a 'technological revolution', featuring computer and communications technologies (eg Stromquist, 2002: 6). At their optimum, these technologies move digitized bits of information around the globe, and into outer space and back, at the speed of light. Digitization compresses both time and space; exchanges and transactions become virtually instant. Space too becomes virtual, redefined in terms of space on a hard disk or other electronic storage medium, or the bandwidth of communication links. (See Harvey, 1989, and Giddens, 1990, for discussions of time–space compression.)

The consequences and implications of this compression are enormous, in all areas of global existence:

- On the economic level, a major feature of global restructuring is the increasing concentration of capital in the hands of a few individuals and organizations. The most significant of these organizations are multinational corporations, which now account for about a third of world economic output and two-thirds of world trade. Around a third of world trade takes place actually within these multinationals, between subsidiaries of the same corporation based in different countries. Other economic features include the growth and influence of international trading blocs and practices favouring private over state enterprises in all sectors of society, including education.

- On the political level, the influence of global organizations is growing, evident in the trading blocs just mentioned, and in the treaties and agreements that regulate world trade and set global standards for human rights and the environment. Concomitantly the state is taking on more mediating than interventionist roles in the regulation of national economies.

- On the material level, certain consumer goods are becoming ubiquitous. Thanks to the reach of the mega-media companies, the global marketing they facilitate, and the effectiveness of franchising and branch-plant manufacturing, the global traveller, at least in the world's capital cities, need never be deprived of deep-fried chicken, cola drinks and beer, the current 'Top Ten' on the pop charts, or the latest Hollywood blockbusters and television sitcom episodes.

- On the cultural level, the technological revolution is giving rise to what is widely termed 'the knowledge society'. Knowledge – or at least information – moves from one spot on the globe to another at the speed of light, and the knowledge and skills needed to capture, manage and use that information become valued resources, emphasized over natural resources and material endowments. In addition, the spread of the items of material culture mentioned above raises the alarm that associated values – the virtues of excessive consumption, individualism, and competition – are also spreading, and indeed threaten to take over and homogenize world culture and values. Analysts of globalization see the rise of nationalist and fundamentalist movements around the world – movements that are as much political as cultural – as a direct response to this threat, struggles to retain or recreate individual and collective senses of self defined by place, language and belief (cf Castells, 1997).

The technological revolution is a material dynamic of globalization. In the ideological dimension, the corresponding dynamic is a neoliberal development agenda that emphasizes the centrality of the market and market forces. Acting on this model, the voices of power call for a less interventionist state in economic and social arenas, and propose measures that include deregulation, decentralization and privatization.

Both dynamics are operating in the arena of education, in complementary and connected ways. The neoliberal agenda for education is being played out worldwide in terms of the following measures (cf Burbules and Torres, 2000; Carnoy, 2000; Stromquist, 2002):

- A shift of public funding for education from higher to lower levels of education (as in the global drive to implement Universal Primary Education by 2015).
- Expansion of secondary and higher education through increased privatization.
- Reduction of public spending on education at all levels, by increasing class size and teacher–student ratios, shifting costs to the user, and encouraging private enterprise initiatives intent on capturing the lucrative 'education market'.
- Decentralization of control over schools to the local level while maintaining centralized control of curriculum (eg the rise of charter schools and voucher systems in US and Canadian schools).
- The drive for 'comparative advantage' in terms of attracting investment, emphasizing the need for labour pools that are at the same time highly skilled and low-waged.
- Regulatory systems that emphasize accountability, giving rise to managerial and business models in school governance and an emphasis on results measured by standard tests at all grade levels.
- Uniform standards with instrumental ends, geared to producing graduates with the skills required by a 'high-tech' labour market (such as the 'back to

the basics' movement that emphasizes maths, sciences and language over literature and the arts).

- Looking to the information and communications technologies that are being produced by multinational companies and used to such powerful effect by finance capital, to work their magic in schools at all levels, in tasks that include delivery of cost-effective programming, facilitation of international and multi-level collaborations, and creation of administrative efficiencies.

Reflections of globalization

What do the chapters in this volume tell us about the impact this neoliberal agenda is having on primary and secondary education?

The two opening chapters make it clear that the discussions of open classrooms that follow are being framed in terms of the technologically derived 'knowledge society' and the requirements it is making of education at primary and secondary levels. Jenkins argues that not only are information and communications technologies setting challenges to educators to prepare children for the knowledge society, if used properly they can also enable schools to meet these challenges. ICTs open classrooms to more flexible modes of delivery and approaches to curriculum that can meet children's individual learning needs and at the same time get them working together both within and beyond classroom walls. Paine continues in this vein, but pushes even further beyond the walls of the classroom, envisioning technologically based schools as learning communities that reach out to their wider community and to the world. Paine is firmly in step with the neoliberal agenda: '[the] knowledge economy is here and to survive we have to make steep changes in the way we do business and educate our citizens or face the horrible economic consequences of failing in the 21st century'.

Bakia steps back a bit from this vision to take a hard look at what it might cost to make it a reality. Dodds steps not so much back as into another reality. Whereas the first three authors are focusing mainly on classrooms in Europe and North America, Dodds's focus is Africa, particularly southern Africa, and what is happening in three countries there in terms of moving schooling at secondary level outside the classroom, and moving the providing organizations outside the centralized control of the state. In terms of the neoliberal agenda, this can be seen as decentralization of control, in the interests of providing greater flexibility and learner-centred programming, and reducing demands on government resources. The creation of such parastatal institutions might also be a move toward privatization of provision, however. In Dodds's view, 'The greatest risk is that, once established as a parastatal agency, such a college will become detached from government involvement and be forced to become increasingly self-financing because starved of government subsidy.'

Marks's chapter takes us back to Europe, but still outside classroom walls. Marks describes how the new technologies, especially in their wireless form, are enabling European Community governments to fulfil their responsibility of making education available to all their citizens, in this case secondary-school-age children of parents whose jobs as fairground and seasonal workers keep them on the move. The involvement of the private sector is essential to this provision, since it is their equipment and partly their expertise that makes this networked delivery possible. Brophy's chapter deals with another, but immeasurably more desperate, case of mobility, that of the world's populations of refugees and displaced peoples. These children also have a right to education as defined in global conventions. However, the UNHCR, the global organization responsible for refugee care and protection, and related charitable agencies face enormous obstacles in providing that education, as Brophy sets out. An obstacle not dealt with by Brophy is financial. Refugee and displaced person numbers are growing, yet funding is declining, as donor nations scale back their funding for UNHCR and other international aid agencies. Despite drastic measures and staff cutbacks, the Commission faces a funding shortfall of tens of millions of dollars (Drumtra, 2001). Funding for humanitarian and related aid does not appear to rank high on the neoliberal agenda.

The next three chapters focus on methods. Interestingly, none of the methods described is reliant particularly, if at all, on the so-called technological revolution. The open schools of India described by Panda and Garg rely primarily on the time-honoured combination of print packages with face to face tutorials and some supplementary media, although continuing planning includes the use of ICTs for some modest networking and administrative support. Butcher describes the care that the South African government is taking not to get unthinkingly caught up in the neoliberal agenda for education by going for 'quick fixes'. The South Africans are intent on educational reform with the aim, in Butcher's words, 'to restore equity and build quality of delivery of education to all of the country's people', but are concerned to build openness into mainstream provision rather than making it a sideline. This mainstreaming will doubtless involve the new technologies – Butcher mentions online curriculum management systems, Web-based portals for curriculum resources, management information systems, and private sector support for ICTs in schools – but the emphasis remains on systematic, mainstream planning.

The Brazilian case, remarkably, focuses on the use of television for a particular audience, out-of-school youth and adults preparing for secondary-level equivalency examinations. 'Old' though the technology may be, it appears to be employed very effectively in the implementation of aspects of the neoliberal agenda, namely, a private sector organization (in this case the ninth-largest media organization in the world) providing nationwide programming focused on skills attainment for the global labour market, as measured by centralized testing and, ultimately, the employability of those who emerge successful.

The closing chapters take us back to the affluent, industrialized world, for a look at online learning at secondary level in Canada, the United States and New Zealand. In Canada, elements of the technological revolution are being put to good use in making advanced courses in maths and sciences available to rural schools too small to make such provision possible. In the United States, the development of 'virtual high schools', in which high school credit courses are taught largely or wholly via various resources on the Internet, is moving ahead apace, funded largely at the level of individual state governments. In New Zealand, the New Zealand Correspondence School, a state-supported, national provider, is moving many of its courses online; at the regional level, electronic interfacing is linking small schools to make specialist subjects available. Government grant funding makes these initiatives possible, but there are plans for an increased national commitment to online learning at secondary level, in which partnerships with the private sector are expected to play a significant role.

Rhetoric and realities

Underlying the move to open classrooms, as evident in many of the contributions to this volume, is the hope that employing the new technologies and increasing the involvement of the private sector in education will enable governments intent on reducing public funding for education to do more with less. The goals of governments in pursuit of the neoliberal agenda are to achieve a 'quality' education, as measured by test results that compare favourably with those of other nation states and by graduates with the skills needed in the labour market, and to do so with the lowest possible expenditure of tax-generated funding. The accompanying rhetoric typically features phrases such as 'enhanced flexibility', 'increased opportunity', 'greater efficiency', 'valuing diversity', 'promoting equity', and, of course, the ubiquitous concern for 'quality'. What do the various chapters in this volume tell us about the extent to which these hopes are being realized by open classrooms?

Jenkins opens the volume with a 'vision of the open classroom' that reflects these hopes: 'reliable and easy access to school learning for all; consistently high quality learning materials and learning support; and a framework to enable learning on the scale necessary for cost effectiveness'. She cautions, however, that 'the jury is still out on a number of issues'. We do not yet know enough about designing open learning that is effective for school-age learners. Open classrooms demand 'deep and complex changes' of teachers, for which they need to be trained, prepared and supported, but for the moment at least teachers 'are being asked to make these changes with no immediate payoff, no guarantee of success, with no guarantee of continuity, with no additional rewards'. Providing training and ongoing teacher support are expensive propositions, and require funding commitments that governments intent on cost reductions are reluctant to make.

Jenkins emphasizes that 'good ODL is not cheap'. Bakia pursues one aspect of this issue in considerable depth, the costs of employing technologies in classrooms. She points to the difficulties of accomplishing cost analyses of computer use in education, and suggests on the basis of existing evidence that until computer applications are as thoroughly accommodated and integrated into classrooms as the print resources and blackboards, 'computers are likely to add to the costs of schooling and may not have any immediate impact on teaching and learning'. The costs are considerable, including acquiring hardware and software, connecting computers to each other and to the Internet, supporting users, both students and teachers, and maintaining the system. Beware the hidden costs, Bakia warns. Two examples: donated computers are not free (they may incur high import duties, and require expensive upgrades before they can be useful); and inadequate technical support costs schools (teachers then have to devote expensive teaching time to trying to fix their own computer problems and providing informal support to their peers). Marks voices concerns about both the pedagogical concerns of open learning for children, and the resource implications of setting up an ICT-based structure for educating travelling children in particular, including in the equation training and support not only for teachers but for parents as well.

Dodds picks up on another dilemma of financing for open classrooms, pointing to the great need for out-of-school secondary education in southern Africa, and at least implicitly doubting the ability of governments to meet this need without continuing and sizeable public subsidies. This runs contrary to the prevailing dicta of reducing public expenditure on education, and raises one of the persistent contradictions within the neoliberal agenda – how to provide inclusive education that reaches out to those on the margins on the basis of the user-pay principles fundamental to private provision. Panda and Garg describe how the National Open School of India makes concessions in admission fees available to 'the weaker sections of society' – scheduled castes, scheduled tribes, ex-servicemen, disabled people and women – from funds it generates presumably from sources such as tuition fees from those who can afford to pay. This increases the unit cost per student, but is necessary if the concerns of equity and social justice that underlie the setting up of the NOS are to be met. South Africa is also engaged in a process of trying to restore equity and build quality of delivery of education to all of the country's people. Unlike India, however, there are no serious open schooling institutions in South Africa, nor, according to Butcher's account, are there likely to be. Rather than create alternative schooling systems, the priority is to integrate alternatives, greater flexibility, and increased efficiency into the mainstream schooling system, a priority that is still at the 'hope' level and far from a reality.

The authors of the chapter on Telecurso make it clear that, although Telecurso is education for the masses, and at least as successful as other equivalency programmes in preparing students for equivalency exams, it is by no means an educational panacea. It accomplishes cost efficiencies because of the scale on which it is offered; television is too expensive as a medium to make it cost-effective for small numbers. Yes, Telecurso is an example of how deregulation in education can be effective in successfully moving at least one aspect of educational provision outside state monopoly. However, it is only a partial solution to the long-standing structural problems within the Brazilian education system.

Neither does the author of the chapter on e-learning in rural Atlantic Canada make claims for e-learning beyond the boundaries of particular populations, namely, students in small rural schools for whom e-learning offers opportunities for advanced science study that were previously available to them only by moving to large urban centres. In New Zealand, however, the application of e-learning appears to be a matter of providing national access to learning opportunities for all, through centrally administered initiatives such as developing online curriculum resources, professional development of teachers and principals, and the spread of national infrastructure, including the enabling of high-speed Internet for all schools by the end of 2004.

In the United States, Roblyer looks at the experience of the virtual high school movement so far in terms of its underlying vision of increasing access to additional education opportunities for more students. Roblyer's conclusion is that this vision is not yet being fulfilled. As is the case with distance education provision in general, drop-out rates in virtual classrooms are higher than in face-to-face ones. Students who succeed are self-motivated and organized. They also need good and consistent access to computers, preferably at home. The 'digital divide' syndrome is at work here, and again points up a contradiction within the neoliberal agenda: those students most in need of these educational opportunities are deprived of them by poverty and location. Efforts are being made to provide access to computers at school, along with special time periods during the school day and before and after school in which students can use them. Economic survival issues may be more intractable, however. Roblyer points out that in order to be sustainable, virtual high schools must offer enough courses that are perceived as needed, and of high enough quality, to enough students to justify the additional administrative costs entailed in running them. And there is no question of these courses replacing teachers: caring, competent teachers are the key to making virtual courses successful and responsive to students' needs. Roblyer emphasizes that virtual courses are not a way of enlarging teacher–student ratios or replacing expensive teachers. Rather, says Roblyer, it may actually be easier to 'overcrowd' a virtual class than a face-to-face one, since virtual classes take much more time to organize and teach than traditional ones. If anything, teacher–student ratios need to be lower rather than higher.

Creating alternatives

Economist Martin Carnoy argues that 'If knowledge is fundamental to globalization, globalization should also have a profound impact on the transmission of knowledge.' But, says Carnoy (citing Harvard educator Noel McGinn (1997)), 'this has generally not been the case. Education . . . appears to have changed little in most countries at the classroom level. . . teaching methods and national curricula remain largely intact' (Carnoy, 2000: 43). I suspect that the authors of the contributions to this volume would not dispute that. The open and out-of-school classrooms they describe are evidence that the technological revolution and the neoliberal agenda that accompany globalization are having at least a modest impact on education at school level, especially at the secondary school level. Nonetheless, the ability of the new technologies, and the various measures arising from the neoliberal agenda, to bring about widespread transformation is still more rhetoric than reality. There are a number of contradictions lurking within that agenda, as we have seen above, that may render such transformation ultimately unworkable. For example, in the virtual classroom (admittedly only one form of the open classroom) teachers appear to be even more necessary than in conventional classrooms, and in greater numbers; they need training and support, preferably not at their own expense; and the students who most need the opportunities offered, at least by the virtual high school, are those least able to afford them. The cost structure of the open classroom, at least in its virtual form, may in the end make it non-viable and keep it on the fringes of educational provision at school level in most countries.

Carnoy also argues, however, that 'there is much more political and even financial space for the national state to condition the way globalization is brought into education than is usually admitted. . . . States can provide schooling access more equally, improve the quality of education for the poor, and produce knowledge more effectively and more equally for all within a globalized economy' (Carnoy, 2000: 58). The various initiatives described in the present volume are also evidence of this. Open classrooms are providing more equal access to at least some kinds of schooling in India, southern Africa, Brazil, rural Canada, and New Zealand, as well as for children of travelling parents in Europe, and for children around the world who have been displaced or forced to flee their home countries by war and oppression. The technological revolution that accompanies globalization is prompting a plethora of educational experiments, particularly in countries of the affluent, industrialized world. This experimentation is forcing those in charge of educational policy decisions to at least consider that there might be more effective ways of organizing educational provision, by putting the power of information and communication technologies to work at classroom level and supporting the kind of 'open pedagogy' that these technologies make not just possible but necessary.

What the contributors in this volume make clear, however, is the reality that in order to provide more equal access to and improve the quality of education, states must be willing to commit public monies on a continuing basis to this cause. User-pay schemes will not close the digital divide. Initiatives such as Telecurso demonstrate that given appropriate circumstances the creativity of the private sector – in this case a world-class, professional media organization – can achieve impressive results in limited sectors of the education arena. As so many of these authors remind us, however, quality education comes at a cost. If quality education for all is to become a reality, education must remain a public good and the neoliberal agenda must be challenged, or at least manipulated in ways that keep that good at the top of global political, economic and social priorities.

References

Burbules, N and Torres, C (2000) Globalization and education: an introduction, in *Globalization and Education: Critical perspectives*, ed N Burbules and C Torres, Routledge, London, pp 1–26

Carnoy, M (2000) Globalization and educational reform, in *Globalization and Education: Integration and contestation across cultures*, ed N Stromquist and K Monkman, pp 43–61, Rowman and Littlefield, New York

Castells, M (1997) *The Power of Identity, vol. 3: The Rise of the Network Society*, Blackwell Publishers, Oxford

Drumtra, J (2001) 50 Years Later: refugee flights on the rise, international support warning, *Refugee Reports,* **22** (5)

Giddens, A (1990) *The Consequences of Modernity*, Blackwell, Oxford

Harvey, D (1989) *The Condition of Postmodernity: An enquiry into the origins of cultural change*, Blackwell, Oxford

Hoogvelt, A (2001) *Globalization and the Postcolonial World: The new political economy of development*, 2nd edn, Macmillan, London

McGinn, N (1997) The impact of globalization on national education systems, *Prospects,* **28** (1), pp 41–54

Stromquist, N (2002) *Education in a Globalized World: The connectivity of economic power, technology and knowledge*, Rowman and Littlefield, Oxford

Index

Afghanistan 94
Africa 55–66, 91–97
    see also South Africa
Africa Educational Trust 95
African National Congress (ANC) 91, 132
    Policy Framework for Education and Training
        123
Albanian Children's Radio Club 95
asynchronous communication 47, 48
Atlantic Canada *see* Canada
audio 42
Australia 20
    Schools of the Air 15, 16

BBC (British Broadcasting Company)
    Afghan Education Projects Unit 94
    Children's Radio Service 94–95
    SOMDEL (Somali Distance Education for
        Literacy) 95–96
Bonfield, Sir Peter 28, 29
Botswana College of Distance and Open
    Learning (BOCODOL) 56, 62–64, 65
Botswana Education Resource Centre
    (ERC) 92, 93
Brand, Dr Jeff 28, 29
Brazil 7, 134–45
    see also Telecurso (2000)
BT (British Telecom) 28, 121

Caldwell, Brian 27

California Department of Education 48
Canada 149–57, 187, 189
    education system in Newfoundland/
        Labrador 150–51
    Web-based teaching 151–53
    See also Vista School District Digital Intranet
Carlos Chagas Foundation 142, 145
CD ROM 43, 79
children of occupational travellers 4–5
Chile 49, 50
Commonwealth of Learning (COL) 4, 8
computers 43–44
    costs 44–50, 188–89
    donated 46, 189
    hardware 44–46
    network 44–45
    software 46–48
    wireless systems 49, 69, 70–71
correspondence education 58
    India 103
cost analysis 41–50
cost drivers 41–42
Costa Rica 50
Covey, Stephen 34–35

'digital divide' 9–10, 190
displaced people 85–98
distance education 2, 58, 59, 88
    continuum 89
    differentiating from open learning 121–23

New Zealand 8–9, 172
  terminology 90
  'third generation' 2
distance learning 4
  India 101–17
  School-level 19
  suitability for young children 86

education
  funding of 185, 188
  future of 29–32
  primary and secondary 39–35
  work and 34
  see also learning
emotional intelligence 34, 36
employers 34
employment
  education and 34
  trends 31
European Distance Education Network
  (EDEN) 4, 8, 16
European Federation for the Education of the
  Children of Occupational Travellers
  (EFECOT) 67–83

FLEX (Flexible Learning Environment
  eXperiment) 69, 74–76, 79
France 16–17
  National Centre for Distance Education
  (CNED) 16–17

Gates, Bill 28, 31
Ghana
  World Links Project 49
globalization 10, 27, 29, 31
  open classrooms and 183–91
GSM data transmission 70, 74, 81

Handy, Charles 34, 35, 36

Imfundo initiative 6
Industrial Revolution 29–30
India 101–17, 187
  education system 102
  National Literacy Mission 109, 114
  National Open School 104–16, 1889
  open schooling 102–07
  student enrolment 107–09
Indian Open Schooling Network (IOSN)
  115
information and communication technologies
  (ICTs) 1, 15, 18, 23–24, 128, 186
  cost-effectiveness 3
  impact on costs 41–51

interactive radio instruction (IRI) 94
Interactive Radio Instruction for Somalis
  (IRIS) 95
internally displaced people (IDPs) 85, 86–87
International Centre for Training in Open
  Schooling (ICTOS), India 115
International Council for Distance Education
  4
International Extension College 2
Internet 22, 24, 28, 33, 43, 48, 116, 149, 159
  access to 29
  cost 42, 48, 49
Intranets 36
  New Zealand 174–75
  see also *Vista School District Digital* 150

Journal of Open Schooling 6

Kaupapa Ara Whakawhiti Matauranga (KAWM)
  project 177–78
knowledge expert 31
knowledge society 3–4, 27, 185, 186
Kosovo 94, 95

learner support systems 60–61, 62, 112
learning
  future models of 31–32
  transformation of 33
local area networks 48

Macedonia 95
MAILBOX 23
Malawi 92
Malawi College of Distance Education/
  (MCDE) 56, 60–61, 63
Mandleson, Peter 28, 29
Massachusetts Institute of Technology (MIT)
  19
Massey University, New Zealand 172
Mexico 43, 134
  see also Telescundaria
Microsoft 28
Moore, Michael 69, 76, 80
Mozambican Open Learning Unit (MOLU)
  91, 92
Mozambique 92
multimedia 2, 22
  impact on costs 41–44
  see also audio, computers, television, video
multinational corporations 184, 186
  see also globalization

Namibian College of Open Learning
  (NAMCOL) 56, 61–62, 63, 64, 65

Namibian Extension Unit (NEU)   91, 92, 93
National Extension College (NEC)   1, 27,
    57
National Open School, India   6, 104–16, 189
    age profile of students   107, 109
    course delivery   112–13
    courses   109–10
    curriculum design/development   110–11
    fees   114
    funding   113–14
    National Consortium for Open Schooling
        114–15
    organizational
    special needs groups   114, 115
    structure   105
    student enrolment   107–09
    unit costs   113–14
New Zealand   8–9, 152, 171–79, 189–90
    computer recycling scheme   176
    Correspondence School   20–21, 172,
        173–74, 188
    Digital Opportunities Programme   177
    e-learning   178–79
    ICT   176
    Information and Communications Strategy   175
    KAWM project   177–78
    online resource centre   175
    open learning   172–76
    regional intranets   174–75
Newfoundland and Labrador   149–57
    see also Canada

occupational travellers   68
online learning   8, 323
    see also Internet
open and distance learning   (ODL) 1, 2, 15–16
    Africa   55–66, 91–97
    basic education   20–21
    benefits for children   20
    Canada   149–57
    children of occupational travellers   67–83
    context   18–19
    cost-effectiveness   21
    cost structure   41–50, 188–89
    displaced people   85–98
    group learning   24
    India   101–17
    New Zealand   171–79
    primary schools   39–52
    rural education   154–56
    school-level   19
    secondary schools   39–52
    South Africa   119–32
    United States   159–69

open classroom   15–16, 19
    access to   191
    cost structure   191
    emergence of   22–23
    globalization and
    see also virtyal classroom
Open Classroom Movement   16
Open Classroom Working Group   4
open learning   2
    definition   120, 123–26
    differentiating from distance learning
        121–23
    South Africa   120–26
Open Learning Agency (Canada)   122
Open Learning Institute (Hong Kong)   122
open schools   6, 36–37
    features of   35–36
    India   101–17, 187
    South Africa   119–32
open teaching   23–24
Open Polytechnic of New Zealand   172,
    173–74
Open University (UK)   17, 91, 122

Pan African Congress   91
parastatal organizations   56, 64, 64–65
    see also Botswana College of Open and
        Distance Learning, Malawi College of
        Distance Education, Namibian College
        of Open Learning
Parent Teacher Association (PTA)   49
parents   70, 77, 80, 81

radio   7, 93–95
    India   111
Radio Education for Afghan Children
    (REACH)   94
    see also BBC
refugees   5, 85–98, 187
Roberto Marinho Foundation (RMF)   134,
    136, 142
    see also Telecurso
rural education   154–56

school level   3
Schools of the Air   15, 16
science classes   151–53
Sesame Street   133, 134
Somalia   94, 95
SOMDEL (Somalia Distance Education for
    Literacy)   95–96
South Africa   7, 119–32, 187
    education system   119–20, 131
    emerging policy recommendations   129–30

information technology 130
open learning 120–32
Open Learning in South African General and Further Education and Training 120, 121, 127, 131
White Paper on Education and Training 124–26
South African Extension Unit (SAEU) 91
South Korea 133
South West Africa Peoples' Organization 92
special learning centres 21
synchronous communication 47, 48, 78, 162
Sudan 88
SOLO programme 91, 92–93

Tapscott, Don 33
Tate, Ormond 172
TCO Project 51
Te Kete Ipurangi 175
teachers 23–24
attitudes 23
role of 19–20, 24, 32, 75, 88–89, 144
Telecurso and 138
virtual classrooms and 153–54
Technical College of South Africa 120, 128
Telecurso (2000) 134–45, 191
audience 136, 143, 145
background 134–36
classroom 138–39
costs 141
drop-out rate 141
educational resources 140
enrolment figures 140–41
examinations 143
open broadcasting 139
organized viewing 138–39
teachers and 138, 144
Telesecundaria 21, 43
television 7, 43
India 111
see also Telecurso (2000), Telesundaria
Tooley, James 34
TOPILOT (To Optimize the Individual Learning Process of Occupational Travelling Children) 69, 70, 71–74, 76
'transactional distance' 69, 79, 80
see also virtual classroom

Trapeze 69, 71, 76–79
travelling children 67–83
Turkey 49

university education 30

video
cost of 42–43, 47, 48
videoconferencing 127
virtual classroom 76–79, 150
'virtual high schools' 8, 47, 159–69, 187–88
background 160
characteristics 160–62
Concord Consortium 160–61, 163, 165
curriculum 161–62
CyberSchool 166
distribution 160
effectiveness 162–63
Florida High School Project 161, 165, 168
funding 167–68
future of 167–69
Hawaii's E– School 166
student motivation 163–64
Virginia Internet High School 166, 168
Vista School District Digital Intranet 150, 153, 154, 154, 155

United States 8, 133, 134, 159–69, 187–88, 1900
Fairfax County 50
University of South Africa (UNISA) 119, 128
USAID 95, 131

work *see* employment
World Bank 59, 60
World Conference on Education for All (1990) 5, 101
World Links Project *see* Ghana
World Wide Web
educational courses and 47
science courses 151
'virtual high schools' 161–62

Young, Michael 1–2, 7

Zambia 92, 93